M000313840

"*Inclusive Leadership, Global Impact* provides
to the topic of global diversity and comes to us at a time when we sorely need it."

— TERRY HOGAN
Former Global Head of Talent Management and Diversity at Citigroup

"*Inclusive Leadership, Global Impact* should be in the hands of every leader and
employee who wants to create an inclusive workplace and achieve better business
results. This book offers various examples and direct, hands-on, practical tools.
There are also great thought-provoking questions which could be used by a
leadership team to read together and then discuss. We can all do more to make
our teams and workplaces more inclusive. This important book educates us and
shows real steps for making this happen."

— HENRIK WULFF
Managing Director, SBR and Head of Pharmaceuticals at Bayer Middle East FZE

"Awareness of effective inclusive practices in both the academic and corporate
spheres has never been more critical. This revised edition of what was already one
of the most robust sources for inclusive leadership is both a timely and timeless
response to this subject. Any leader, especially those engaged in motivating
and inspiring others across cultures, should use this book as an integral part
of developing and implementing actionable strategies that will have positive
impacts on their bottom line."

— BRETT D. PARRY
President SIETAR USA (Society of Intercultural Education, Training and Research)

"The authors' experience in business, academic and cultural anthropology shine
through in this latest body of work. Having worked and partnered with Dr.
Williams for more than 10 years, I find it wonderful that she is able to share
her profound knowledge, experience, and wisdom. I continue to learn from
her. My latest read from Dr. Williams and Dr. Gundling, *Inclusive Leadership,
Global Impact*, is spot on."

— RICHARD S. SPADA, MA
PCC, President and Principal Consultant, Aspire International LLC; Former Global Executive
Director, Diversity and Inclusion Center of Excellence, Novartis International

"*Inclusive Leadership, Global Impact* is a wonderful contribution to the DEI
field and global inclusion initiatives. Ernest Gundling's practical, developmental
approach answers key questions and specifies a clear path for improvement."

— JOYCE OSLAND
Senior Partner, Kozai Group; Professor Emerita, San Jose State University

"With this book, we finally have a truly useful resource that digs deeply into the thorny questions leaders must wrestle with, while providing highly practical advice on what leaders can actually do to create workplaces that are more inclusive, and that unleash massive organizational potential that too often lies dormant. This book will challenge you in all the best ways. Every leader who aspires to be more inclusive should read this book."

— JASON D. PATENT, PH.D.
Director, Robertson Center for Intercultural Leadership, International House Berkeley

"*Inclusive Leadership, Global Impact* is a real contribution to organizations seeking to improve inclusion on a global scale, but also to the intercultural field as a whole. No one else is providing analysis that is so thorough and so practical."

— DR. GEORGE RENWICK
President, Renwick & Associates

"As a leader in the medtech industry having led diverse, cross-border teams for over fifteen years, I find *Inclusive Leadership, Global Impact* a thoughtful and balanced resource to help further my impact and coach my team to achieve even better performance. This book contains many practical examples of putting inclusive behaviors into action to drive innovation and improve business results. A great read to bring you up to date on the main tenets every leader should know including creating psychological safety in your organization, developing diverse talent, and building a high performing organization that gives every employee the opportunity to excel."

— TISHA BOATMAN
Managing Director, Nordic and Baltic Countries, Siemens Healthineers

"I highly recommend *Inclusive Leadership, Global Impact*. The book is academically sound—based on research, proven techniques, and practical ideas. The use of models, charts, and graphics throughout make it easy to grasp key learnings. There's something for everyone to learn given its focus on what the individual can do to promote 'everyday inclusion' and the systemic changes that need to be addressed at the organizational level."

— JULIE O'MARA
Author and Co-author of DEI books and The Global Diversity, Equity, and Inclusion Benchmarks; Board Member, The Centre for Global Inclusion

"My students LOVE this book! The content is timely and presented in a very engaging manner. Not only do my students claim that their understanding of Diversity & Inclusion has been expanded by the examination of implicit and explicit bias, their understanding is moving them to take meaningful action."

— KATHRYN HOLLYWOOD, PH.D.
Chair of Doctoral Programs—College of Business, DBA, Ed.D./Ph.D. in Organizational Leadership & Sports Leadership; Professor, Doctoral Faculty, Leadership, Concordia University, Chicago

"I have had the great fortune to partner with Dr. Williams on prominent Diversity, Inclusion, Equity and Belonging initiatives over twenty years. Cheryl is an expert in crisis communications, global cultural insights, and maintains a high BIPOC acumen. I highly recommend this poignant book as a core and practical guide to foster inclusivity, build organizational capabilities, and improve employee performance."

— GINA GALASSO
Executive VP & Chief HR Officer at ocV!BE Sports & Entertainment (parent company of Anaheim Ducks, The Rinks, Honda Center); Former Head of HR for the LA Dodgers

"*Inclusive Leadership, Global Impact* provides a great perspective that will help develop your Diversity Equity and Inclusion lens globally. Having the ability to see and support marginalized groups in your workplace is pivotal to a team dynamic. The tools on how to become an inclusive leader that are provided in this book are second to none! A good read and highly recommended."

— TYRONE WISE
Associate Director of Student Experience, Haas School of Business; Chairman, Black Staff and Faculty Organization; Co-Chairman, Veterans Staff Organization; Advisor, NAACP Youth and College Division; University of California, Berkeley

"Dr. Williams and Dr. Gundling have written a must-read primer for anyone considering working in the global diversity, equity, and inclusion field. Read this book—and learn from two of the best."

— JACOB A. O. PREUS, TH.D.
Former President, Concordia University Irvine; Executive Vice President for Mission Advancement, Bethesda Lutheran Communities

"*Inclusive Leadership, Global Impact* is required reading for any leader who is truly passionate about developing the skills required to create inclusive cultures. Leading successfully in a globally diverse world demands nothing less."

— ALAINA LOVE
CEO, Purpose Linked Consulting; 2021 International Thought Leader of the Year; Member, Marshall Goldsmith Top 100 Coaches; Former Executive Director, HR, Merck & Co., Inc.

ISBN: 978-0-578-91328-5

INCLUSIVE LEADERSHIP, GLOBAL IMPACT

Dr. Ernest Gundling and Dr. Cheryl Williams

TABLE OF CONTENTS

PART FOUR: DEVELOPING INCLUSIVE LEADERS

ACKNOWLEDGEMENTS

Writing a book on the topic of inclusion creates a new appreciation for the value of a diverse set of contributors. The authors would like to acknowledge a number of people who have contributed their ideas and input during the writing process. Adwoa Osei, Anthony Greco, Ashley Coombs, Christie Caldwell, David Abebefe, Ebenezer Amuasi, Freeda Fernandes, Jason Overton, Jason Patent, Karen Cvitkovich, Mercedes Martin, Michael Nadeau, Mike Greto, Morten Skov-Carlsen, Mui Hwa Ng, Pamela Leri, Rachel Korah, Simone-Eva Redrupp, Ted Dale, and Theresa Kneebone all provided valuable comments on the manuscript along the way. Thanks to each of them and to many other colleagues at Aperian and in our field for their insights, advice, and dedication to a shared purpose.

Our wonderful, hard-working book production team of Adilah Rahim, Michelle Mascarenhas, Nicole Ury, Sarah Cincotta, and Theresa DiCenzo has seen this complex project through from start to finish. We appreciate their persistence, creativity, positive energy, and faith that we would eventually get this project done! It's been a pleasure to work with each of them, and special thanks to Michelle for her work on formatting and graphics. Kay Jones has been a disciplined and systematic editor, helping us to rein in our sometimes-ungrammatical enthusiasm for this topic with both humor and concrete support in clarifying our intended message.

Dozens of clients and colleagues in the field have also provided various forms of input, encouragement, and opportunities for direct contact with current inclusive leadership challenges. We have mostly omitted reference to specific individuals and organizations out of respect for confidentiality, but would like to express our deep appreciation nonetheless. It has been our pleasure and privilege to work with them in every region mentioned in the book: Europe, the Middle East, sub-Saharan Africa, Asia-Pacific, and North and South America.

Finally, we are grateful for the patience, persistence, and encouragement of family members, especially Kacey and Kenny, who watched us wrestle with the writing process and how to bring the practice of inclusion to life in our own work by incorporating several rounds of feedback and commentary. The sharpest criticisms were often the ones that resulted in the greatest improvements to our original draft, but we also took a lot more time on this project than originally promised.

In addition to the many people who have contributed already, the authors welcome feedback, updates, and examples from readers. Feel free to reach out to us and provide your comments at **contactus@aperianglobal.com**. Although we can't promise to incorporate every contribution in future revisions given the extremely wide range of views on the topic of inclusive leadership, we will read every comment and consider carefully the views that you share with us.

PART ONE:
SETTING THE CONTEXT

Introduction

Inclusion Trends

Inclusive Leadership: Dealing with Difference

01.
Introduction

Inclusion has the most powerful impact when it is not just an initiative, a corporate principle, or a required training program.

The practice of inclusion is relevant to everyone, particularly those in leadership roles. Inclusion has the most powerful impact when it is not just an initiative, a corporate principle, or a required training program. There is increasing recognition that all employees—CEOs, middle managers, new hires, cafeteria workers—have a role to play in making inclusion an integral part of the organizational fabric.

Inclusion is most viable when it is not the goal of a single department or the passion of a particular executive, interest group, or category of people. It is not "mine" or "theirs," but "ours," and is linked to core values such as human dignity, freedom, opportunity, meritocracy, and pragmatism. Inclusion brings a sense of joint commitment and real belonging to each person, going beyond the buzzwords to the implementation of practical plans.

Too often, however, companies that aspire to become more inclusive find themselves heading in the opposite direction. The sign below was recently posted on the break room walls of a large organization after discussions between employees with different political, religious, and socioeconomic backgrounds and beliefs had turned into heated workplace quarrels.

Figure 1.1: Avoid Controversial Discussions

In contrast to the uneasy quiet of this break room, where employees co-exist but do not co-create, truly inclusive organizations are easy to identify because they are buzzing with energy and collaborative discussions. This atmosphere is readily evident from their office or virtual meeting rooms to their lunch and break rooms; such places have a magnetic attraction for talented individuals from any background.

Although there is not a simple program or recipe to move from divisive quarrels or an uneasy truce to shared enthusiasm and creativity, the path does involve moving from one-dimensional stereotypes of others to a fuller and more complex sense of who they are and how they understand themselves. Deeper mutual understanding makes it easier for people from different backgrounds to join in the service of common goals, and having shared goals, in turn, becomes an impetus to strengthen bonds of trust with each other.

Leaders in any organization must consider where they are now, where they want to go, what kinds of changes will stick, and what goals might be too lofty. Individual leaders have their own comfort levels with the topic of inclusion, and it is important for them to recognize where they are and start from that point. **We will provide a general roadmap and practical recommendations for individuals, teams, and organizations to become**

If anyone, no matter who, were given the opportunity of choosing from amongst all the nations in the world the set of beliefs which they thought best, they would inevitably—after careful considerations of their relative merits—choose that of their own country.

– Herodotus[1]

more inclusive, with resources for leaders at various points in their own inclusion journey.

WHY GLOBAL INCLUSION?

Current ideas and practices related to "inclusion" are culture-bound. They have originated within specific cultural contexts, particularly Western Europe and the U.S., and may not be easily transported elsewhere. Although there is a common impulse to broaden inclusion initiatives that have been formulated at headquarters, when taken abroad, they often run into obstacles: puzzlement, resistance, apathy, or misuse. **It is ironic and unfortunate when inclusion efforts fail because their terminology, applications, or learning methodology are unwittingly ethnocentric.**

This book's authors are both from the U.S. and have lived and traveled extensively in Asia-Pacific, Europe, Africa, and South America over several decades. We enthusiastically endorse the values that underpin inclusion in its present form and also acknowledge its historical roots in our own country's long struggle to counteract racism and to expand the rights of minorities and women. We acknowledge the perspective of those who argue for cultural relativity—that is, understanding the beliefs and actions of others within their own cultural context—but also believe that inclusion does have cross-cultural merit when carefully adapted to local contexts.

The forms that inclusivity takes in different parts of the world are likely to surprise headquarters-based experts. Wider global exchanges could potentially spark mutual learning and even lead to a far richer and more nuanced global perspective. In some countries, for example, race is a fundamental inclusion issue while in others it is not; there might be one main ethnic group or a thousand; religion may or may not be an important factor; the next step for women could be greater executive suite representation or security from physical violence. Government ideology and inspirational slogans—"Liberté, égalité, fraternité"—are often belied by the realities on the ground. No country is a flawless paragon; everyone has further to go, something more to learn. Our focus combines a commitment to social justice on a global scale with practical business impacts in terms of employee engagement, innovation, and serving diverse marketplaces.

KEY QUESTIONS

Many well-intentioned leaders are still struggling with the question of what they themselves can do—how to take **practical actions that will create a more inclusive work environment**. This book addresses a growing set of questions we are hearing from executives in a variety of industries and countries around the world:

- What are the major *inclusion trends* that we should know about?

- How can we *deal with differences* without increasing mutual grievances among employees?

- Is there a concise, memorable approach to understanding and addressing *unconscious bias*?

- What are the *everyday skills* that leaders, managers, and employees need to become more inclusive?

- Are there *new boundaries* to cross and new forms of inclusion that each of us needs to learn about?

- How can leaders serve as *champions* and as effective models of inclusion?

- How can inclusion be linked with getting better *business results*?

- What is the impact of increased inclusiveness on *team performance*?

- Are inclusion challenges the same everywhere, or are there differences across *world regions*?

- *Are race and ethnicity universal issues* that employers should be addressing with a common approach?

- What are the value and limits of current *neuroscience-based approaches* to inclusion and diversity?

- How can inclusive leadership be incorporated into programs for *developing current and future leaders*?

- What kinds of systemic *organizational changes* are essential to support inclusion?

- Is it possible to *measure progress* toward a more inclusive work environment?

AN INFLECTION POINT

The topic of inclusion now carries a palpable sense of urgency because our global society has experienced a rolling series of simultaneous crises: the accelerating impacts of climate change, a global pandemic, the growing strength of anti-democratic, authoritarian politicians and regimes, and stark socioeconomic inequalities accompanied by calls for greater social justice. The Black Lives Matter movement in the U.S. and its reverberations in many other countries have brought wider acceptance for the need to reconsider what "equity" means and how to address systemic issues that hold back those who have been marginalized.

MAMA

I feel fortunate to have been born black. 'Black' to me represents the strength of a people who have a history fraught with terror, a perseverance for justice and values grounded in family love, and the belief in a higher power that unconditionally welcomes all.

Much of the world has viewed the horrific video footage of George Floyd, a black man, being murdered in broad daylight, in clear public sight, by a white police officer. Reminiscent of black folks hanging from trees as their breathing stopped during pre-civil rights era days, this scene evoked in me a sense of horror when I saw Mr. Floyd's breath being cut off by the white cop who kept a knee on his neck until he was no longer breathing.

My formal education and my personal values usually allow me to proffer a mature, non-emotional response to confrontational situations. When the pain hits my children and grandchildren, however, the 'sheep throws off her clothes,' exposing the wolf. Here is what my wolf looks and feels like in real-time.

What struck me even more deeply than Mr. Floyd's now famous cry, "I can't breathe," was that he also called out, "Mama." This hit me so deeply that anger and resentment leaped into my soul. It brought out the "Mama" in me, the blackness of me, the humanity in me, and an ardent cry for social justice. I wanted to call my pack, to howl and to hunt together for the human decency, basic fairness, and justice so long denied.

No one has any say about how they will show up after passing through the birth canal. Your existence outside of your mother's womb begins when you take your first breath. Breathing is our most fundamental need in life. It connects living beings to the world. The air we breathe is essential for plants, animals, and humans to co-exist. To deny or take away this basic need conjures up an illness that is sickening and deadly, which is the way I think of racist, hate-filled behaviors.

The loss of breath means to die, to lose that most basic and precious gift of birth that "Mama" gave us. As an asthmatic, I have felt this fear and profound need to get air at any cost. For the brief moment it takes for me to reach for the nebulizer that helps to recover my breath, I can imagine Mr. Floyd's final moments. Mr. Floyd had no nebulizer to reach for and no relief for his pain. There were bystanders, upstanders, allies, advocates, and strangers who witnessed it all.

However, there is a glimmer of hope that Mr. Floyd did not die in vain, that he was not 'just another black man' in a long line of blacks whose lives have been diminished or cut short by the disease of racism. The world is listening, some people more than others. Now more are acknowledging the presence of individual, institutionalized, and systemic racism than at any other time in history. It is visible! Former naysayers are recognizing it, speaking out, and willing to take action.

We need each other. Mothers, fathers, and all members of our extended human family must insist that an inclusive, proactive way forward is mandatory for our continued co-existence. Even or especially when our internal wolves are howling, we have to do whatever it takes to dismantle or hurdle racist barriers and bring about sustainable equity through peaceful means.

Cheryl Williams, Co-Author

This book is intended for people who want to do something about the lethal impacts of racial bias and other forms of exclusion, both in their local environments and on a more global scale. In addition to the destructive effects of racial discrimination, a host of other forms of exclusion can and do affect a variety of groups and individuals around the world: ethnic minorities, women, immigrants and refugees, religious believers, indigenous people, LGBTQ+ individuals, the disabled, and so on.

Exclusion occurs in ways that are spoken, unspoken, internalized, or embodied by personal conduct and organizational systems. Inclusion in a broad sense starts with identifying insider/outsider dynamics wherever they exist, along with the ways in which the exclusion of those perceived as outsiders leads to unearned disadvantages, unfounded prejudice, and forms of social oppression, whether by neglect or by design.

Inclusive organizations seek to transform all of their employees into insiders, regardless of their backgrounds, in joint service of a worthwhile mission and common goals, and to create an environment where each person can thrive and feel they belong. Companies need internal alignment and high levels of employee engagement in order to best serve their customers and to achieve their business goals, and they can sometimes be a positive force for change even when other social institutions are not.

ORGANIZATIONAL VITALITY

What is at stake with inclusive leadership is, in fact, nothing less than organizational vitality. Corporations generally have a center and spokes, as does a wheel. There are myriad variations in organizational structure, and some are designed to have multiple centers, but they all need a healthy flow of ideas and information among people and places. John Kotter, one of the best-known scholars of leadership and change management, emphasizes that **a strong organizational culture can be a blessing or a curse**—a powerful asset so long as it is suited to the surrounding marketplace, but a fatal flaw when there is no longer a match between this culture and its changing environment.[2] Organizations with a one-sided flow of information, whether this is top-down within the same office or between headquarters and subsidiaries, are likely to stagnate and fail to meet changing environmental circumstances.

Unhealthy organizations, including governments as well as corporate autocracies, find **scapegoats**, singling out individuals or groups—usually those who can be labeled as different in some way based on their appearance or their ideas—to blame for poor performance results; these people are then chastised and cast out while the real perpetrators claim the problem is solved. The ultimate form of exclusion is ostracism from the tribe, which in the ancient world meant almost certain death. But sooner or later, underlying issues that have not been addressed through blaming and excluding resurface, and then the hunt is on again for a new scapegoat. This social pattern—which is found in every civilization, ancient or modern—can lead to a recurring cycle of exclusion and underperformance, with a spiraling descent into ruin.

Autocratic leaders are seldom inclined to embrace inclusion and diversity, and there is nothing inevitable about social change in a dictatorship other than lethal battles for succession. Leaders may indeed decide that it is politically expedient to blame, persecute, or expel those who appear different or who fail to sing a one-party anthem with sufficient gusto. Pitting "them" against "us" is a convenient way to distract national or corporate citizens from problems that are actually self-inflicted. More inclusive forms of governance, on the other hand, must bridge divergent interests, however imperfectly, to create a more productive and vibrant union.

Rather than blaming others who are different and casting them out as scapegoats, inclusive leaders connect people at various levels and locations. They inspire collaborative problem-solving, keeping the organization's culture current with the times while seeing themselves clearly enough in the mirror to take responsibility for problems that they themselves have caused. Individuals who might previously have been candidates to become scapegoats may turn out to be innovators, inspirational trend-setters, and future leaders.

INCLUSIVE BEHAVIORS: FIVE DEVELOPMENTAL STAGES

So how can individuals and organizations surmount bias and realize the full benefits of inclusion—both at home and on a global scale—while avoiding the temptations of simple yet ultimately destructive solutions such as scapegoating? The recent emphasis on coupling awareness with action has also driven a move from learning events to a learning journey.

Building new patterns of behavior strong enough to counteract entrenched habits and even our primal, atavistic impulses to wall off those perceived as outsiders requires creating a shared language, numerous touch points, and multiple forms of reinforcement.

The ultimate goal for many current inclusion champions is to create a transformative, high-performance organizational culture that also serves as a greenhouse for developing inclusive leaders. Inclusion is neither a cure-all for every business problem nor a ticket to utopia. It will not erase historical injustices, and it cannot completely eliminate distinctions between people based on power, privilege, or hierarchy. Inclusive leaders can, however, seize the inherent possibilities in the present to work toward a better future that offers equal opportunities to all, regardless of their background.

1. Learning About Bias
How aware am I of my own biases, and how do I begin to learn about others who are different?

2. Building Key Skills
What critical baseline skills do I have for acting in a more inclusive way?

3. Working Across Boundaries
How successful am I in working with various aspects of diversity such as gender, generational, functional, cognitive, or cultural diversity?

4. Becoming a Champion
What does it mean to champion inclusion, and am I doing what it takes?

5. Getting Results
How well do I link inclusion to business results?

Figure 1.2: Five Stages of Inclusion

Figure 1.2 outlines a progression that we often see in inclusive leaders and their organizations. These five stages are not strictly sequential but flourish in mutually reinforcing cycles. Each stage creates a foundation for those that follow—"Building Key Skills," for example, is a gateway to "Becoming a Champion"—and yet each also remains an ongoing project, including "Learning About Bias." Leaders are never done with the work of inclusion and able to cross this item off their task lists, but they can make enormous changes over time, especially when they exert steady efforts on a daily basis. Inclusivity is an essential feature of a "growth mindset,"[3] enabling leaders to get beyond fixed, outdated perceptions and to engage employees from any background, access new information, and respond to fresh trends. The chapters that follow, particularly those in Part Two, provide a guidebook for aspiring inclusive leaders to make every one of these stages come alive, and to move from awareness to action to business impact.

CHAPTER OVERVIEW

The chapters in this book address the questions about inclusive leadership listed earlier. We also incorporate newer themes such as intersectionality, third-culture kids, cultural neuroscience, and psychological safety, along with data from empirical studies on global leadership. Although our primary focus is on individual development, the book outlines key organizational levers for systemic change as well. Here is a brief description of each chapter that follows:

Part One: Setting the Context

Chapter 2: Inclusion Trends

Describes major trends in the field of inclusion and diversity: Awareness to Action, Digitalization and Demographics, Global Principles & Local Knowledge, Compliance Challenges (Again), Competitive Advantage, and Commitment to Equity.

Chapter 3: Inclusive Leadership: Dealing with Difference

Covers the hazards and benefits of addressing differences in race, ethnicity, gender, function, culture, cognitive style, and other aspects of a diverse workforce, while providing a clear model for proactively leveraging differences.

Part Two: Five Stages of Inclusion

Chapter 4: Inclusive Behavior: Learning About Bias

Examines the renewed urgency for inclusive practices in current workplaces and how organizational values are being tested; describes the simple and memorable CIAO model that defines four key types of unconscious bias using everyday examples; highlights empathy as the doorway to inclusive action.

Chapter 5: Inclusive Behaviors: Building Key Skills & Working Across Boundaries

Provides practical recommendations for cultivating key inclusion skills in areas such as listening, feedback, meeting facilitation, and conflict resolution; challenges leaders to expand their inclusive actions to incorporate new and unfamiliar groups of counterparts.

Chapter 6: Inclusive Behaviors: Becoming a Champion & Getting Results

Offers guidance for leaders on how to move beyond their immediate work teams and contribute to the broader organization as inclusion champions through one-on-one interactions or process improvements; identifies specific means by which inclusive practices can be leveraged to create better performance results.

Part Three: Global Applications

Chapter 7: Global Teams

Takes the concept of unconscious bias beyond the realm of individual awareness; demonstrates how bias can create a downward spiral of mistrust and underperformance in a diverse, dispersed team context unless proactively addressed using the full range of inclusive behaviors.

Chapter 8: Regional Inclusion Challenges

Explores regional differences with illustrations from several geographies; suggests ways that those who are leading inclusion initiatives should be questioning basic assumptions and adapting their approaches.

Chapter 9: Race and Ethnicity: A Global Perspective

Examines the topic of race and ethnicity through the lenses of several global examples—the U.K., Brazil, Nigeria—to illustrate both common themes and ways in which this topic must be approached differently in each country to be locally relevant.

Part Four: Developing Inclusive Leaders

Chapter 10: Brain-Based Leadership: What's Missing?

Highlights the deficit of cultural knowledge in common neuroscience-based approaches to leadership development, as well as ways to address this by incorporating the findings of "cultural neuroscience."

Chapter 11: Inclusive Leadership Development

Offers a diagnosis of why leadership development programs tend to fall short of their objectives due to fatal flaws such as headquarters-centrism and the "parade of professors"; spells out alternative practices that provide current and future leaders with first-hand experience in the markets of the future along with a trusted network of global peers.

Chapter 12: Five Organizational Levers

Provides recommendations for how inclusive leaders and their organizations can build a culture of inclusion using five critical change levers: recruitment; executive engagement; coaching and mentoring; key performance indicators; and policy and process.

02.
Inclusion Trends

Against a background of rapid, unprecedented change on a global scale, inclusion is now a requirement for continued relevance in most industries.

The field of inclusion and diversity has changed considerably over time, and there is wide disparity among organizations. Some are still seeking to build a baseline awareness, while others have moved on to broader change initiatives. Before considering how leaders can contribute to an inclusive organizational culture, it is important to take stock of the current inclusion landscape. **In our work we have encountered six major inclusion trends**.

1. AWARENESS TO ACTION

The concept of unconscious bias has gained widespread acceptance, in part because research now suggests that rather than being a personal character defect, bias is a common human phenomenon—we all hold biases of varying types and degrees. Bias is now seen as being linked with the habits, or default shortcuts, that the human brain takes to ensure that attention and energy are used efficiently. Although most leaders working in diverse environments recognize that it is important to become aware of biases that shape exclusionary actions, many efforts to unwind such biases have become mired in complex terminology and finger-pointing.

"Bias fatigue" may set in when people hear long lists of possible biases that are difficult to grasp and retain, while some individuals or groups feel that they are being singled out for blame. The concept of unconscious

There is a growing trend to tie awareness to action—leaders and employees not only face the challenge of how to think inclusively, but also how to act in more inclusive ways as well.

bias seems to entail a kind of infinite regress because unconscious biases are inexhaustible and must be continually revisited. There is a growing trend to tie awareness to action—leaders and employees not only face the challenge of how to think inclusively, but how to act in more inclusive ways as well.

Another way to address bias is through engaging in deliberate acts of inclusion. Psychological research tells us that action can shape attitudes, just as the reverse is also true.[1] This method is at least as old as Aristotle, who noted in his Nicomachean ethics (circa 340 BC) that virtue is cultivated through the practice of good habits. New behaviors, however awkward they might feel at first, stimulate the development of related mental patterns that in turn provide further support for such behaviors. Insights quickly dissipate without follow-up actions, but a mutually reinforcing cycle of insight and action can become a powerful personal and organizational change agent. Although some might claim that focusing on inclusive action is a way to avoid talking about unconscious bias, it may have the opposite effect by generating experiences that make the presence of bias and the need to address it more tangible.

Over the past decade, it has also become common to reverse the term, "Diversity and Inclusion," to "Inclusion and Diversity," reflecting the aspiration to move beyond awareness of differences to cultivating inclusive behaviors across the workforce over time (although some still argue that diversity logically comes before inclusion). Experts and practitioners in this field have made great strides in defining what inclusive behaviors look like and how leaders can evolve from basic awareness of unconscious bias to becoming workplace champions and role models.[2]

2. DIGITALIZATION AND DEMOGRAPHICS

Powerful social currents are likely to keep driving urgent calls for more inclusive leadership. An approach favored by some executives has been to hunker down and wait for the inclusion movement to blow over and be replaced by some other faddish trend. Others make a show of supporting initiatives while going through the motions of minimal compliance, with little enthusiasm for anything further. But both technological innovation and demographic trends make such a head-in-the-sand approach unrealistic.

Digital technologies now connect people across oceans, mountains, and deserts and are able to magnify negative or positive interactions almost instantly; twice as many people on the planet are connected to the internet now as there were a decade ago, with rapidly increasing bandwidth. A simultaneous transformation is occurring in the location of future customers, employees, suppliers, and fast-growth markets. Several key underlying demographic changes are not only roiling global markets, but also transforming the headquarters operations of almost every major multinational.

- *Population Growth*: *We've more than tripled the planet's population in the last seventy years,* from 2.5 billion to almost 8 billion, and this has affected every region of the world. Almost all of this explosive population growth is occurring in emerging markets,[3] with billions more people on the way over the rest of this century to reach the earth's projected peak population of 9 to 11 billion. 90% of the world's children under the age of 15 currently live outside the developed economies of Europe, North America, and Japan.

Differences in birth rates are leading to major changes both between and within countries. The highest birth rates globally are in sub-Saharan Africa (e.g., Niger, Uganda, Zambia) and in South Asia, with the lowest rates being in northeast Asia and in Europe (e.g., Taiwan, Japan, Germany, Italy). To provide an illustration of how marked these contrasts are, in a recent year approximately the same number of babies were born in Niger, with a population of 21 million, as in Japan, with a population of 126 million. In the U.S., although non-Hispanic whites currently comprise two-thirds of the nationwide population, this ratio is predicted to shift to less than half of the overall country population in 2050 due to comparatively lower birth rates, in spite of a recent decline in minority births.

- *Urbanization and the Middle Class*: *The expansion of new cities is driving two-thirds of the world's GDP growth*, with millions of people moving to cities each month from rural areas in search of new opportunities. Hundreds of additional cities will be required to house all of these people, and, in addition, the citizens of each new city will need to purchase manufactured goods, transportation, food, and energy. Many of these people are still living in acute poverty. At the same time, there is a huge and rapidly growing new urban middle class of consumers that will soon number a billion people or more. Its members in Asia, Africa, the Middle East, and South America desire many of the products and services enjoyed by residents of the current high-consumption markets.

- *International Migration*: *Migration across national borders has increased by almost 50% since the year 2000*, with the primary flow of people moving to high-income countries. Millions of people emigrate every year to escape from poverty, conflict, or natural disasters.

A United Nations study notes that the number of migrants as a fraction of the population residing in high-income countries has risen from under 10% to almost 15% on average. Three-quarters of these migrants are of working age, and they normally seek to join the workforce as quickly as possible in their new locations.[4]

Whether your job is with a global team or in a local office with limited opportunities to travel, **chances are that your workplace and the tasks you are engaged in will involve a more diverse range of counterparts from this day forward**.

3. GLOBAL PRINCIPLES, LOCAL KNOWLEDGE

More than ten years ago we published *Global Diversity: Winning Customers and Engaging Employees within World Markets.* In that book, we pointed out that it is essential to view diversity through a local lens, exploring this topic in eight countries: China, India, Egypt, Mexico, Japan, Russia, the U.K., and the U.S. Organizations had been reporting that their attempts to roll out global inclusion initiatives were falling flat or generating unanticipated resistance. The primary reason for such failures was that they were based on headquarters' perspectives and experiences, and the concepts and practices they conveyed often did not resonate with local employees and their issues.

While some organizations have learned from earlier trials and are working hard to integrate the priorities of both headquarters and regional markets, others have continued to discover the hard way that imposing one set of culturally-based assumptions on employees and customers elsewhere is a dependable recipe for failure, and a violation of vital inclusion principles. Even when an initiative is supported with the best of intentions, negative outcomes are especially likely when it is deeply rooted in the original home country's distinctive history and business environment. This can occur whether the initiative's focus is gender, race & ethnicity, age, sexual orientation, unconscious bias, team performance, developing future leaders, or another aspect of a company's diversity and inclusion agenda.

More successful efforts usually highlight a short list of core principles while at the same time leaving room for adaptation and interpretation based on local circumstances. Beyond national cultural orientations, it is essential to understand "cultures within cultures," or the astonishing diversity that exists within each country as well.

Clifford Geertz, renowned for his meticulous anthropological field work and his respect for the cultures he encountered, emphasized the value of "thick description"—that is, knowing a place well enough to grasp how people understand themselves and their own world. He asserts:

> The next necessary thing…is neither the construction of a universal Esperanto-like culture…nor the invention of some vast technology of human management. It is to enlarge the possibility of intelligible discourse between people quite different from one another in interest, outlook, wealth, and power, and yet contained in a world where tumbled as they are into endless connection, it is increasingly difficult to get out of each other's way.[5]

Geertz's observation is important for practical businesspeople as well as for academicians to consider: **ongoing discourse to increase our knowledge of one another is essential**.

For better or worse, the world's cultures appear to be diverging in some respects, just as they may be converging in others. If anything, for example, global trends toward democratic government and science-based reasoning once thought to be inexorable have slowed or even reversed. Mutually hostile autocracies, defined along ethnic and tribal lines, now commonly claim to have characteristics that make them superior to their neighbors.

Meanwhile, fundamentalism, blossoming under a variety of lethal banners, looks to literal interpretations of sacred texts rather than to science for policy guidelines.

4. COMPLIANCE CHALLENGES (AGAIN)

Progress in blending global inclusion principles with local knowledge has been accompanied by a renewed emphasis on compliance challenges. Many of these have come as a painful surprise even to global firms proud of their brands and their prior image as progressive employers. Inclusion experts once predicted an enlightened advance from legal compliance efforts to more sophisticated organizational processes designed to leverage diversity for product innovation, employee engagement, or new market entry. However, with heightening political polarization in many locations concerning hot-button issues such as terrorism, immigration, and gaps between rich and poor—often fueled by inflammatory rhetoric—compliance has become, if anything, more important than ever.

For example, major commercial and academic institutions in the U.S., including Uber, Google, and Harvard University, have been hit with charges of discrimination based on race, gender, or political views, taking them back to basic compliance measures such as conducting mandatory training and establishing standard grievance processes. Accusations of sexual harassment are reported regularly in the news. Corporate leaders have discovered that workplace actions or even tweets of individual employees or

of CEOs themselves can quickly go viral and spark legal and public relations firestorms that incur enormous costs.[6]

Compliance requirements have continued to be a corporate priority for other reasons as well. A number of European countries, including Norway, France, Germany, Spain, Italy, and the Netherlands, have mandated quotas for public companies to have a minimum representation of women on their boards—companies that fail to comply with these quotas risk penalties such as the nullification of existing boards. Meanwhile, strict European privacy laws have set off a new compliance scramble by companies worldwide that do business with European counterparts and customers. Google has already been fined $57 million by France's data protection agency for alleged failure to comply with the EU's General Data Protection Regulation (GDPR).[7]

In addition to avoiding discrimination against individuals or groups based on specific characteristics, now organizations in Europe must comply with procedures to protect the privacy of their unique data and individual preferences expressed online. Inclusiveness in the form of personal data collection through surveys or other means may be defined as intrusive, and it is necessary for internet service providers to preserve a clear and simple right to "opt out."

So, at the same time that inclusion has become a much more universal topic, with global initiatives now being driven by companies based in the EMEA and Asia Pacific regions as well as in North America, results have been mixed. "Two steps forward and one step back" and the legal equivalent of "whack-a-mole" seem to be common patterns for companies that seek to move beyond focusing primarily on compliance.

5. COMPETITIVE ADVANTAGE

Some early approaches to "diversity" involved keeping the topic in a corner removed from the real business while checking compliance boxes provided by corporate counsel and thereby limiting exposure to risk. This approach has turned out to be inadequate even for risk mitigation. Simplistic approaches such as just hiring more people from underrepresented backgrounds have also proved inadequate: "Having people from various identity groups 'at the table' is no guarantee that anything will get better;

in fact, research shows that things often get worse, because increasing diversity can increase tensions and conflict."[8]

There is an expanding body of evidence for the competitive advantages of work environments that are both diverse and inclusive. Claims regarding the business benefits of inclusion are still challenged and have many silent doubters: "How is an inclusion initiative going to help me meet my sales goals?" The research data connecting diversity and inclusion with significant business benefits do generally demonstrate correlation rather than direct causality, but this evidence continues to accumulate.

Against a background of rapid, unprecedented change on a global scale fueled by demographic shifts, inclusiveness is now more likely to be a requirement for continued relevance in many industries. No matter where a company is headquartered, promising growth market opportunities are often situated in distant and relatively unfamiliar places. McKinsey predicts that as the center of the global economy continues to shift, nearly half of Fortune 500 companies will be headquartered in emerging markets by 2025—up from just 5 percent in 2000.[9]

Specific benefits linked with diversity and inclusion in various studies are innovation, success in growth markets, better business outcomes, and the acquisition and retention of top talent worldwide. Such positive outcomes are best achieved through targeted inclusive actions that build a climate of trust and mutual learning, while harnessing the forces of "divergence" and "convergence" in diverse workplaces. Here are sample statistics that support the business case for both diversity and inclusion:

THE BUSINESS CASE: SAMPLE STATISTICS

- Companies with above-average diversity on their management teams reported innovation revenue that was 19 percentage points higher and EBIT margins that were 9% higher than companies with below-average leadership diversity.[10]

- Employees of firms with diverse leadership teams are 45% more likely to report a growth in market share over the previous year, and 70% likelier to report that the firm captured a new market.[11]

- Inclusion is tied to a 17% increase in team performance, a 20% increase in decision-making quality, and a 29% increase in team collaboration.

- Organizations with inclusive work cultures are twice as likely to exceed their financial targets and six times more likely to be innovative.[12]

- Companies with ethnically diverse leadership teams are 33% more likely to outperform their competitors.[13]

- Two-thirds of job seekers consider a company's diversity when making decisions about where to work.[14]

- Employees at companies with high levels of both diversity and inclusion report a 12% higher level of discretionary effort, and a 19% higher level of intent to stay with their current organization (discretionary effort and retention are the two primary indicators of employee engagement); they also report significantly greater team collaboration and commitment.[15]

- Women will control 75% of discretionary spending worldwide by 2028.[16]

Leaders still not persuaded by such research will probably see the wisdom in avoiding the expensive compliance disasters mentioned previously; in fact, this is a topic of quiet discussion in many boardrooms. Costs of settlements and legal defense fees for a single incident—not to mention the distractions that crisis management poses for those who should be running the enterprise—can easily run into tens of millions of dollars, and other expenses may be incurred through boycotts, mandatory training, government-imposed fines, damage to brand reputation, and so on.

Charges of anti-Semitism, anti-gay bias, discrimination based on race, or inequitable treatment of new fathers have been made in recent years against companies and industries as disparate as Delta Airlines, the Italian pasta maker Barilla, the Al Jazeera news network, and Estée Lauder, the French cosmetics giant. Many organizations have dozens if not hundreds of such pending claims that they are facing simultaneously, with costly in-house legal staff and/or external counsel (billing in 15-minute increments) dedicated to defending them.

After a single alleged racial discrimination incident in a Philadelphia store, for instance, Starbucks lost an estimated $12 million in sales when it shut down all of its U.S. stores for an afternoon to put 175,000 employees through racial-bias training. The full cost of this incident was probably double or triple the reported sales loss if other expenses are tallied: legal counsel, public relations, training delivery, employee wages, and the confidential settlement payment made to the plaintiffs. In a separate event, an engineer formerly employed at Lockheed Martin charged the company with age discrimination after he was laid off at age 66, and was awarded a $51 million settlement.

Regulatory sanctions or class-action suits can be even more expensive than the costs for a specific event, and some lead to public charges against executives. Possible compliance issues vary from country to country; they may be based on strict labor and union rules as well as laws that forbid discrimination against protected classes. Some governments make a practice of cracking down on relatively minor violations by foreign companies as an example to domestic firms and also to give their local players a bit of an edge—all the more reason to proactively avert legal or regulatory claims by creating an inclusive organizational culture in addition to following the letter of the law.

6. COMMITMENT TO EQUITY

In the wake of the Black Lives Matter movement and related cross-border efforts, there is a more intense focus on the obligations of major organizations to serve causes such as equity and social justice regardless of the direct business benefits. Intensive social discourse is sparking calls for systemic change, and many companies as well as other institutions are now responding because making a significant commitment to equity is seen as the right thing to do.

Yet there are many different definitions of equity, both implicit and explicit, and people holding different definitions often find themselves at odds with each other. Such confusion can lead to initiatives that lack widespread buy-in and encounter unexpected backlash. Cross-border initiatives may encounter employees who know the dictionary definition of equity as "fairness," but are unsure of its implications in a corporate context. Here is a spectrum of contrasting definitions that range from providing *equal opportunities* to achieving *equal outcomes*:

Figure 2.1: Equity: Opportunities or Outcomes

- **Hiring**: Some organizations focus on equal opportunity employment, seeking out candidates from underrepresented sections of society to bring their talents into the workforce. A point of view expressed by many executives is that "If we hire for diversity, we are inclusive." Equitable hiring practices can be one important step for fostering greater inclusivity, although they must usually be augmented by other measures such as exploring new recruiting channels or rewording job postings.

- **Access**: Another approach to equity is to focus on what happens after new employees are hired—whether they have fair access to developmental opportunities. Are some individuals getting more developmental feedback from their managers than others? Does everyone have meaningful opportunities to succeed, or is there an uneven approach to making opportunities and resources available to rising talent? Is the performance management system calibrated to recognize a broad range of skills and abilities? Does the promotion pipeline tend to weed out people who are different from corporate norms?

- **Support**: At various junctures in their career paths, employees from backgrounds that are not present in the current leadership group may need additional forms of support in order to make progress. Whether their minority status is based, for example, on race, ethnicity, nationality, gender, or a combination of such factors, an organization is more likely to retain minority talent and best leverage individual capabilities by offering timely coaching, mentoring, or sponsorship. Particularly when there are few role models with similar backgrounds in the executive suite, it can be helpful for minority employees to learn from leaders who have "been there and done that." Visibility and relationships within informal social networks are also important, and mentors or sponsors can often open doors for their protégés to receive recognition and fresh opportunities.

EQUITY: A GASTRONOMIC DEFINITION

Matthais, a French manager struggling with how to understand and apply the concept of equity in his organization, offered an analogy which falls in the category of "support":

> *If I want to order food for the people in my office, I can't just ask for 10 pizzas. I have to take into account different dietary requirements – vegetarian, no pork, etc. – as well as eating customs. There may even be employees who are fasting for religious reasons, for example, or who just don't like pizza.*
>
> *Equity means I have to find different ways to support each person with their roles and responsibilities by learning what will work best for them. It is difficult to know exactly what to do, but I am trying to create the right menu.*

- **Targets**: Many organizations are now setting specific targets that could include hiring, retention, engagement, and promotion of underrepresented employees. For instance, if an organization is aiming to develop a leadership pipeline that is comprised equally of men and women, but their workforce is comprised primarily of men, they will need to implement measures focused on attracting, retaining, and developing women. A common challenge is to set goals that are both ambitious and realistic based on the available talent pipeline and the performance of industry peers.

- **Compliance**: There are various approaches worldwide to implementing regulatory and/or corporate mandates. A number of countries (e.g., South Africa, Malaysia, Nigeria, India, Canada), as well as companies, have established affirmative action requirements in areas such as education, hiring, promotion, equity ownership, procurement, government jobs, or board composition. Such requirements are typically in place as a means of including people who have been historically marginalized, with the intention of creating a workplace that is more reflective of the general population. These measures can be seen as controversial and have been criticized by some as undermining merit-based standards. Detractors cite negative consequences for employers as well as for employees who are either promoted or left behind by overly rigid requirements. Several related questions are part of ongoing compliance discussions in many organizations:

  - Do we establish a pool of candidates who are "qualified" and then select from this pool, or look for the "best" candidate, especially if this latter criterion is influenced by fit with the current culture and the status quo?

  - Is our approach to equity simply meeting a requirement—"As soon as we hire them, we've succeeded"—or is it to continue looking for areas of growth where there is an opening for a person with the right experience and ties to a new market?

  - What is our message to other employees who are not addressed by a given requirement? They might think, "I no longer have a chance here regardless of my performance because others will be favored." Or they could say, "We're committed to building an inclusive organization, and my day may come tomorrow if I continue to perform well." How can we convey the intent of new policies in a way that is accurate and does not produce unintended consequences?

Leaders now under pressure to make a commitment to greater equity must consider what to prioritize and where to invest limited resources—"What is our 'why' for equity, what are we trying to achieve, and how are we going to get there?". Depending on a company's unique characteristics, they may choose to focus on one or more of the forms of equity listed above. Achieving clarity and alignment about the type of equity that fits one's own organization provides the best starting point for practical action.

The six trends described in this chapter are prodding many organizations to step up their inclusion efforts. Whether these efforts are driven, for example, by the promise of better business results, required as a risk mitigation strategy, or implemented as part of a renewed commitment to equity and social justice, the value of strategically-crafted inclusion initiatives has become increasingly compelling. They influence an organization's ability to compete in the global marketplace and can also have an immensely positive impact on the lives and careers of people who were previously excluded, underutilized, or lost to other employers.

Figure 2.2: Inclusion Trends

03.

Inclusive Leadership: Dealing with Difference

Trendy forms of "micro-," "bite-sized," or even "snack-sized" learning... offer carefully curated yet ultimately minor insights.

How can we deal with differences without increasing mutual grievances among employees?

Inclusive leadership has increasingly come to blend issues previously considered to be either "cross-cultural" or aspects of "domestic diversity." Proponents and practitioners of this fused brand of inclusive leadership development have expressed fresh concerns about the potential hazards of overexposure to differences. Is examination of the full plethora of cultural, racial, ethnic, regional, linguistic, cognitive, generational, and other differences within a diverse multicultural work environment more likely to lead to understanding and alignment—or fuel a heightened sense of separation and grievance?

Learning modalities that produce a sense of mild discomfort, followed by a quick reintegration to consolidate key learnings and restore comfort, comprise a classic instructional methodology. However, diverse groups can be explosive if "discomfort" ignites anger or resentment. Comments from program participants such as, "You will never understand my life experience," or "I feel like I'm being blamed for something I didn't do" are the bane of facilitators, and may escalate into serious conflicts if not expertly handled.

Better to highlight common organizational objectives and set aside differences, some would say, including both educators and practitioners informed by neuroscience. They advocate making learners a bit uncomfortable, so their brains are stimulated to make new neural connections and to retain what they have learned, but prefer not to take people very far out of their comfort zones, often finding solace in the dubious proposition that differences around the world are gradually melting away amidst the global deluge of social media.

It is better to focus on what we have in common.

Cultures are converging in the digital age.

However, such a cautious approach is insufficient to cultivate leaders who are mature, seasoned, and steeped in global experience. The doctrine of safe and cheerful incrementalism focuses on common goals, shared language, and experiences of mild to moderate discomfort—such techniques are all useful in building awareness and skills for everyday use. Yet this approach brings with it risks of its own. If relied upon too much, it can result in papering over real differences, muffling important voices that seek to be heard in languages of their own, and shaping leaders who are oblivious to the rigors and potential rewards of life on the remote edges of their organizations.

"I want our leaders to have a real experience of what it is like to be excluded," some learning professionals say, and their instincts are well-founded. Both research and practical experience confirm the value of "crucible" experiences that take leaders through the fire of intense trials to forge new and creative approaches to their work. Learning journeys that include mild unease and incremental learning can be part of this approach, but are normally insufficient to produce profound personal transformation unless they also involve rigorous, gut-wrenching experiences.

DIFFERENCES THAT DIVIDE

In the expanding world of training on diversity and inclusion, now often mandated by companies and even governments, there are many ways to alienate participants rather than to facilitate meaningful conversation and mutual learning. In addition to the involuntary aspect of certain programs that is off-putting from the start, terminology that may make sense in the abstract can be perceived as offensive by some would-be learners.

Every human society has forms of privilege along with those who are excluded from the inner circle of power. The term, "white privilege," for example, points to the fact that in countries such as the U.S., skin color shapes access to lifetime opportunities as well as basic physical security— references to the faux crime of "driving while black" symbolize the extra police scrutiny and fear experienced by many black people even while pursuing lawful everyday activities.

Corporate employees who have benefitted from privileges of one form or another are often willing to acknowledge this and to address historical wrongs that have resulted from social pathologies such as racism and discrimination. However, they may respond quite differently to the suggestion that they are in their current roles based on unearned advantages.[1] Training methods perceived to involve "blaming and shaming," compelling participants to respond in a certain way to acknowledge and make amends for their privileges, often backfire by producing overt or covert forms of resistance.

Broad concepts such as white privilege appear less monolithic when individuals reflect on or share their own life stories: "I was born with a speech handicap"; "My father died when I was seven years old"; "After my mother lost her job, we had nothing"; "As the only woman in my department, I've had to work twice as hard as others to get promoted"; "I became addicted to pain medicine"; "I come from a multicultural background."

Few people who have been in their jobs for several years or more, especially if they have begun to take on leadership roles, feel that their roles and responsibilities, let alone their salaries, are unearned. "I have worked very hard to get where I am," most people would insist. Even leaders born with the proverbial silver spoon in their mouths tend to develop impervious rationales for why they have earned their places in the organizational hierarchy. Perceived questioning of a person's work ethic and accomplishments is more likely to produce resistance and even rage rather than an open mind and heart.

Likewise, "targets" for the hiring and promotion of minorities and women sometimes begin to sound like quotas—which are, in fact, legal requirements in some countries—and engender a sense of unfairness. Correcting a historical imbalance doesn't necessarily feel right in the present moment to employees who believe that they have been or will be passed over in favor of others who appear to be less qualified, although this may be absolutely justified in the eyes of those who want to build a more equitable future.

As pointed out in Chapter 2, there is also an increasing sense of unconscious bias fatigue in many organizations. The list of potential biases, now well over a hundred and continuing to grow, seems elusive and impossible to master. These biases are by definition unconscious to begin with; dealing with subtle biases is like the legendary task of Sisyphus to roll a rock uphill only to have it come rolling down again. How can leaders possibly remember a functional list of biases, let alone apply them in their daily work? Who wants to be blamed and yet feel that there is no way to emerge from a cycle of attempted redress and recurring complaints?

At worst, a clumsy focus on differences creates a shared climate of hypersensitivity and drives groups of people apart with a heightened sense of mutual injustice. These tribal divisions can be reinforced by stereotypes and labels that paint the other tribe with broad, threatening brushstrokes. Far from finding common organizational goals, the new focus becomes payback to right supposed wrongs, and a conviction that the others will never "get it." Sociopolitical factors may spark combustible resentments within various groups, with extreme political viewpoints and social commentary providing the tinder for heated emotional exchanges and little real listening.

THE BREAK ROOM: COFFEE CLASH

In the office break room two employees were discussing recent news over coffee. They shared the same political views and were nodding in agreement with each other. Another employee wandered in and overheard their conversation. After listening quietly for a couple of minutes he began to question the two colleagues sitting at the table, and a difference of opinion quickly emerged.

As the conversation continued, the tone started to become more heated. A fourth person entered the room, and she began to challenge the first two as well. It became clear that the four people in the room had voted for different political candidates and were receiving their news from different, conflicting sources. There were racial and ethnic differences in the group as well. In fact, there was little that the members of this group had in common besides working for the same organization in the same location and taking a break at the same time.

Referring to the gaps between them, one person said in frustration, "You just don't get it, and I'm not sure you ever will." The person to whom the comment was directed replied, "I don't think you understand me very well either," resulting in a very uncomfortable standoff.

> *After a pause, the last person to enter the room commented, "It's a free country. We don't have to agree, or to embrace everything about each other all the time. Don't we just want to create a place where we can all do our best to contribute?" With this statement the atmosphere of the room shifted. What had seemed like a long and potentially dangerous conversation only lasted for ten minutes, and everyone soon headed back to work, but a residue of mutual antagonism remained.*

Figure 3.1: "You don't get it."

DIFFERENCES THAT STRENGTHEN

So why encourage open exploration of real differences when this could lead to trouble? Why not simply avoid differences or at most consider them only in small, safe doses if they can take us down a dark and divisive path? What is it about experiencing difference that is so crucial for aspiring leaders?

Although exposure to difference is challenging and potentially hazardous, the most successful global leaders frequently report that their "fish out of water" experience in a new country, business, or function—and the struggles and failures that came along with it—was their most formative career phase. Research from multiple sources corroborates this assertion, highlighting the effects of such experiences in shaping key leadership capabilities.

The Corporate Executive Board (CEB), for instance, in one of the largest empirical studies ever carried out on the topic of global leadership development, with more than 11,000 survey respondents across many companies and industries, concludes that passage through demanding "crucible" experiences is closely correlated with the ability of leaders to exert the critical skill of influence. They recommend that "organizations should focus on providing leaders with development experiences that push them outside of their comfort zones and in unfamiliar environments."

Such experiences include tackling new roles outside of one's functional area of expertise, working in a new market, or running a new business. They can also consist of leading the turnaround of an underperforming project or team or managing a critical project on a fast cycle. The most effective leadership development experiences of all, according to the CEB study, are "crucible experiences that occur in an international context."[2]

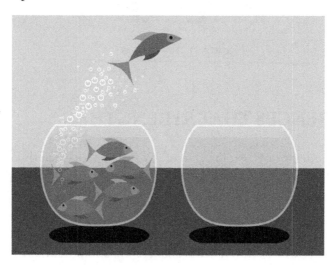

Figure 3.2: "Fish out of water."

In a similar vein, INSEAD researcher William Maddux has found a strong link between living abroad and increased creativity. Study participants who had lived abroad scored significantly higher on an established test of creativity than did others without this experience, and the longer people had lived abroad, the higher they scored. Shorter-term travel abroad did not produce the same effect:

> The more people had adapted while they were abroad, the more creative they were… Not only does the time matter, which can explain why living abroad matters and not traveling abroad, but also the psychological transformation that you might go through while you are abroad.

Furthermore, Maddux notes, even "priming" participants to remember their fish-out-of-water experiences in other countries led to more creative responses than when participants were not primed in the same way. He cites a similarly significant correlation between time spent living abroad and entrepreneurial activity. Building barriers between cultures, he concludes, could stifle innovation.[3]

Crucible experiences, although they can be more or less effectively supported, are not consistently pleasant or contained. Some careers do not survive or are sidetracked by this experience, and family solidarity is often tested. According to seasoned leaders, the underlying reason why a crucible of some kind was so vital to their development is that it forced them to make a wrenching reassessment of previous patterns of success that turned out to be dysfunctional in their new environment. Proud and previously successful people taste real failure, perhaps for the first time in their lives, learn humility, and scramble to understand their new context and how to become effective in it. They must make new personal connections, ask for help, question fundamental assumptions, and try novel strategies and tactics. "Fall down seven times and get up eight" is an expression for the resilience that such leaders discover and come to value along the way. Through experiencing adversity, they also learn to empathize with others who are going through struggles of their own, including colleagues from very different walks of life.

These difficult and even excruciating lessons are unlikely to occur through other increasingly trendy forms of "micro-," "bite-sized," or even "snack-sized" learning, which offer carefully curated yet ultimately minor insights. By way of contrast, one former expatriate reported, "My whole team in our Bangkok office quit within my first six months as their leader because they could not accept my more direct, aggressive, and results-oriented leadership style." This was a riveting crisis that challenged his sense of competence and personal efficacy, and the leader who went through this painful process wound up hiring a new team, altered his style to become more effective at managing and coaching employees in his new context, and now heads up a major function back at headquarters for a Fortune 100 company. "The most effective managers often suffer the most severe culture shock," notes Nancy Adler, one of the most respected scholars of expatriate effectiveness.[4]

In addition to a large body of empirical research, myths and legends from various cultural settings tell us that great leaders gain wisdom and courage by embarking on journeys, encountering many obstacles, and ultimately facing existential, fire-breathing threats. No mythical hero slays a tame, carefully curated dragon. Sacred texts from many traditions share similar lessons. The patriarch Moses, who is recognized by Judaism, Christianity, and Islam, lived through a lengthy exile in Egypt before starting the journey back to the Promised Land. He named his son Gershom, sometimes translated as "exile," commemorating the experience of being a "stranger in a strange land."[5] Moses became a stronger and more capable leader through the trials he encountered during a life in exile.

Figure 3.3: The Crucible Experience

DISTILLING DIFFERENCE

The choice doesn't have to be between a flight to safe (but narrow) common ground or encounters with differences that heighten conflicts and divisions. As the Corporate Executive Board study suggests, a crucible experience can take on a variety of forms, and it is not essential to send every employee on a lengthy assignment abroad for them to encounter and learn from real differences.

Warren Bennis defines this experience as "a trial and a test, a point of deep self-reflection that forced (leaders) to question who they were and what mattered to them." He affirms that crucibles appear in numerous forms, noting that these may involve encounters with prejudice at home or abroad, working with a demanding mentor, or handling a crisis.[6]

Targeted career growth experiences could thus include moves to different functions, business units, or particularly challenging projects. The mythical journeys upon which heroes used to embark are also now available down the hallways or in the virtual meeting spaces of many domestic organizations, which hold myriad people and voices from around the world. These can be a rich source of new experiences and perspectives for individuals who seek to learn.

Home is Not Homogeneous

Exclusion is a universal human phenomenon, and there are likely to be those in our everyday environments who are confronting this experience firsthand.

FEEDBACK FOR LATISHA

Latisha is in her first year on the job in the marketing department at a major U.S. manufacturing firm. She entered as a mid-career hire, having specialized in marketing in school and at her previous company. She likes her current employer and has been working hard to continue building her professional career, but has been frustrated by the lack of feedback from her manager thus far. Her manager seems to spend a lot more time talking and laughing with other team members, and Latisha has also heard her making comments and offering advice to them on their reports and presentations.

Inspired by a recent "Growth Mindset" training event put on by her company that encouraged employees to reach out and request feedback, Latisha decided to ask directly for the feedback that she hadn't been receiving. Normally a shy person, she mustered the courage to ask her manager: "Do you have any feedback for me? I'd really like to know what I can do better." After a few seconds of reflection, her manager responded, "Well, one thing you could do is to smile more. You need to make the people around you feel more comfortable."

Latisha was amazed and disappointed by this response, as it seemed so far from her own self-image. Her mind was full of thoughts that she didn't want to say out loud to her manager for fear of putting a good job at risk. "Oh, so just because I'm trying to put on a serious professional face at work, you're afraid of some angry black woman stereotype that you have in your mind and you want me to smile more? Don't you know that my name actually means 'joy'? What about some concrete feedback on the quality of my work or the ideas I've been raising at meetings? I've already been feeling like I can't bring my whole best self to work, and now you're telling me to paste on a pretty smile? If you're uncomfortable with me, is that my responsibility or yours? My family and friends, who have always worked in blue collar jobs, say that they hardly recognize me when I dress up for work, and now you tell me that you're not comfortable with me here on the job! I feel like I'm not black enough for my family, and not white enough to be working here. Where does that leave me?"

Latisha's manager may never hear her unvoiced thoughts, and perhaps she would be disappointed but also a bit relieved if Latisha leaves for another job. But what if she did get to know Latisha better and learn to understand her background, her concerns, her

Why leave behind the seat that exists in your home and go aimlessly off to the dusty realms of other lands?[7]

challenges, and her potential? Wouldn't this be stepping into a different world for her as well? Not only could Latisha benefit from feedback that would actually help her to improve her performance on the job, but the manager could overcome stereotypical images and unfounded fears that may be influencing her own perceptions while learning to work more effectively with a valuable employee. There are dragons for this team leader to slay in her own mind, and she doesn't need to journey far to encounter them.

Accelerated Learning

While crucible career experiences are not guaranteed to be safe, and there are bound to be casualties along the way, the insights they produce are life-changing rather than tepid, and the leaders who emerge are far better prepared to tackle today's swirling VUCA forces: volatility, uncertainty, change, and ambiguity.

Crucible experiences, along with structured learning and development, can all be supported to produce positive results at an accelerated pace with the help of skilled managers, facilitators, coaches, and mentors. Here are some common principles:

- Use tools and techniques to encourage and reinforce **self-awareness** of one's psychological and cultural background.

- Equip the learner with **baseline skills** for reserving judgment and engaging in proactive inquiry when encountering unexpected differences.

- Provide periodic opportunities for structured **orientation, reflection, and course correction**.

- Enable **network-building** among learners going through similar experiences who can share key learnings with each other and provide mutual assistance.

- Bring learners into contact with mentors and coaches who help them make sense of their experiences and **support experimentation** with new approaches.

Structured learning programs augment on-the-job encounters with difference by offering exposure to a diverse mix of people and ideas. They ideally feature a wide array of viewpoints from less well-known parts of the organization, balance participation so that it doesn't favor either the most fluent or the most strident, and introduce simple, reliable frameworks for explaining differences and helping leaders to understand "the why behind the behavior." Such programs can also enable people to move beyond readily visible differences to discover unexpected similarities—for instance, a common military background, children of identical ages, or previous experience in the same country—which foster trust in a way that is less feasible if differences are ignored or downplayed. Action learning that focuses on identifying and resolving practical issues also generates common ground for participants through shared trials and joint problem-solving. Inviting organizational leaders to recount their own developmental journeys lets others know that it is okay to struggle while facing severe trials, reassuring them that they are not alone.

Cultural Competence

The underlying framework for such learning is straightforward, moving from self-awareness to knowledge about others to techniques for building bridges in practical ways. This is, in fact, the core definition of "cultural competence," and it applies to crucible experiences both at home and abroad.

Know yourself	Know others	Know how to bridge differences and build on similarities

Figure 3.4: Cultural Competence: Three Steps[8]

Hannah de Zwaan from the Netherlands learned these lessons the hard way after moving to the Czech Republic and taking on a factory general manager role there.

HANNAH THE FACTORY MANAGER

Hannah describes her original leadership style as "very much engaging in open, democratic discussion and involving staff in decisions." She soon discovered, however, that, "You need to be able to step outside yourself and get into the other person's head. Your way of doing things is just one of many... Where I came from, people want to be informed about everything, but when I was in the Czech Republic, at first I really over-informed employees and they were bored, sleeping through meetings. I was used to democratic management, but this did not work at all in the Czech Republic.

The most difficult task was being responsible for eighty blue-collar workers who spoke no English. At the beginning I had a warehouse manager, but he left and then I had no one, so I needed to deal with employees myself. I had to go out on the warehouse floor, take a box, show exactly how to pack it, and tell them to finish by 3:00 P.M. It felt like being in the army to be giving such specific directions. They immediately respected me and did what they were told to do. Because of the cultural differences I had to change my leadership style and become stricter, more directive, and provide clearer deadlines." As time went on, Hannah also discovered that she had to differentiate between working with her production manager and with local blue-collar workers, becoming more or less directive in her leadership approach. "You have to be able to switch as needed to get results."

Many aspects of Hannah's leadership role were not easy, including her dealings with vendors outside the company. "I was the first woman general manager. I had to deal with the manager of a local company who was not cooperating. He saw me as a naïve female, and tried to slow things down and give me an unfair price. You have to be tough and not just accept people trying to fool or cheat you." She also struggled with the Czech language. "I ended up speaking a mixture of Czech and English to communicate. I tried to learn Czech, but it is a very difficult language. So I learned what I could and used it, and they respected me for this."

Hannah eventually found herself sharing her hard- won understanding of both sides of the cross- border interaction. "I had a lot of colleagues from headquarters come down to deliver training in the Czech Republic. They kept saying that Czech people are so different, but I would respond, "From their standpoint, you are very different. You are in their country so you are the one who is different."

Hannah developed great affection and respect for her local colleagues. "I learned a few lessons about Czech culture and history. This helped me to understand the reasons for why they are the way they are. The lack of initiative, for example, is linked to the communist period in their history. This is how you had to act to survive." As her own understanding and ability to adapt to local circumstances deepened, she found that a significant part of her job became managing others' expectations. "A lot of my time was used in setting the right expectations of people in other parts of the company, including headquarters. It is difficult for them to imagine what it is like, what is possible, what the price levels are, how the culture works. Being a bridge-builder and aligning expectations took a lot of time."

CRUCIBLE LEARNING: THE IMPACT

Hannah's journey from self-awareness to understanding her colleagues to bridge-building not only made her a far more effective expatriate factory manager, but it also gave her hard-won leadership lessons that have stayed with her. She is now running a diverse multicultural team at headquarters.

After moving back to the Netherlands, she was put in charge of a team that included six managers, all of different nationalities. Hannah notes, "I felt that it was so easy to get to know them, to start a dialogue and engage in small talk because I can easily imagine how they feel being here, what kind of problems they have being new to this country and not knowing the language. I can put myself in their place. I have more empathy." Her frame of reference, or perspective, as a leader has broadened, and she has become flexible enough to devise solutions for business problems by leveraging more than one perspective. "Sometimes I look at issues from the Czech point of view now."[9]

Other types of crucible experiences produce similar learnings, whether the distance between participants is defined by national borders or the gap between the assumptions and expectations of people from different backgrounds within the same country. For example, managers in the Czech Republic today, both expatriates and locals, note that they must respond to motivational differences between different generations if they are running a multi-generational team. These differences have been most strongly shaped by pre- and post-communist environments, depending on whether people were born before or after a communist-era baby boom that lasted until the early 1980s. Workers born in the communist period generally tend to be more risk-averse, hierarchical, and comfortable with structure, while younger workers who have grown up in a very different environment are more adventurous and entrepreneurial than the previous generation.[10] So a Prague- based project manager may need to ignore assumptions from elsewhere about the characteristics of "Gen X" or "Gen Y," as well as lessons acquired from handling the prior generation of workers, and learn how to build employee engagement and performance with younger employees in local terms.

Those who go through crucible experiences of one kind or another report, like Hannah de Zwaan, that they must become clearer about their own background and assumptions, learn more about the people in front of them—including their individual personalities and predilections—and find ways to build ties of mutual understanding, trust, and practical action. Through the journey from self-awareness to other-awareness to bridge-builder, such experiences tend to foster several key capabilities that underlie inclusive leadership.

- **Empathy**: sensing the emotions of others, including reactions to exclusion
- **Perspective**: taking a broad and objective view of self and others
- **Flexibility**: altering behavioral patterns that are exclusionary and ineffective

Such critical leadership lessons are not easily spoon-fed or doled out as pre-packaged insights that can be weighed and measured, meanwhile shielding the learner from frontal exposure to real differences. They must be deeply learned and felt. Once absorbed, however, they often become enduring characteristics of successful leaders.

ADDRESSING UNEARNED DISADVANTAGES

Differences are generally most volatile when they intersect with access to power. For example, people who are members of minority racial or ethnic groups, non-native speakers of the organization's primary language, or female employees in a setting where women executives are few in number face many disadvantages.

SHAUN'S NEW OFFICE

Shaun, a middle-aged black manager, was promoted from his job in the R&D lab to a new executive role, with an office on the top floor of the headquarters building. He was the first and only black employee in his company's history to work at this level, both in terms of his rank and his location on the building's famous "14th floor," where important decisions were made regularly affecting company operations worldwide.

During Shaun's first week in the new role, a steady stream of people arrived from other floors via the elevator doors near his office, but nobody who was walking by stopped in to say hello or to offer congratulations. Shaun found this puzzling and a bit hurtful. Although he had worked hard for this promotion and believed that he deserved it, he also still felt himself to be a temporary resident in his new office with a fine view of the city, and wondered if he really belonged. Shaun was accustomed to working in a much smaller cubicle, and had moved into the 14th floor office with just a mobile phone—no pictures or

> *other decorations—until he showed his new office to his mother during a phone call with her, and she took the initiative to send him a large office plant to help him feel more at home.*
>
> *It turned out that most of the employees who were passing by Shaun's office thought he was probably from the IT department or maintenance services. They assumed that he was making arrangements for another person to move in who would look like a bonafide top executive. Until Shaun was formally introduced at an executive meeting the following week, many of his fellow executive team members on the same floor had been thinking the same thing.*

Shaun's example demonstrates a relatively benign form of bias in comparison with more deliberate or vindictive ones. Nonetheless, a person whom others literally cannot imagine as an executive faces built-in disadvantages, including basic skepticism about their suitability for such a role. Shaun is gradually adjusting to his new job thanks to enthusiastic sponsorship by the company's CEO, who knows his track record well and has since positioned him carefully within the executive team. Nonetheless, the jury is still out on whether the other 14th floor residents will fully embrace and extend the transformation that he represents.

Exclusion is not just an objective outcome of workplace interactions. It can also become internalized in the minds and hearts of people who have experienced its effects:

 ## STAY IN THE CAR

> *Two very young African-American girls had an aunt who did domestic work for a white family. Periodically the aunt would drive to her employer's home to pick up her paycheck. One of the girls, who had lighter complexion and straighter hair, was usually invited by the aunt to enter the house, while the other girl was told, "you stay in the car."*

We can only imagine how the girl with the darker skin tone and curly hair felt about this, and how it affected her feelings about herself and her cousin. Such experiences based on what we now call "colorism" or "hairism" can affect people for their whole lives.

In an earlier era, the African-American community had ways of differentiating skin color that influenced the attitudes of people I grew up with. These included the "brown paper bag test" (whether your skin was lighter or darker than a brown paper bag) or the "blue vein test" (the blood veins of lighter-skinned individuals appeared to be blue rather than darker).

Those with darker skin color who failed to pass such tests were denied entrance into some African-American social clubs, fraternities and sororities, or even churches, not to mention being treated differently by other family members in ways that persist today. And black children learned the lyrics of the song by blues musician Bill Broonzy:

"If you was white, you's alright, If you was brown, you could stick around, But as you's black, hmm, hmm, brother, get back, get back, get back." [11]

While some leaders accustomed to being part of a dominant group may bristle at the notion that they are enjoying unearned advantages, many of these same people are quite willing to consider the negative impact of "unearned disadvantages." This is especially true when they learn about discrimination so pervasive that its toxic residues have become embedded in communities, families, and individual psyches.

Crucible experiences tend to engender a particularly keen appreciation for the consequences of exclusion, plus a readiness to address unearned disadvantages. The fire of a crucible role, like the one that Shaun's CEO went through for several years in a company subsidiary abroad, or the one that Shaun is now experiencing as a stranger on the 14th floor in the same building where he has worked for many years, becomes a searing, make or break growth experience for any high-potential leader. The profound and disorienting pain of separateness, of not belonging, of being a stranger who must build trusting relationships with new people in order to get things done—under these circumstances, even people without previous experiences of exclusion learn to confront it first-hand themselves and in support of others.

Those with access to institutional power and authority have a special responsibility to lead by example and to draw out the talents of colleagues who are on their own journeys. Bridge-building only works when it is practiced in concert with others, and employees closely watch those in positions of power and take their cues from them.

The empathy, perspective, and flexibility developed through crucible experiences foster a strong sense of kinship and future possibility across an organization. They are also indispensable ingredients for handling all forms of exclusion effectively, whether these are based in the past or the present. Perceptive leaders have a keen sense of an expanded present that contains both the legacy of many histories—"history is literally present in all that we do"[12]—and the potential for a better shared future.

PART TWO:
FIVE STAGES OF INCLUSION

Inclusive Behavior: Learning About Bias

Inclusive Behaviors: Building Key Skills
& Working Across Boundaries

Inclusive Behaviors: Becoming a
Champion & Getting Results

04.
Inclusive Behavior: Learning About Bias

Each of us has to extract ourselves from the box of assumptions that can keep us walled in and impervious to the ideas and capabilities of others.

Is there a concise approach to understanding and addressing unconscious bias?

Learning About Bias Building Key Skills   Working Across Boundaries   Becoming a Champion   Getting Results

Asim is a manager for a high-tech company who has been living in the U.S. for most of his adult life. He considers it his home—five years ago his employer sponsored him for a green card, which he cherishes. He is originally from India and is Muslim, although he does not practice all the tenets of the faith, such as praying five times a day.

WHO IS ASIM?

I have lived in America for fifteen years, ever since coming for graduate school, but now for the first time I am afraid. I love America and it has given me and my family many opportunities. People were so welcoming when I first came to this country, and I made wonderful friends. Maybe it's just my perception, but at work now I feel that some colleagues are looking at me in a different way and worrying that I am a terrorist, although 9/11 was many years ago. I am afraid they look at my wife and children that way too. And it has become more difficult to travel back to India to visit my parents and return—in the airport now I am often 'randomly' selected for extra questioning, and on our last trip even my wife and children were held in a room and questioned. It was humiliating. Worse yet, we have heard recently about Sikhs from India who were heckled, beaten up, or had hot coffee thrown in their face right here in California, based on the mistaken assumption that they are Muslim. The people who are attacking them do not seem to realize that they are followers of a different religion.

INCLUSIVE BEHAVIOR #1: LEARNING ABOUT BIAS

Now more than ever leaders must serve as role models for inclusive behaviors. **Inclusive leadership involves self-awareness, careful listening, outreach to people with different perspectives, and persistent, stubborn**

efforts to find common ground. It is founded on mutual respect—a consistent pattern of trustworthy behavior is also vital because trust is the basic currency of inclusion.

This is often easier inside an organization than across a whole nation, as employees of any organization ultimately share the common objectives of growing in key markets, becoming more efficient, and attracting and retaining competent and highly skilled talent. Inclusive corporate leaders build self-awareness of their own cultural backgrounds, invite unexpected information from employees and from new markets, and become catalysts for solutions that integrate diverse contributions.

Before any bridge-building can begin, however, each of us has to extract ourselves from the box of assumptions that often keeps us walled-in and impervious to the ideas and capabilities of others. "We can be blind to the obvious, and we are also blind to our blindness," notes the Nobel-Prize winning economist Daniel Kahneman.[1] Unconscious bias is a pervasive feature of the human brain, ultimately grounded in natural tendencies such as daily habits and instincts for self-preservation.

> **National or organizational cultures, which embody shared knowledge and are themselves a collective means of survival, can also support forms of bias that are hard to detect...**

Psychology and anthropology, now augmented by neuroscience and its access to functional magnetic resonance imaging (fMRI) data, have identified brain-based patterns of human behavior—"fight or flight," for instance—that are linked to survival and tend to reinforce bias. National or organizational cultures, which embody shared knowledge and are themselves a collective means of survival, can also support forms of bias that are hard to detect: "Culture hides much more than it reveals, and strangely enough what it hides, it hides most effectively from its own participants."[2]

Here are four general types of unconscious bias, with examples of how they can inhibit productive interactions among employees of the same organization. Those who learn about such biases are likely to spot them almost immediately in their own daily interactions, as they are powerful and mutually reinforcing elements of most people's lives.

| Confirmation Bias | Insider Bias | Attribution Bias | Overconfidence Bias |

Figure 4.1: Unconscious Bias: Four Types

1. Confirmation Bias

"*We see the world as we are*"—Anais Nin

Humans are creatures of habit, and much of our day is spent on autopilot, carrying out routine tasks. Our expectations are shaped by our previous life experience, and the automatic reactions we have as a result of these expectations—say, driving forward through a green traffic light with the assumption that other vehicles will remain stopped while their light is red—make it possible for us to get through each day in a way that is functional, efficient, and safe.

However, even when our expectations are based on insufficient information and/or faulty assumptions, the same mental process still tends to run in the background, "confirming" that we have seen what we expected to see. This may include the expectation that co-workers are friends or foes, competent or incompetent, suited or not suited for particular roles, or should be more or less closely managed because they are perceived as belonging to particular categories.

Because Asim is from South Asia and a Muslim, if he grows a beard, for example, other employees from different backgrounds may almost imperceptibly begin to feel that he has taken on radical beliefs because he now looks a bit more like those terrorists in the news. The real explanation may be that his wife thinks he looks better in a beard, that he finds it warmer to have facial hair during a rainy winter, or that he has taken on more responsibilities at work and is cultivating a new leadership image. Unless Asim's colleagues take the time to question their assumptions, they may find themselves avoiding him in the cafeteria or hesitating to endorse him when he is put up for promotion.

> **Recommendation**: *One way for a leader to approach confirmation bias would be to reach out to Asim—inviting him to meet instead of avoiding him—and learn more about him, asking about his interests, goals, and aspirations, just as a good manager might do with any other employee. In the process, it is important not to make Asim feel singled out for being "different," as this could make the situation worse instead of better. Learning more about Asim is likely to reshape assumptions about him based on more pertinent information, and thereby to recast daily perceptions of his actions. (Perhaps Asim is growing a beard because he lost a bet to his cousin that his favorite Bollywood star would get married this year).*

2. Insider Bias

"Beware of strangers."

For most of its history and prehistory, the human race lived in tribal units. Cities, countries, and corporations are relatively recent inventions. Our brains are wired to recognize and respond to threats to our survival and to immediately recognize subtle cues regarding whether another person is part of what we regard as our "in-group," or a dangerous "out-group."

Asim speaks English with a British accent, visits India over the holidays, and knows more about cricket than baseball. Even though he has lived in the U.S. for many years and is a legal resident, there are still aspects of his appearance that could seem "foreign" to some U.S.-born workers who have not traveled widely. In a corporate context, inclusive leaders must actively counter the deep human instinct to distinguish insiders from outsiders.

> **Recommendation:** *Widen the "in-group" by creating new markers of membership such as clothing with the company logo, team pictures, birthday celebrations, invitations to corporate events, honors and awards, and so on. It is difficult to be suspicious of a person who just received a nice award for his tenth anniversary with the organization.*

3. Attribution Bias

"Sorry I'm late. The traffic was terrible."

More than sixty years of psychological research into "attribution theory" has provided insights into the ways in which humans explain behavior and events. When there is a problem, we tend to explain our own flaws in terms of circumstances, and attribute the mistakes of others to character defects; the reverse is true when the outcomes are positive. We attribute success to the positive character attributes of ourselves or our close associates, while providing circumstantial explanations to rationalize successes of others who are seen as outsiders.

Negative Outcome: If Asim is late for a team meeting, for instance, a counterpart might leap to the critical judgment, "He is not very well organized" (character), without noticing that Asim's previous meeting ran over because the business unit director wanted to address a customer issue on the spot (circumstance).

Positive Outcome: Conversely, when Asim's project team completes its project on time and under budget, this could be attributed to a terrific set of team members (circumstance) and not to his leadership style (character).

> **Recommendation:** *Question character judgments, particularly regarding those who might not be perceived as insiders, by asking about mitigating circumstances. "Is he frequently late or was this an exception? Did he have a prior meeting?" Likewise, question whether attributions to circumstances (the team performed well because of its members) are obscuring real talents or demonstrations of character.*

4. Overconfidence Bias

*"**All the children are above average.**"*

Another enduring aspect of the human psyche is that we have greater subjective confidence in our judgments than an objective assessment would warrant. We also tend to overestimate our own performance relative to that of others. No one is exempt—generals, doctors, politicians, professors, students, and corporate leaders can all fall victim to overconfidence. So in that nine-box succession planning meeting during which a colleague confidently asserts that "Asim is a high performer, but not a high-potential," it is important to ask for more evidence. Is this assertion based on the fact that Asim has a management style that is grounded in his cultural background? How has he responded to previous opportunities for professional development? Is he more suited to a technical track than a management track? How will you know?

> **Recommendation:** *Test confident assertions, both your own and those of others, for signs that they are grounded in solid evidence. Systematically incorporate multiple perspectives and forms of evidence into processes such as succession planning to better ensure that assertions are examined from various points of view using balanced sources of data.*

For those who find mnemonics useful, the Italian word CIAO has a dual meaning. It can signify greeting or departing, hello or good-bye. Each encounter that a leader has with fellow employees can be a greeting that is open to new information and possibilities, or a hasty act of avoidance due to faulty, unexamined assumptions. Remembering and running through the first letter of each of these forms of unconscious bias—Confirmation, Insider, Attribution, and Overconfidence—is one way of building greater awareness and ensuring that neither individuals nor their organizations fall victim to such bias. Once leaders can identify their own possible sources of bias, reexamine their perceptions, and seek alternative perspectives when needed, they are then able to make informed and flexible choices.

EMPATHY: THE DOORWAY TO ACTION

Addressing unconscious bias requires genuine effort. During the course of any given day, how can a leader with positive intentions but limited time cultivate a personal commitment to action? Building greater empathy offers fresh insights and helps to make what has been previously unconscious or neglected newly visible.

Daniel Goleman's work on emotional intelligence highlighted the value of empathy for people in leadership roles.[3] Noting the neurological basis of psychological states such as fear and other forms of "emotional hijacking," Goleman attempted to explain why talented leaders sometimes fail, even though they may be technically gifted or have crafted a brilliant business strategy. Employees respond to their own managers in ways analogous to the manner in which patients evaluate physicians based on their "bedside manner." Physicians with equal medical acumen tend to either be regarded positively by patients or sued more frequently for malpractice depending on how effectively they listen and respond to their patients' emotional states. Similarly, leaders who are able to perceive and respond to the emotions of others are more likely to build real trust, engage team members, and accomplish their overall objectives.

So what does empathy look like in a diverse workforce context? Most people will agree with the principle of equal opportunity for all, with advancement based on merit and performance. They are also usually willing to support others who have disadvantages stemming from factors difficult for them to control, such as poverty, race, gender, educational opportunities, nationality, or other elements of an individual's life circumstances. Leaders who also invest the effort to understand the challenges and the feelings experienced by a fellow employee like Asim are most often inspired to take action—hearing a vivid, first-hand account from another person of their own experience tends to arouse shared sentiments and a sense of solidarity.

Here is a sampling of the surprising range of comments made by employees who are struggling to succeed in a diverse workforce environment.

Figure 4.2: Employee Comments

Cultivating empathy toward workplace colleagues provides surprising dividends in return. For those who find it difficult to sit and contemplate how unconscious bias may be clouding their judgment or affecting their daily conduct, an advantage conferred by increased empathy is that it offers meaty possibilities for perceiving immediate and perhaps unintended responses to one's own actions. **Empathy not only dials us into the**

general emotional state of others, but it also allows us to see where we may have caused real damage ourselves.

It could have been "me," for instance, who assumed that another person is motivated in the way that I am, who failed to reach out to a new employee, who internally scoffed at a tattoo, or who mistook one colleague for another with the same ethnic background. Maybe "I" forgot to ask others for their ideas (even though they were bursting to share them), felt impatient with a colleague's heavily accented speech, didn't offer recognition where it was due, ignored the challenges of a single parent, or made an insider joke that caused some people to feel left out. Leaders with a genuine desire to become more inclusive can learn quickly from their own mistakes through a positive feedback loop of empathy, reflection, and insight. Each reinforces the other, unlocking deeper empathic skill.

Figure 4.3: Empathy, Reflection, & Insight

Our workplaces may promote either exclusion or inclusion. Nearly everyone has felt excluded at some point in their lives. Moving to a new school, being chosen last for a playground team, making the wrong wardrobe choice, encountering a physical or verbal bully, not hanging out with the popular kids, or doing poorly at math or art—these are all ways that people may feel like outsiders as they are growing up. Some are made to feel like

The stakes become far greater when exclusion is not only permanent, but also translates into tangible disadvantages in workplaces or communities...

perpetual outsiders based on aspects of their lives that they cannot change, such as gender, age, skin color, and so on. The stakes become far greater when exclusion is not only permanent but also translates into tangible disadvantages in workplaces or communities, whether this means limited educational or employment opportunities, few chances for pay raises or promotions, or inadequate access to quality healthcare.

Inclusive leaders provide personal examples through their daily actions, setting the tone for their organizations and team dynamics. If we seek to harness the full energy, enthusiasm, and potential of each individual in a diverse workforce, it is vital to cultivate genuine empathy and find ways to better understand and include employees such as Asim along with others who have similar but different life stories: Manuela, Marwan, Ayo, Sachiko, Leotie, Sergei, or Louise. Each name has a meaning, often unknown to co-workers, that only begins to point to the complexity of the person. It is essential for leaders and teams to be alert to the mental prison shaped by unconscious bias, and to recommit to the basic principles of listening, bridge-building, and finding common ground.

LEARNING ABOUT BIAS: SUMMARY

- Demonstrate curiosity when interacting with persons with different backgrounds and cognitive styles.

- Check for bias in yourself and others: Ask, "Are we relying on obsolete information or stereotypes?"

- Flip it and test it: Take your response to a situation and test it by checking to see if you would act in a similar way with a different person. If not, ask yourself if your immediate response was suitable.

- Ask open-ended questions: Encourage discussion and actively listen for new perspectives and experiences.

- Check "Intent / Impact": If what you said had a different impact on another person than intended, explore why and what you could have done differently.

- Surprised by an answer? If someone reacts in a way that you did not expect, ask what they are thinking and why.

- When discussing sensitive topics, don't judge until you fully draw out the other person's point of view. What Information do you lack?

- Request input: Ask someone from a different background or culture about what to expect and what advice they have.

- Build empathy by seeking to understand the experience of others who may have been excluded through no fault of their own.

05.
Inclusive Behaviors: Building Key Skills & Working Across Boundaries

Practical actions taken on a daily basis can address forms of exclusion that might otherwise affect the performance of individuals, teams, and entire organizations.

What everyday skills enable people to become more inclusive?

Are there new boundaries to cross and new forms of inclusion that each of us needs to learn about?

Learning About Bias

Building Key Skills

Working Across Boundaries

Becoming a Champion

Getting Results

This chapter examines two further stages in the inclusion journey from awareness to action to impact. Each stage builds on prior ones, although the journey described here is not necessarily linear. Leaders who focus on taking relatively simple inclusive steps may find that these become a catalyst for deeper insight into their own unintended biases; such insight can then enable more thoroughgoing action and behavior change.

INCLUSIVE BEHAVIOR #2:
BUILDING KEY SKILLS

The most critical inclusion challenges for those in management or supervisorial roles tend to occur with common tasks such as bringing on new team members, providing feedback, and running meetings. Focused efforts on skill-building to address each of these topics are likely to produce practical results. Leaders who learn about their colleagues and develop empathy toward those who are experiencing some form of exclusion become better equipped to apply key inclusion skills in a targeted and effective manner. Perhaps the best way to illustrate how to respond to such employee concerns is to consider specific examples.

ONBOARDING A NEW EMPLOYEE

Carla is a relatively new employee in her current workplace. Her parents had an elementary school education, and she is the first person in her entire extended family to be working in a professional white-collar setting. Carla's biggest current issues are confidence and a sense of belonging—even after a year of employment at her new company, she still doesn't have the sense that she quite belongs, and often feels left out of discussions that involve humor she doesn't understand, unfamiliar acronyms, or banter among long-time team members.

Carla has reached out to make friends and has tried to learn quickly about her role and about her new work environment, but has been hesitant to assert herself with more senior colleagues because she is worried that she might be perceived as being overly aggressive. Some days are better than others, but today was a particularly difficult one because Carla realized during a team meeting that she had been unaware of a serious technical issue that everyone else on the team knew about and had been discussing informally already.

There are many possible avenues for Carla's co-workers—both her direct supervisor and peers at the same level—to act more inclusively in this situation. Beyond organization-wide programs for new employee onboarding, there is typically an extended period required for new employees to get up to speed in their roles and to feel like they truly belong, particularly if they have entered a work environment that seems "foreign" based on their prior experience. Actions that any co-worker can take based on a modicum of self-awareness and a sense of what could be helpful to a new colleague include simply reaching out and introducing oneself, initiating a conversation at the water cooler or coffee station, inviting Carla to join a group lunch, or offering to help her with an unfamiliar task. Each of us has a daily routine along with tasks to complete, and it may require a conscious effort to alter this routine slightly to include a new person.

"When I look around the office, I don't see a lot of persons like me – I don't feel that I belong here…"

"Yesterday was my best day so far. A few colleagues asked me to join them for lunch."

Carla's supervisor should take additional steps to ensure that she is effectively integrated into the team and able to fulfill her new role:

INTEGRATING NEW TEAM MEMBERS

- Learn more about the new employee as a person to find out about professional aspirations, perceived strengths, and key motivators, along with possible concerns.

- Position this employee with other team members by sharing aspects of her prior background and experience (enough to make other team members feel welcoming yet not resentful of a new "golden child").

- Create a learning path with the new employee to build a sense of confidence and direction.

- Ensure that initial milestones are clear and reasonable, and check in frequently during the startup period to confirm understanding and progress.

- Translate acronyms, technical jargon, and insider humor to facilitate a sense of belonging.

- Provide feedback in an even-handed way to ensure that the new employee can continue to make performance improvements.

- Extend invitations to team social events, and act as a role model for including this recent hire in conversations on such occasions.

- Ensure that the new person gains access to information longer-term employees are receiving through informal channels.

INCLUSIVE MEETINGS

Maksims is an engineer, originally from Latvia, who is currently working in his company's European headquarters in Belgium. He was brought in as a mid-career hire, and is now concerned that the move he made with such optimism may turn out to be career-limiting. Maksims

> *has a relatively introverted personality, and is a careful thinker who is slow to speak out not only by nature but also by choice—his motto is to think three times before saying something in order to ensure that his comments are both correct and considerate of others. His own Latvian cultural background has reinforced this, with long pauses in conversations being common among his family members and others from his home country.*
>
> *Maksims was always better at engineering than at English during his university career. Although his foreign language skills are adequate, he finds that it is very difficult to contribute to team meetings with co-workers who are fluent English speakers and seem to enjoy debating and expressing their opinions vigorously. Maksims finds it distressing to listen to technical discussions that are apparently based on insufficient data or shaky assumptions. He is a gifted engineer with an incisive critical mind and creative ideas to offer, but he has not yet found a way to make a useful contribution to these meetings.*

Nearly every company has the problem of one-sided meetings, with a few people doing most of the talking. A simple goal for leaders who seek to create more inclusive teams is to make every conversation multi-directional, with anyone present who could make a useful contribution able to join the discussion. Facilitating an inclusive team meeting is a skill that includes monitoring the conversation for contribution levels, noticing who could still provide useful input but has not, and asking more active participants to leave room for others while drawing out the views of those who have been slower to speak up.

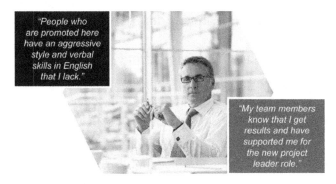

Given that their team includes non-native language speakers and divergent communication styles based on cultural and/or personality differences, Maksims' colleagues clearly need to implement a comprehensive set of best practices for team meetings if they want to leverage the full value of his engineering expertise (see also the list of recommended teamwork practices in Chapter 7).

The following graphic provides suggestions for what the members of this team can do before, during, and after team meetings in order to ensure that their meetings are inclusive. It includes multiple means of ensuring that team members who are normally reticent have ample opportunities to speak.

Figure 5.1: Effective Team Meetings

Barriers to Inclusion: Micro-inequities

Another general skill-building area for anyone who seeks to act inclusively is to become aware of so-called "micro-inequities" that undermine positive intentions. Many otherwise talented workplace leaders find it easy to overlook or underestimate the impact of small behaviors of their own that others may perceive as exclusionary. In contrast with the "isms" (racism; sexism) that are more readily identified and linked with specific language or behaviors, micro-inequities tend to be relatively subtle and subject to different interpretations.

WELCOME TO THE CLUB?

In my family, going back several generations, education was instilled as a fundamental value to be realized at all costs. The way up and out of the "ghetto" was to get a good education for yourself and on behalf of the community at large. Talk about school and education were part of every family gathering and celebrated at every milestone, from nursery school graduation to doctoral commencements. Educational achievement, demonstrated in a professional title like Doctor, Attorney, or Judge, was a source of respect and pride for each of us and for the family as a whole.

Upon earning the title of full professor, I was asked along with several others to be a university executive committee member. I felt a new sense of pride to join this inner circle, albeit as the only person of color. I thought I was finally being 'included,' accepted, and was ready to engage and add value. However, when an announcement about the council was made to the university community at large, the publication had everyone's name, title, and academic honorific listed except for mine. Just my first and last name were given. The only visible difference between the others and myself was that I was black.

On the surface, this may not seem like much, but the fact that no one noticed this omission or made any mention of it was appalling and embarrassing to me. Not wanting to create an uncomfortable conversation for someone, I said nothing, but wondered what this omission could have possibly meant. Was it just a careless mistake, an example of unconscious bias, a deliberate slight, or an indication that my presence on the committee was a token gesture and not taken seriously?

In hindsight, I am sorry I did not speak up. Instead, for some time I was disengaged and no longer felt valued or inspired to go the extra mile. I did just what was needed to be a full employee, no more. My lifetime belief in the value of the education that I had worked so hard to receive had been undermined, and I went through a period of personal doubt and questioning.

Cheryl E. Williams, Ph.D., African-American, Baby Boomer, Her-Hers-She, Parent, Wife, Grandmother, Professor Emeritus, and Global HR Executive

Micro-inequities sometimes overlap with behaviors that in other contexts might be regarded as thoughtless, rude, or inconsiderate. Contextual factors that differentiate micro-inequities from everyday boorishness and poor manners include conduct on the part of people in positions of authority that limits input from those who are seen as outsiders, foreigners, subordinates, or juniors. Seemingly minor actions may be perceived as loaded with symbolism, and also taken as cues by other employees who begin to mimic this conduct. An accumulation of micro-inequities creates a workplace environment that feels benign or even friendly to some but pervasively hostile to others. The good news for leaders who aspire to be more inclusive is that many of these behaviors, once noticed, are fairly easy to reverse or correct, and such positive actions have meaningful symbolic significance as well. Here is a list of sample micro-inequities and the unintended exclusionary messages they may convey, along with suggestions for how to address them.

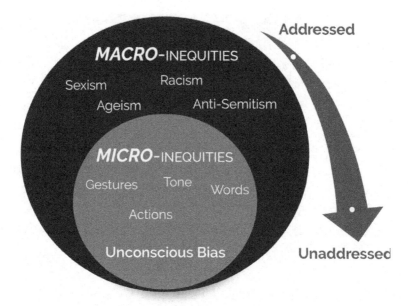

Figure 5.2: Micro-inequities vs. Macro-inequities

Sample Micro-inequities and Possible Antidotes

- **Checking a smart phone during an important conversation**

  Perceived message: *The person whose text the manager is reading is more important than I am.*

  Possible antidote: Put the phone down and turn off the sound, or at least apologize if you have to take a call or respond to a text: "Sorry, this is a text from my son whom I've been worried about. Would you mind if I send him a quick response?"

- **Greeting one person more warmly than others**

  Perceived message: *My manager has a favorite employee, and it's not me.*

  Possible antidote: Greet each person in the room or in the workplace in a similar way, except in unusual cases such when a person has returned from a long trip.

- **Introducing one person with glowing accolades, and another with only a name**

  Perceived message: *My manager values that person more than me.*

  Possible antidote: Make a conscious effort to introduce people in a similar way.

- **Omitting someone from an important e-mail or other form of communication**

  Perceived message: *They don't feel the need to include me.*

  Possible antidote: Make a habit of taking one more step before you hit the send button to ask yourself who else should be included as a team member with something to contribute. (It's also important not to overdo this and copy others unnecessarily.)

- **Excluding an employee from socializing opportunities**

  Perceived message: *I'm not part of the inner circle of this team.*

  Possible antidote: Consider whether there are others who would appreciate an invitation from fellow team members.

- **Taking credit for someone else's work or idea**

  Perceived message: *Even when I have a good idea, I'm not going to be recognized for it.*

  Possible antidote: Offer credit where it is due. (This will make you look like a better leader as well.)

- **Cutting off a colleague in mid-sentence**

  Perceived message: *They are not interested in what I have to say.*

  Possible antidote: Let the person finish, even if their communication style or language skills are different from yours.

- **Repeatedly canceling meetings with a colleague**

  Perceived message: *Meeting with me is not a priority.*

Possible antidote: Ask yourself why, apologize, and schedule a meeting for which you are fully present.

- **Using acronyms that others do not understand**

  Perceived message: *They have a special language for insiders here and I don't understand what they're talking about.*

  Possible antidote: Explain the acronym you're using just like radio hosts explain unfamiliar terms used by guest speakers; if there are numerous acronyms that are difficult for new people, then create a list.

- **Exhibiting impatience because of a colleague's accent**

  Perceived message: *I have a permanent disadvantage in this organization, no matter how good my ideas are.*

  Possible antidote: Try learning a foreign language yourself for a dose of humility and consideration. Practice speech without slang, idioms, or acronyms while modifying your pace of speaking; check periodically for questions and confirmation of understanding.

- **Only considering people with styles similar to yours for recognition or attractive opportunities**

  Perceived message: *Certain types of people are recognized and developed here, and that's not me.*

  Possible antidote: Ask yourself if the only high-potential individuals are those who are already closest to you.

- **Expecting others to accommodate your time zone**

  Perceived message: *They assume that their schedule and family life are more important than ours, or they don't really want me to attend anyway.*

  Possible antidote: Share the pain; acknowledge and thank others when they do.

- **Inviting a person to attend a meeting or function based on appearance rather than on substance or potential contribution.**

Perceived message: *Looks like I'm the token minority at this event; they don't really want me to contribute.*

Possible antidote: Ensure that an invitation to attend includes a meaningful role.

In addition to the general list of micro-inequities that almost anyone can engage in without negative intent, the most crucial micro-inequities for managers and supervisors tend to cluster in five primary areas. Focused efforts on skill-building to address each of these topics are likely to produce the best results. As with other aspects of this topic, many of the effects are unintended, and deliberate attention accompanied with straightforward actions can produce quick improvements.

Employee Engagement: Key Motivators are Assumed
"My supervisor said, 'I think you'll be really excited about this project.'"

Feedback: Conversations that Do Not Occur
"It seems like my supervisor is avoiding me."

Meetings: Unbalanced Meeting Participation
"The same people do all the talking."

Decision-Making: Not Consulted
"Nobody asked me."

Delegation: "Throwing Things Over the Wall"
"I don't have enough information, and I am getting responsibilities thrown at me without having the opportunity to agree/disagree!"

Figure 5.3: Managers and Supervisors: Common Micro-Inequities

Some micro-inequities have large-scale career impacts. For example, a leader's well-meaning assumption about what is right for an employee in terms of personal motivation or family circumstances may convey the message that this person is no longer on the fast track to an executive role. Such a misunderstanding could potentially be avoided by scheduling a conversation to explore the topic together.

A SOFT LANDING?

An executive group was considering the best candidates for a new project team leader position. This role would involve considerable travel to a variety of locations in Asia-Pacific. The two top candidates under discussion were Luis and Karin, who both had strong track records.

Another candidate was discussed briefly: "What about Tina? She is just coming back from maternity leave, and has been a star performer." A senior leader responded, "You're right. She's very capable, but I think it would be too much to ask her to do all that travel. Better to put her in a job where she can have a soft landing and not jump into such a demanding role right away."

The team returned to discussing Luis and Karin, ultimately deciding on Karin for the role. Afterwards, it turned out that Tina would have appreciated being considered seriously. "At least they could have asked me what I wanted rather than assuming that they knew. My husband's work is flexible, and we both have parents living nearby who are happy to help with childcare. It feels like I've just been shifted from the fast track to the slow track in this company."

The examples provided thus far illustrate how practical actions taken on a daily basis can address forms of exclusion that might otherwise affect the performance of individuals, teams, and entire organizations. Below is a more comprehensive list of key skills for creating an inclusive workplace. Both leaders and individual contributors will be able to identify many actions that they can take. We recommend starting with one or two that feel most accessible, and generating momentum with these.

BUILDING KEY SKILLS: SUMMARY

Relationship Building

- How well do you know the people around you? What could you do to get to know them better? Express a sincere interest in learning more about them, listen carefully to what they say, and set a comfortable tone of discussion to draw them out further.

Communication

- Commit to being an active listener, aware and mindful of potential differences in communication style.

- Monitor your role in workplace conversations; consider whether you contribute too much or too little.

- Consider whether your non-verbal messages—conveyed through tone, body language, gestures, mobile phone usage, etc.—are consistent with your intent and take into account differing norms and preferences.

Engagement

- Create opportunities to ask or to observe what motivates others. Reflect on the differences between key motivators for yourself and others, and how to best address what motivates the latter.

- How can you draw out untapped skills or interests of your colleagues so they feel more engaged at work?

Feedback

- When providing feedback, are you even-handed with everyone, regardless of their background?

- Consider how often you seek feedback on your own actions from a peer, mentor, or "cultural guide."

> **Teamwork**
>
> - Actively consider diverse competencies and profiles when building teams.
>
> - Provide meeting agendas and materials in advance so that non-native language speakers have time to prepare.
>
> - Structure meetings with devices such as turn-taking, opportunities for written input, etc. so that each team member with something to contribute can join the conversation.

INCLUSIVE BEHAVIOR #3: WORKING ACROSS BOUNDARIES

While having an awareness of unconscious bias and a baseline set of inclusion skills in place often produces visible positive results, there is sometimes a tendency to declare victory too early. Heightened awareness and building key skills can lay the groundwork for further inclusive actions. Even for organizations that have achieved important statistical milestones—for example, increased retention of minority employees, or higher percentages of women in managerial roles—there are far more ways to be inclusive.

People who have begun to build capabilities for working with colleagues from different backgrounds often encounter opportunities to interact with a wider range of counterparts representing additional diversity factors such as race, gender, age, nationality, function, cognitive style, and so on. Skills acquired for working with one set of colleagues may transfer easily to other types of relationships, or they may need to be modified. Diversity experts like to portray a "diversity wheel" with concentric circles that fan outward from characteristics that are inherited to those that are acquired over a lifetime. One such version, adapted from the work of Gardenswartz and Rowe,[1] is depicted in Figure 5.4:

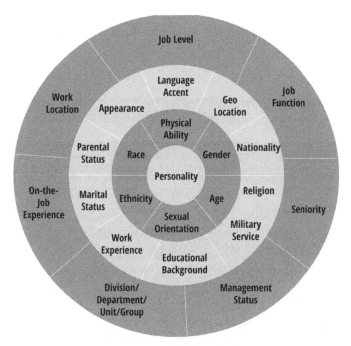

Figure 5.4: The Diversity Wheel

For those who seek to become truly inclusive, it is worth examining the current scope of their everyday business relationships and asking where it would be useful to try crossing a visible or invisible boundary that separates them from other groups. For instance, are cognitive styles or technical skills that happen to be outside of the organizational mainstream valued and incorporated? (This could mean "blue sky" thinkers in a data-driven culture, or research and development scientists in a company built on marketing strength.) Are there individual personality differences, socio-economic gaps, or racial and ethnic distinctions that cause employees to feel excluded in a way that affects their level of engagement?

Some boundaries, particularly those related to deep-rooted historical differences in access to power and resources, are more emotionally loaded and difficult to traverse. Others, such as organizational divisions between functional roles, have been aspects of the human experience for millennia,[2] but are shifting as technology changes. Here is an example of a company that has encountered obstacles based on functional and geographical differences:

SUPERSTARS VERSUS EVERYONE ELSE

At a U.S. west coast-based information technology firm, employees complained about the bias that existed between technical employees in computer science or engineering functions and non-technical functions such as sales, finance, marketing, or human resources. Non-technical employees felt that they were being treated as second-class citizens. They wanted strategies for how to overcome this, yet the sources of bias were deeply ingrained.

The company had grown quickly through a series of hit product innovations. As it expanded throughout the world, the company's leaders recognized that their global presence had brought them a diversity of thought that could be a huge advantage in continuing their tradition of innovation and high performance. Many technical employees, even at headquarters, were originally from other countries, adding further complexity.

These were smart, ambitious, and forward-thinking people, so what was getting in the way of their truly being able to leverage the ideas and creativity of their entire workforce? The problem seemed to be behavioral habits that were grounded in the company's own original DNA and reinforced by its successes over time.

Employee interviews uncovered a culture in the organization that was open only to the ideas of those technical "superstars" who had been successful previously in product development, and who were primarily based in the United States. Most participants in the system considered themselves to be open-minded and without any particular bias—but there was a pervasive yet largely unconscious bias against those who weren't among the acknowledged superstars. Proposals from employees outside of the company's technical elite were viewed with skepticism, regardless of their value. In principle, people agreed that "we want an environment where all ideas are considered," but in reality, this was not happening.

Fifty employees gathered together, and those who identified themselves as technical workers were asked for adjectives they would use to describe nontechnical colleagues. They used words like illogical, fuzzy, uniformed, uneducated, ignorant, and useless. Similarly, non-technical employees described their technical peers with terms like socially inept, passive-aggressive, self-absorbed, arrogant, territorial, and black-and-white thinkers. The starkly negative perceptions each group held of the other highlighted the importance of better integrating this functional dimension of diversity within the organization. Functional differences were clearly linked with an unhealthy dynamic that was impeding collaboration among different parts of the company. Surfacing negative stereotypes sparked intense and constructive discussion about how to foster cross-functional innovation by improving collaboration and generating ideas based on different perspectives.[3]

In this example, the barriers to innovation and higher levels of performance were primarily functional (technical vs. non-technical) but also cultural (home country vs. everywhere else). These barriers were further reinforced by widely held negative stereotypes that deepened divisions among conflicting factions and made attempts at collaboration seem pointless; loaded terms such as "illogical" or "arrogant" added fuel to the flames of mutual antipathy. To turn this situation around, employees in all parts of the world, including top executives, had to adopt boundary-crossing skills for approaching their counterparts with a new openness to mutual learning. The successful change effort that took shape over time incorporated a fresh organizational narrative—"We need each other to grow"—with an emphasis on positive examples of collaboration between technical and non-technical employees as well as those from different cultural backgrounds.

Global Boundaries

While organizational boundaries can be found wherever there are differences of any kind (race, gender, function), the most literal boundary lines are, of course, those between countries. Do global colleagues who are remote from headquarters have an equal chance to advance based on their performance? Are they included in product development discussions that will affect their markets and their customers? Are they able to fully contribute their knowledge and capabilities to global team projects?

Physical distance, time zones, language barriers, and the limitations of virtual means of communication all reinforce national boundaries. In addition, culturally-based differences in leadership, communication, and problem-solving styles create even more significant gaps that global team members frequently underestimate or ignore. The dimensions of culture depicted in tools such as the GlobeSmart Profile[SM 4] are based on many years of research and a very large database of survey responses. Knowing how one's personal cultural profile compares with those of global counterparts, customers, or team members is an excellent way to identify and bridge workstyle barriers, especially when the process takes into account the profiles of real people rather than broad country-level generalizations. In an increasingly mobile world with large waves of immigrants and refugees, it is more important to consider cultural differences within diverse local workplaces as well.

Global organizations offer yet another challenge for well-intended inclusion initiatives, as each country has its own unique constellation of diversity factors and priorities rooted in history and demographics. In a separate book, *Global Diversity*,[5] we have compared the diversity profiles of eight different countries, highlighting the factors that are most prominent in each location.

In the absence of country-specific knowledge, it is easy to make false assumptions such as, "Gender issues are the same everywhere," and to impose solutions from one's own social context onto another location where such measures may appear to be irrelevant or wrong-headed. Companies based in Europe, for instance, tend to highlight their own version of gender issues along with employment challenges associated with ageism, while in Australia, it is more common for organizations to wrestle with how to promote inclusion of indigenous people as well as immigrants.

A leader who seeks to become more inclusive on a global basis will find it worthwhile to consider the current social challenges and aspirations of employees in each major market. The table below outlines four country examples.

United States	India
• Race and ethnicity	• Socioeconomic status
• Gender	• Regional origin
• Political affiliation	• Religion
• Immigration	• Gender
• Sexual orientation	• Language
Japan	**United Kingdom**
• Age	• Immigration
• Gender	• Race and Ethnicity
• Regional background	• Socioeconomic status
• Organizational affiliation	• Educational background
	• Language and communication

Figure 5.5: Contrasting National Diversity Profiles

Personal Boundary-Mapping

A way to begin to identify where our own boundaries are drawn is by mapping our "go-to people" in the workplace. This exercise involves considering the people that we interact with most regularly in getting things done, analyzing how diverse this network is based on a number of factors, and considering whether business objectives could be achieved more readily by including people from different backgrounds. This exercise is described in Figure 5.6:

INSTRUCTIONS:

1. Write your name in the middle of a blank page with a circle around it.

2. Outside of the circle with your name, write the names of other key people at your company who are your "go to" people for input, strategic advice, delivery of critical projects, and thought partners. Note those who are in your most tightly held circle at your organization.

Individually:
Using different color markers or types of lines (solid, dotted, etc.), analyze the diversity dimensions of your "go to" people and draw connection lines using the factors below or others you select:

- **Black** = Different division
- **Green** = Different race or ethnicity
- **Red** = Different job level (at least 2 levels +/-)
- **Blue** = Different nationality and/or geographic region
- **Yellow** = Different age (at least 10 years +/-)
- **Purple** = Different gender
- **Orange** = Different regional and/or linguistic background

Figure 5.6: Go-To People Exercise

Leaders who seek to expand their "go-to network" based on this activity can ask themselves several questions:

1. How could you reach out to meet people from different backgrounds?
2. What could do to learn more about the people you would like to meet?
3. How might you adapt your own style to be effective in your work together?

At the same time as we attempt to reach across boundaries to broaden our network and perspectives, it is vital to get to know real people rather than stereotypical categories, even revisiting labels that may appear to be familiar.

THE "WHITE MALE" CATEGORY

Those who celebrate diversity sometimes ironically perpetuate a stereotype of white males. Whether the context is North America, Europe, Latin America, or the Middle East, a modicum of reflection reveals that this category incorporates a very heterogeneous mix.

People identified as white males may include, for example, individuals from radically different cultures and even bitter historical enemies: French, Germans, English, Scots, Croats, Serbians, Greeks, Turks, Italians, Spaniards, Algerians, Saudis, Israelis, Russians, Argentinians, and so on. White males are adherents of every major religion: Christianity, Judaism, Islam, Hinduism, Buddhism, etc.

There are white males who are politically conservative and those who are radical, a mix of different sexual orientations, members of at least five different generations, native speakers of dozens of languages, city-dwellers and farmers, some who are well-educated and others who didn't finish high school, rich and poor, tall and short, factory workers and athletes, astronauts and homeless people. The traces of history still present within their everyday lives come from thousands of distinct social units, with memories, stories, poems, and songs echoing back to countless ancient campfires.

The fine lens of complexity that is so carefully applied by inclusion practitioners to other hot-button categories should be applied even-handedly to achieve a new and richer form of inclusiveness.

To further illustrate the practical steps involved in working across boundaries, it is worth examining another example.

A NEW TEAM LEADER

Lily works in her company's customer service call center in Chengdu, a city in southwestern China, where she is a newly promoted manager. She has now been placed on a project team that will require working with colleagues in the southern city of Shenzhen as well as a call center in the Philippines. Several of the Manila call center workers whom Lily will now be managing have been with the company for more than ten years and are significantly older than she is. Lily is open to this new management role but is feeling unprepared as she has no prior work experience outside of Chengdu. Some of her new Chinese colleagues in Shenzhen are native speakers of Cantonese, a different dialect that is difficult for her to understand, and she suspects that whatever perceptions she has about Filipinos are probably wrong.

In this scenario there are several types of boundaries that Lily will need to be able to cross in order to perform effectively in her new role: cultural, generational, and linguistic. Here are a few recommendations as she begins to manage her new team:

- Proactively build relationships with team members in other locations; learn about their backgrounds and the reasons behind their actions.

- Schedule initial one-on-one meetings as well as team sessions.

- Travel to Shenzhen and Manila to meet in person with the employees now reporting to her if this is at all possible budget-wise.

- Build a regular schedule that dedicates equal time to team members who are co-located and to those who are remote; reach out periodically to remote team members informally as well as formally.

- Learn everyday expressions in Cantonese, English, or Tagalog as a way to demonstrate interest and build ties with other team members.

- Handle long-term Filipino employees with respect based on their tenure with the organization, and ask for their advice on subjects in which they have special expertise.

- Refrain from making hasty judgments about team members based on insufficient information when problems arise, or when there is tension in a conversation.

- Find opportunities to give and receive feedback with colleagues in all locations.

For leaders who want to move beyond "Building Key Skills" and discover ways to apply their skills in an expansive workplace context, there are a number of pragmatic steps they can take, such as the ones recommended for Lily above. Organizational goals and personal job objectives are likely to drive boundary-crossing priorities. However, we often find that broad networks created based on genuine interest and friendships, without necessarily having an immediate task or goal in mind, can also offer significant personal and professional dividends over the long-term.

WORKING ACROSS BOUNDARIES: SUMMARY

- Examine your network: Whom else can you reach out to in order to add more diversity to your network?

- Consider those from other functions, ethnic groups, generations, and so on.

- Create personal stretch goals: Identify a group with which you are relatively unfamiliar (e.g., people from a different function) and learn more about those individuals. Monitor your biases and stereotypes (e.g., regarding "engineers" or "salespeople"). Seek to discover different self-perceptions and/or patterns of behavior.

- Pay attention to communication patterns based on gender, generation, national culture, cognitive style, career experience, social class, etc.

- Transfer skills: If you have been successful in working with one group, try to transfer your skills to working with other kinds of people while being open to learning new skills as well.

- Consider job switching, job shadowing, and job-sharing exchanges to broaden your experience.

- Create an inclusive physical work environment: Redesign your workspace to be less "siloed."

- Join diverse work teams for exposure to different perspectives and to learn from each other in an inclusive team environment.

- Seek input (both formal and informal) to gauge the effect of your current inclusion practices on groups that you do not know well; invite suggestions for improvement.

- Organize and/or attend company-wide meetings, celebrations, seminars, workshops, or retreats that bring together people from groups who do not normally come into contact with one another.

Personal Action Plan

Select at least one of the following diversity dimensions, or another aspect of diversity you think is important in your place of work or study, and write down personal action steps you are willing to take in order to expand your own approach to inclusion.

- Race/Ethnicity
- Generation
- Gender Identity
- Culture
- Job Function
- Cognitive Style

- Disability
- Sexual Orientation
- Socioeconomic Status
- Educational Background
- Religious Belief
- Political Affiliation
- Other

Keep the following questions in mind as you write down the action steps you will take below:

1. How could you reach out to meet people from the group(s) you have selected?

2. What could you do to learn more about the people you would like to meet?

3. How might you adapt your own style to be effective in your work together?

Figure 5.7: Personal Action Plan

06.
Inclusive Behaviors: Becoming a Champion & Getting Results

Managing global innovation means leveraging diversity from every possible angle to drive the innovation process all the way from inception to execution.

How can executives serve as champions and effective models of inclusion?

How can inclusion be linked with getting better business results?

Learning About Bias   Building Key Skills   Working Across Boundaries   **Becoming a Champion**   Getting Results

Many leaders have responsibilities that extend beyond the immediate business objectives of their own team. They must evaluate team members' performance and development potential, contribute to cross-functional or interdepartmental meetings, interact with peers running other teams, deal with internal or external customers and suppliers, and manage upward to influence decisions made at higher levels in the organization. Beyond the inclusive behaviors covered previously—foundational skills for working inclusively with fellow team members and proactive extension of one's network to include a more diverse range of colleagues—there are ways that leaders can expand their organizational influence.

Human resources departments are usually in charge of providing a framework to manage and develop talent while enforcing compliance with legal standards; however, nearly everyone serving in a leadership role is involved in implementing multiple phases of the talent life cycle.

Figure 6.1: Talent Life Cycle

INCLUSIVE BEHAVIOR #4:
BECOMING A CHAMPION

Becoming a champion of inclusion involves recruiting diverse talent, building engagement among all employees, assessing performance and dispensing rewards fairly, retaining and rewarding high-potential individuals from any background, and developing future leaders— even people who don't fit current executive team member norms. Examining specific examples helps to illustrate how leaders can become champions of inclusion along the way.

RETAINING TALENT

Dr. Katarzyna Bankowski is a senior oncologist in a large hospital in Warsaw, Poland. In addition to her medical expertise, which is much admired by colleagues, she has a reputation for being an excellent listener who runs departmental meetings effectively. Her team consistently receives positive, even grateful feedback from patients as well. She did some of her previous medical training abroad, and therefore has experience with medical practices in several different countries.

Katarzyna has observed a retention problem at the hospital. Many young, newly qualified doctors who join the staff leave after their first year for medical residencies in the U.K., the Netherlands, Austria, and Germany. Based on conversations with departing physicians, she has learned that they often perceive the "old guard" of established physicians as being overly rigid and unwilling to adopt new patient care practices. Katarzyna wants to make the workplace more inclusive so that these young physicians feel they can build their careers in Poland rather than abroad.

Katarzyna's institution is experiencing the classic talent life cycle issue of how to retain high-potential employees, with a generation gap between older and younger physicians. If younger physicians continue to depart in large numbers without returning, the facility will suffer a talent drain that affects the workload of remaining physicians and the quality of patient care. Katarzyna could take steps such as the following to address the larger organization issue of excessive turnover:

- Better understand the perspectives of the other senior physicians.

- Learn what motivates the younger doctors, including which changes they feel are most important.

- Recommend and model the creation of "reverse mentoring" pairs of senior and junior doctors who seek to learn from each other.

- Challenge the senior medical staff to improve the engagement and retention of younger physicians through a change initiative.

Each of these steps builds on prior stages of inclusive leadership. Katarzyna is already an effective, inclusive team leader with a diverse informal network of friends and contacts within the hospital. If she chooses to take these steps, she will have also moved beyond her own specific job description to tackle a broader organizational issue linked with the talent life cycle.

Inviting senior and junior doctors to enter into mentoring roles with each other while challenging senior medical staff colleagues to improve the engagement and retention of young physicians entail possible career hazards. However, Katarzyna is likely to succeed in being a catalyst for change not only because of the esteem in which she is held as a medical professional, but because she has already learned how to become more inclusive in other ways.

SUPPORT FOR WOMEN

Dinesh is a purchasing manager based in the high-tech city of Noida, India, close to Delhi. He has a reputation for being skilled at motivation, problem-solving, and hands-on instruction, which is exactly the right recipe for his relatively young team members. Dinesh has also built a strong network throughout the Noida site and with his counterparts at headquarters in London thanks to rotations through previous job assignments and a short expatriate stint at the worldwide purchasing department headquarters in the UK.

Dinesh has noticed that women employees at his site tend to advance slowly, with men occupying most of the key management roles. Some managers have a tendency to "talk down" to their subordinates, especially women. There are also workplace cliques based on different linguistic, ethnic, and educational backgrounds within India that at times leave both men and women feeling isolated or left out of workplace conversations.

It appears that assessment and development of talent are inconsistent at Dinesh's location, and that there may also be bias related to gender or other background factors. Dinesh has been considering several countermeasures that he personally could take, each of which will require a degree of courage on his part to go against current trends. On the other hand, during informal conversations he has had with managers who are his peers, several have agreed with his assessment and shared his willingness to promote changes. Dinesh has recently resolved to take three specific steps:

- Support high-potential women candidates during promotion discussions by providing examples of his interactions with them.

- Speak with one particular colleague he has observed "talking down" to or appearing to demean others, finding a time for a private conversation to share his observations and to ask the colleague about his intent.

- Model outreach to employees from different backgrounds in the lunchroom to diminish the potentially divisive influence of workplace cliques.

A Range of Options

Leading a systemic change effort will strike many people as a daunting and risky task. It is true that driving organizational change in areas such as the talent cycle requires political savvy, experience, and possibly seniority as well—not to mention a sustained commitment of energy. Serving as an inclusion champion, however, can take many forms, including small-scale everyday actions such as the final item on Dinesh's list of steps above.

A good place for many leaders to start is seeking to understand their colleagues from different backgrounds in a fuller way that goes well beyond initial impressions. This simple step may hold surprises regarding a person's unique qualities, life experiences, or emotions. The growing literature on allyship also suggests that leaders, in particular, are well-positioned to share the organizational platforms that have given them visibility, providing others with chances to grow and garner recognition.[1]

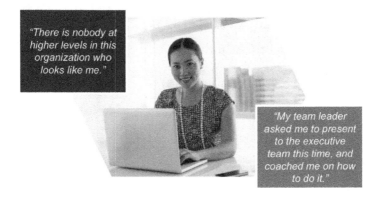

When leaders observe inappropriate workplace behaviors, they can also choose to "see something, say something," or "call out" such actions, either publicly or privately. In so doing, they serve as a role model for employees and may even find that their comments, if made in a careful and considerate way, result in a "thank you" rather than in the receiver being offended or alienated—many people are simply not aware of the impacts they have had on others. Comments phrased as questions are sometimes easier for the other person to digest and respond to constructively:

- When you were texting during the meeting, did you notice how the others who were present reacted?

- I know that you were excited and wanted to contribute, but how do you think Sonya felt about the way that you interrupted her?

"Pick your battles" is probably good general advice in deciding when to champion the cause of an inclusion effort or when to hold back. Returning to the theme of empathy highlighted in Chapter 4, one way to choose how best to act is to learn what forms of exclusion are most troubling to team members and conversely, what opportunities they would find most exciting, and then respond accordingly. This could mean serving as a champion on a smaller scale or on a grander one, depending on how deep-rooted or systemic the underlying issue turns out to be.

Daily acts of coaching, mentoring, or outreach to others may contribute to substantial changes over time. Another positive action that tends to have a ripple effect is to note examples of inclusion as they occur, and to spread these success stories to others; authentic local anecdotes make inclusivity seem more accessible.

BECOMING A CHAMPION: SUMMARY

The following list of recommendations includes a range of options from lower to higher risk and impact:

- Ask colleagues from different backgrounds how you can support them.

- Offer to mentor or coach others who appear to be struggling in your work environment; share the "unwritten rules" on how things are done in your organization.

- Seek out mentors who can provide you with broader perspectives.

- Adapt your leadership style and give on-the-spot coaching and developmental support where needed; keep in mind different motivators and feedback approaches.

- Actively build a work environment of trust, respect, and psychological safety that enables people to speak up without fear of criticism or penalty.

- See something, do something: Be alert for hurtful, disrespectful, or unjust comments or decisions—either your own or those of others. Constructively address these to ensure that people can make amends and create a more inclusive environment.

- Brainstorm ways to keep the topic of inclusion dynamic and alive. Be open to new approaches—others are likely to see this and to feel more comfortable taking action themselves.

- Create opportunities for talented persons from diverse backgrounds to work on visible projects; share your platform and network with others.

- Advocate for highly capable colleagues, even when their styles diverge from corporate culture norms. For example, when told that a person with a unique work style is "not ready" for a new assignment, important project, or promotion, question the evaluation for bias.

- Be an organizational change agent when needed: Explain the business case for inclusion and serve as a role model in terms of inclusive behaviors. Address aspects of the talent life cycle (recruiting, engagement, performance assessment, rewards & retention, talent development), finding ways to make them more inclusive.

INCLUSIVE BEHAVIOR #5: GETTING RESULTS

Leveraging diversity to innovate and to grow the business is the ultimate goal for most leaders who strive to be inclusive. Inclusive leadership can be justified in a broad moral and historical context as a matter of social justice; organizations that answer to shareholders must also scrutinize investments of time and resources for their practical efficacy—inclusion initiatives are no exception. Rhetoric about the effects of diversity on innovation is often not backed up by skilled innovation leadership and positive business results. How, specifically, can diversity be leveraged to achieve more effective performance, and where could it be an obstacle as well as an opportunity? Ultimately workplace inclusion needs to produce practical results in order to be seen not only as "the right thing to do" but as a real business driver.

Mitigating the potential risks of legal actions is, of course, a significant advantage in itself. Exclusionary actions, even those that are unintended, can be costly, distracting, and damaging to employee engagement. Beyond the very real risks that need to be addressed, though, there are major opportunities as well. The following example demonstrates how inclusive leadership is likely to be an essential ingredient even for viable product development.

PRODUCT DEVELOPMENT TEAM

Deion is a seasoned leader with a Fortune 100 manufacturer. He recently relocated to Shanghai, far from his company's U.S. headquarters. His assignment is to head up a regional team that will take the lead globally in developing a new product for which the Asia-Pacific region is now the largest market.

Deion is a skilled listener and a veteran manager with a reputation for providing fair and balanced feedback. As an African-American, Deion thought that he was well aware of the meaning of diversity and inclusion and had been an active member of an employee resource group at an early stage in his career.

Now in Shanghai, given the unfamiliar diversity elements among local employees within his office, Deion has been uncertain about how best to lead his team. He still feels culturally awkward, as he can spot unexpected reactions from his local colleagues, but doesn't yet fully understand what they are thinking and feeling. Nonetheless, he needs his team to deliver outstanding results.

Deion is in a new market with a new team. In order to lead his product development project successfully, he must cultivate a deep understanding of regional customer needs, competitors, supply chain capabilities, and the resources available within his own local organization. Although he is a company veteran with extensive engineering expertise and prior experience in this product line, trying to replicate what has previously worked in North America is unlikely to produce a good product fit for Asia-Pacific. There are substantial market differences, including the types of customer solutions the product must address, the most desirable features, the pace of development, local standards for the size of the product footprint, acceptable price points, financing arrangements, and expectations for follow-up service.

Although Deion's team members regard him as an expert and are willing to follow his instructions, he is going to need to tap their expertise and insights from the very beginning of the project. Building upon other inclusive leadership behaviors discussed thus far, here are a few of the many steps that Deion could take to create an inclusive, high-performing team:

- Establish a diverse network of relationships, both with team members and across the regional organization, to build his knowledge about colleagues, the organization, and the market.

- Adapt his communication style to draw out ideas, to confirm understanding and/or agreement, and to read subtle messages from team members who prefer indirect communication methods.

- Learn how to inspire and elicit the best contributions of team members from different backgrounds based on deep understanding of their skills and potential.

- Leverage the knowledge of local team members to ensure that their insights into the needs of regional customers are accurately reflected in the product design.

- Balance customization that is truly required to meet unique local or regional needs with global standardization for maximum efficiency.

The need for a recently arrived expatriate such as Deion to be inclusive in order to achieve his team's objectives is relatively easy to perceive, although many international assignees actually do fail by ignoring local input and attempting to repeat past patterns of success in other markets without modification. Beyond the realm of expatriates, greater inclusiveness can enhance the quality and quantity of innovation organization-wide.

Innovation Cycle—Generate, Plan, Implement

Leaders of successful innovation efforts tap diverse perspectives and capabilities of team members through several stages of innovation: idea generation, planning, and implementation. Companies have various innovation platforms and processes, but all must traverse the broad path from divergence to convergence, or from early-stage ideation to go-to-market implementation.

Figure 6.2: Innovation Stages

Generate

During the idea generation stage of an innovation effort, diverse teams have the potential to perform in their full glory. They can accomplish this through a combination of all the stages of inclusive behaviors described in this chapter and in previous ones. Inclusive team leaders systematically leverage the many perspectives that their team members offer, and draw in even more when needed.

At the idea generation stage, a useful starting point is to have all team members consider who their normal "go-to people" are when they approach a problem likely to require an innovative solution (see Chapter 5). Once they have mapped the individuals to whom they turn most often, they can then analyze these contacts to consider how broad or narrow their reach might be. Team members are thereby able to determine how to broaden their network of contacts if needed to fulfill their objectives.

Inclusive leaders not only expand their team's network, but they also strive to seek out and incorporate novel ideas in an objective manner. On an everyday basis, whether at home or abroad, there are frequently team members and other colleagues who have useful ideas to offer, but for some reason—communication style, gender, nationality, age—their potential contributions have been ignored or discounted.

The following anecdote describes an innovation leader who found that his organization was falling prey to a surprisingly regular form of unconscious bias against valuable engineering ideas, and sought to counteract this trend.

SOURCING NEW IDEAS

Wolfgang, a director for a large high technology company based in Europe, heard concerns expressed by a variety of people—customers, employees, fellow executives—that his organization was losing its innovative edge. Moreover, the company had made a strategic decision to expand its portfolio of product offerings for fast-growth markets in other regions. Employee survey results suggested that management practices might be an impediment to innovation. More specifically, there were comments that technical managers had been ignoring ideas from individuals whom they assumed were less qualified than others: "Our European engineers had a tendency to ignore the ideas of our engineers in India."

Inspired by the practice of blind orchestra auditions, which has resulted in far more female musicians being selected for open orchestra positions when judges are unable to identify gender based on appearance, Wolfgang instituted a blind audition process for new ideas. All participants in a company-wide drive to generate product improvement ideas received nicknames so that no one who was assessing the ideas could associate them with a particular region or country.

> *The results of this relatively modest experiment were impressive. Far more ideas were selected and implemented from engineers outside of Europe than had previously been the norm. Wolfgang comments, "The new process made us see the possibility of innovation through diverse thought in our own organization. It made us listen to one another in new ways, without our normal filters, and it powered a real shift in the organization."[2]*

Plan

Once creative ideas have been generated, most teams go through a planning or design thinking process that involves testing ideas, setting priorities, and formulating a strategic plan. Edward de Bono became famous for his "Six Thinking Hats" approach to developing ideas. He suggested that team members recognize the cognitive stance that they would normally take— passionate advocate (red hat), data-driven analyst (white hat), habitual critic (black hat), process controller (blue hat), etc.—and learn to wear these hats purposefully and in a collaborative manner.[3] Beyond this valuable application of different cognitive styles to cultivate ideas, there are other useful filters which apply the "lenses" provided by different dimensions of diversity, such as generation, race and ethnicity, or gender.

DIVERSITY LENSES
- Cognitive Style
- Generation
- Race & Ethnicity
- Gender
- Culture
- Function

Figure 6.3: Diversity Lenses

For example, the automotive industry has become increasingly focused on the changing attitudes of a younger generation of consumers in the U.S. and Europe. In contrast to older drivers who took their driving tests on the first possible date of eligibility and for whom car ownership was a significant life milestone, younger consumers tend to be indifferent about car ownership, nervous about learning to drive, and more concerned than their elders about the dangers posed by distracted drivers. Automakers have unexpectedly discovered that certain autonomous vehicle features that they are testing—autonomous parking, lane control, blind spot sensors, automatic braking—can become attractive current selling features to these younger buyers who are accustomed to deploying high-tech fixes in other aspects of their lives, in contrast to their elders who probably retain the habit of looking over their shoulders when changing lanes. A fresh generational perspective has led automotive marketing and R&D teams to prioritize such features and to plan how to leverage their appeal to younger drivers.

Diverse teams often flounder when it comes time to hammer out and commit to a strategic plan in order to get things done. Would-be inclusive leaders often feel a gravitational pull toward complexity, ambiguity, and confusion—the natural outcome of having many different working styles and points of view. Leaders of high-performing global teams regularly consider several questions about their decision-making process that are highly inclusive, while remaining focused on business objectives and not just inclusion for its own sake:

- **What** information should we be looking at together?

- **Who** should be involved in this decision?

- **How** can we share ideas in a way that everyone is able to contribute?[4]

Using a disciplined process such as this one enables a team to continue to leverage its diverse resources but not be distracted by forces that will require it to go back to the beginning and start over. Even the classic Deming cycle of "plan—do—check—act" can go astray if it does not address these three questions. It is vital to define the breadth of information the team requires (the What) and the right people to engage in the planning discussion (the Who). Then, when the right people are together in the same physical or virtual space, it is just as important to have a process in place (the How) that enables everyone to express their points of view. Likewise, the team must have a clearly defined decision-making process—whether this is democratic, consultative, or directive—that enables it to move toward closure.

MISSING LENSES

Global managers with long memories probably recall disaster stories of product names and advertising slogans that backfired due to lack of cultural knowledge. Less well-known is the fact that such fiascos continue unabated, at considerable expense to the organizations involved. Here is a list of relatively recent, high-profile consumer goods controversies that could have been averted by more diverse and inclusive marketing teams:

- *Nivea: The "White is Purity" slogan coined for this brand's deodorant campaign was accused of endorsing white supremacy and had to be hastily withdrawn with an official apology just as it was being embraced by supremacist groups.*

- *Tesco: The U.K.'s largest supermarket chain set up a product promotion for Muslims during Ramadan. While this is a common practice, unfortunately the product selected was smoky bacon-flavored Pringles, a violation of Muslim customs that forbid consumption of pork products.*

- *Urban Outfitters: The company's Kent State sweatshirt with a pattern that looked like bloodstains unintentionally revived older U.S. consumers' memories of the death of four student protesters at the hands of Ohio's National Guard.*

> - *Zara: A new line of children's shirts with stripes and a star that resembled the uniforms of Nazi concentration camp victims was discontinued after intense online criticism.*
>
> - *Qiaobi: In its advertisement for a laundry detergent, an Asian woman shoves a detergent pod into the mouth of a black worker, pushes him into her washing machine, and sits on the lid; the person who comes out of the washing machine after the cycle is an idealized Chinese male.[5]*
>
> *Such public relations controversies are not confined to any particular industry or country; the products listed above are from companies based in Germany, the U.K., the U.S., Spain, and China. In addition to the direct cost of wasted planning and production efforts, companies must also consider the less easily quantified but perhaps more significant toll of brand damage from negative consumer comments that go viral. Regarding one of the examples above, a consumer remarks on Twitter: "Shame, Shame, Shame on you. Fire your marketing person and anyone who approved this ad."*

Implement

Tom Kelley of the renowned design firm Ideo wrote a book called *The Ten Faces of Innovation* in which he describes different roles people can take to move a project toward completion.[6] Inclusive leaders know how to tap diverse team members for their particular skill sets or working styles in the implementation process. Members with specific functional skills can obviously contribute their specialized expertise in areas such as engineering, finance, or marketing. In a business environment where companies are vying for innovation leadership, it is also worth considering, for instance, how the cultural profiles of different individuals could be utilized for the benefit of the team as a whole.

A team member who is status-oriented may have unique insights into customer expectations in a hierarchical society such as China or India, and could be designated as the "Master of Customer Care." Or to evaluate the pros and cons of product rollout timing options in different global markets, it might be useful to pair a more risk-oriented individual with a person who is more certainty-oriented. A relationship-oriented person from a culture where building amicable and trusting relationships is an art form could be designated as the "Teambuilder," while a task-focused team member could be assigned to some of the most time-sensitive deliverables as "The Enforcer." Such labels can be playful, intentional, and practically useful at the same time. They also help to keep the members of a heterogeneous team focused on implementation rather than reverting back to idea generation, which comes more easily.

The potential of a diverse workforce will only be fully unleashed when it is tapped to innovate and grow the business. This means far more than a rich brainstorming session which generates attractive ideas that then falter or fall flat when it comes to implementation. Managing global innovation means leveraging diversity from every possible angle to drive the innovation process all the way from inception to execution. This is easier said than done, but the steps outlined here—generate, plan, implement—provide a partial guide. Leaders who adopt these practices or invent their own methods for eliciting contributions from diverse team members will discover plenty of reasons to celebrate diversity.

Developing Future Leaders

Getting results requires more than blending the best ideas from different sources to create superior products or services; it also means recruiting, retaining, and developing a diverse array of leaders who can drive future growth. An important aspect of the talent life cycle depicted at the beginning of this chapter is discernment in evaluating future potential. We tend to look for ourselves in the mirror when identifying future leadership prospects, and this approach is fundamentally flawed in organizations with a diverse global workforce.

Sometimes the source of bias is primarily linguistic. People may be promoted into leadership roles because they have the language skills to communicate well with executives, but lack technical capabilities, customer knowledge, or the respect of fellow employees. In other cases employees might be misjudged, for example, based on more deep-rooted racial, ethnic, gender, or cultural biases that shape the conclusion, "This person is just not leadership material." Current leaders who implement an open-minded and insightful approach to evaluating talent are generally both welcomed by employees and respected for doing the right thing for the business:

A NEW LEADER

Recently a new global leader who is very good at judging people took over our line of business. It was so exciting to see her listen carefully to each person on her team, speak to other employees, and go on customer visits, even when she had to communicate mostly through an interpreter. We gradually began to open up and tell her who is really capable, and she has begun to promote them, including one local salesperson who doesn't speak other languages well but has won a lot of business with customers and is very much respected by employees.

Once high-potential talent has been identified, leaders must be able to follow up with flexible developmental practices that may differ from their own preferred norms. For example, a manager who is normally hands-off— "I hate to be micromanaged myself and imagine that others dislike this as well"—might discover that a hands-on style is required with a promising team member. Standard delegation practices that work in one environment could be regarded critically as "delegate and disappear" in another.

The emerging patterns of leadership exhibited by employees based on their own life experiences may be both unexpected and unlike those of executives previously held up as role models. As one respected leader comments, "I had to give others the chance to prove themselves in ways that no one had been successful before, and to utilize their own values and styles to succeed."

Inclusive leadership development thus produces several kinds of positive outcomes. Employees are open in sharing their best ideas, and customers are well-served. High-potential employees are retained and ready to take on future assignments with greater responsibilities. Beyond these effects, close relationships with a diverse range of employees can provide current leaders themselves with valuable feedback while eliciting a level of commitment and performance that is otherwise difficult to achieve: "If you are honest with people and show them you are trying to help their career, they will give you everything they've got."

GETTING RESULTS: SUMMARY

- Proactively seek out ideas, approaches and perspectives from people who do not think like you do. Express appreciation for their input, even when you disagree.

- Explore the suggestions of others before introducing your own proposals.

- Seek out internal and external customers that you could learn more about in order to understand their needs deeply, tapping the insights of employees whose backgrounds are similar to those of the customers.

- Experience unfamiliar markets directly by sampling competitors' products, living in a local residence, riding the subway, or spending a week in the factory.

- Consider the blind solicitation of new ideas to ensure that proposals are judged on their own merits. Be alert to new ways of achieving results and solving problems.

- Learn to distinguish between real agreement and polite responses that do not signify understanding or commitment.

- Establish processes that enable team members to analyze challenges from various angles and to build new ideas or proposed solutions together, using relevant diversity lenses.

- Examine workplace habits or systems that may benefit from inclusion. Check "the What, the Who, and the How" of key team processes. What changes could bring improved results?

- When making decisions, allow time for consultation and meeting preparation. This fosters more open discussion and allows for the expression of differing opinions.

- Continue to leverage diverse team member backgrounds during the implementation phase, considering their cultural profiles when determining key roles.

- View the talent life cycle as an additional means of producing results. Are you looking for yourself in the mirror or are you willing to sponsor leaders with different backgrounds and styles?

- Make a genuine commitment to developing the careers of others with leadership potential, even if they have a radically different style compared to yours.

- Be prepared to modify your developmental approach to high-potential employees based on their real needs.

- Seek feedback on the efficacy of your own leadership style so that you can continue to develop in addition to developing others.

PART THREE: GLOBAL APPLICATIONS

Global Teams

Regional Inclusion Challenges

Race and Ethnicity: A Global Perspective

07.
Global Teams

Inclusive global teams set in motion a positive spiral of trust, cultural competence, mutual learning, and high performance.

What is the impact of increased inclusiveness on team performance?

Unconscious bias is generally described and viewed through an individual lens. Learning programs focused on bias typically provide a list of potential biases, with explanations and examples of each, and ask participants to reflect on how bias of one kind or another may be affecting their own conduct. However, bias acquires its most powerful forms in complex interactions—social, political, economic—in which an individual's views and behavior impact others and are impacted in return. Social media is rife with biased commentary that can echo and grow, provoke harsh clashes, or consist of people talking past each other; there is often little real dialogue between people with different perspectives, and seldom any resolution. Another manifestation of such biased interactions, with vital implications for organizational performance, takes place within global teams.

Diverse global teams offer fertile ground for the propagation of bias due to a number of reasons:

- Remote team members may not have the chance to get to know each other well.

- Virtual communication and cultural differences in communication style make it easier for misunderstandings to occur and to fester.

- Team members are often dealing with "foreigners," or people far from their immediate in-group who look and talk differently.

All of these factors affect a team's prospects for developing shared trust as well as alignment among team members. It is not surprising that research on the performance of diverse teams shows mixed results. When they are inadequately managed, such teams tend to perform poorly, as differences and distance create strong centrifugal forces that pull them apart. On the other hand, teams perform at a higher level when they are managed in ways that enable their members to both "diverge," or draw out the creative potential of different perspectives, and then "converge" by aligning around shared goals, clear roles, and a joint commitment to action.[1]

So how might bias affect a global team, and what is the best way to address this? Self-awareness is a contact sport, and biases are readily aroused when people come into contact with others from different backgrounds. Here is an example of how the biases of team members can interact and result in mutual incomprehension and negative judgments.

EXAMPLE: THE ASIA-PACIFIC TEAM MEETING

A meeting has just occurred in which the members of a product service team were brainstorming solutions to an urgent regional client issue in a series of rapid-fire exchanges. During the meeting, headquarters-based participants in London, including an experienced team member named Alex, did much of the talking, while the team members based in Singapore were mostly silent. Here are the post-meeting impressions of the team leader at headquarters, followed by a contrasting set of impressions from one of the Singapore team members:

THE VIEW FROM HEADQUARTERS

I know that my colleagues in Singapore are less experienced. They usually don't have much to contribute to our meetings. I was disappointed but not surprised when they didn't say anything during our lively team discussion. On the other hand, I was impressed by the meeting contributions of my team member Alex, whom I've known for many years—we used to work in the same product group together when I was in a previous role. Alex had a lot to say during this meeting because he is an expert. Several of the other participants were too passive and should have spoken up more. I felt that we had a good meeting overall, and identified solutions that would be effective throughout Asia-Pacific.

THE VIEW FROM SINGAPORE

We knew that the team leader wasn't really interested in our opinions. She never gave us time to speak. People based at headquarters have a very limited understanding of our local clients and their needs. We could contribute more if they would study the data we send them in advance, and then run meetings in a way that we can join in the discussion. Alex seems to like to hear his own opinion—he feels that he is the only expert, but he is just the one with the loudest voice. It is unlikely that solutions similar to those from other regions will work in Asia-Pacific.

ANALYSIS: BIAS ON A GLOBAL TEAM

Global team veterans are likely to recognize many of the challenges that this team is facing. Before leaping to best practices that this team could implement, it is useful to analyze team member interactions for possible forms of unconscious bias, as this can illuminate why they have become so unproductive. In Chapter 4, we outlined the **CIAO model of unconscious bias**, which is summarized here:

- **Confirmation Bias**: We see what we expect to see. With limited information, our brain fills in the blanks based on prior experiences and beliefs.

  Example: *Both men and women tend to evaluate female candidates for technical roles more critically than they do male candidates.*

- **Insider Bias**: Genetic programming for "signs of danger" divides us into either friends (insiders) or enemies (outsiders or foreigners).

  Example: *Managers tend to favor employees from the same university, region, or ethnic group as themselves.*

- **Attribution Bias**: We "attribute" different causes—circumstance or character—to similar events based on whether someone is an insider (ourselves included) or an outsider. There are two opposite forms of attribution depending on whether the results are positive or negative.

  Example: *(Edward is a close friend of the manager, and Gwyn is not.)*

  Manager commenting on a positive outcome: Edward's team is doing well because he is a strong team leader (character); Gwyn's team is performing well because she has a terrific set of team members (circumstance).

  Manager commenting on a negative outcome: Edward's team is struggling because he just doesn't have the right mix of team members (circumstance);

Gwyn's team has problems because she is more tactical than strategic (character).

- **Overconfidence Bias:** We are overconfident about our own judgment and about our competitive standing relative to others.

  Example: *Over ninety percent of college professors believe that they are in the top half of teaching performers.[2]*

| Confirmation Bias | Insider Bias | Attribution Bias | Overconfidence Bias |

"CIAO" in Italian can mean either "Hello" or "Goodbye"!

Unfortunately for the members of the Asia-Pacific team described above, the CIAO model fits their interactions quite well. The comments of the two team members are revisited below with a breakdown that depicts these four biases in action on both sides:

The View from Headquarters

Confirmation Bias: *I know that my colleagues in Singapore are less experienced. They usually don't have much to contribute to our meetings. I was disappointed but not surprised when they didn't say anything during our lively team discussion.*

Insider Bias: *I was impressed by the meeting contributions of my team member Alex, whom I've known for many years—we used to work in the same product group together when I was in a previous role.*

Attribution Bias: *Alex had a lot to say during this meeting because he is an expert. Several of the other participants were too passive and should have spoken up more.*

Overconfidence Bias: *I felt that we had a good meeting overall, and identified solutions that could be effective throughout Asia-Pacific.*

The View from Singapore

Confirmation Bias: *We knew that the team leader wasn't really interested in our opinions. She never gave us time to speak.*

Insider Bias: *People based at headquarters have a very limited understanding of our local clients and their needs.*

Attribution Bias: *We could contribute more if they would study the data we send in advance and then run meetings in a way that we can join in the discussion. Alex seems to like to hear his own opinion—he feels that he is the only expert, but he is just the one with the loudest voice.*

Overconfidence Bias: *It is unlikely that solutions similar to those from other regions will work in Asia-Pacific.*

TEAM MEMBER BIAS: THE DOWNWARD SPIRAL

The cumulative effect of such team member biases when they occur in combination is powerful and pernicious. First of all, the CIAO elements themselves are mutually reinforcing. Because some team members are perceived as relative outsiders (insider bias), it is likely that those who consider themselves insiders will expect and perceive negative outcomes from the others (confirmation bias), blame these outcomes on character flaws or lack of capability (attribution bias), and be convinced that their own judgment is correct (overconfidence bias).

This lethal intermingling of biases is further compounded when the negative views within different team factions reinforce patterns of unproductive behavior, further strengthening the biases that are fueling such behaviors in the first place. **A tail-chasing cycle of biased assumptions and actions makes everyone on the team less likely to seek out new information or to act in a way that would disconfirm their basic assumptions**. Deeply entrenched views on both sides can make it harder to anticipate or to notice positive intentions or to elicit potential contributions, with slim prospects for change. Bias hardens into a wall of mutual antipathy that causes teams to head into a downward spiral of misunderstanding, misjudgment, blame, and mistrust, all confirmed and deepened by poor performance.

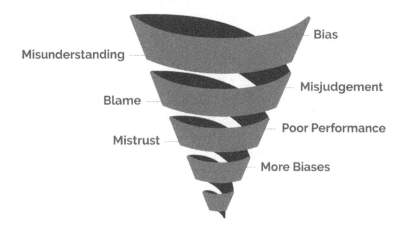

Figure 7.1: Bias and the Downward Spiral

INCLUSIVE LEADERSHIP BEHAVIORS: APPLICATIONS

So how can teams avoid this frightening descent into mutual animosity and blame, creating instead a positive, upward-moving cycle of shared insight and high performance? The Asia-Pacific team described above would benefit almost immediately from applying all five of the inclusive behaviors outlined in previous chapters. Below is a brief summary of sample ways that team members, starting with the team leader, could put inclusive behaviors into action:

Learning About Bias: The team leader in London and her regional counterpart in Singapore need to make a joint commitment to identifying and addressing bias, unconscious or conscious, beginning with evident symptoms such as the insider/outsider dynamics occurring between the two primary locations. Their first joint resolution could be to consciously act as "One Team," with the intent to have all team members in both locations interact as fellow insiders. Scheduling more informal one-on-one interactions outside of team meetings and exchanging personnel between London and Singapore for short-term assignments, for instance, will help team participants to build more personal bonds and greater mutual understanding.

Building Key Skills: The team should implement right away the global meeting best practices described in Chapter 5. These include asking for input in advance on agenda items; sharing information and documents beforehand; structuring turn-taking for speakers during meetings, with opportunities for written input as well; and following up informally after meetings to request feedback and to confirm the next action steps.

Working Across Boundaries: A key cultural dimension affecting team interactions is direct versus indirect communication style preferences. Building conscious awareness of cultural differences and skills for how to bridge them will help everyone. Team members in London will become better able to interpret messages they are already receiving from their APAC colleagues, and Singapore-based team members will learn to contribute in a style that their counterparts in the U.K. are more likely to recognize and value. Potential actions for bridging communication style differences are to require that all team members read meeting documents in advance, and to let Singaporean colleagues know they will be expected to offer their own recommendations in the next meeting—then giving them time to speak without interruption.

Becoming a Champion: The London-based team leader could serve as a mentor for the Singaporean regional lead, who aspires to a higher-level role and would probably appreciate the leader's advice on how to work more effectively with headquarters counterparts. Periodic "reverse mentoring" sessions, during which the Singaporean counterpart offers specific insights regarding the needs of regionally-based customers, would also expand the London-based leader's global perspective.

Getting Results: This team must be able to balance headquarters' strategic direction and available resources with keen insight into the needs of regional customers. It can only achieve this if team members have a shared awareness of each other's circumstances and use their collective knowledge nimbly to problem-solve and to innovate. More deliberately leveraging the diverse perspectives and capabilities of all team members—not just national cultural differences but also perspectives based on function, gender, generation, and so on—will produce better results.

HIGH-PERFORMING TEAM CHARACTERISTICS

Diverse global teams have distinctive challenges as well as potential advantages. In contrast with other, more homogenous teams, they need to counter the divisive effects of distance, cultural differences, and even matrix organizational tensions in order to perform at a high level. Survey data we have collected from the members of more than 1,300 global teams[3] highlight the **particular importance of establishing and maintaining strong team foundations**: shared goals, clarity regarding roles and responsibilities as well as the interests of key stakeholders, and trust among team members.[4]

Our experience over several decades of working with global teams has been that inclusive behaviors create a foundation of trust, a vital foundational element. Strong trust among global team participants is usually accompanied by several related features: psychological safety, cultural competence, and mutual learning. These team characteristics are in turn conducive to further inclusive actions.

1. Psychological Safety

One way to define psychological safety is as a form of applied trust: "I trust that if I speak up, my voice will be welcomed and I will not be punished." A sense of trust or psychological safety can become a vital tonic for a diverse team because it counteracts several forms of bias simultaneously, supporting the creation of a new set of linked mental habits. We are more inclined to anticipate and "confirm" positive contributions by trusted members of our team, which widens the circle of "insiders," discouraging negative character "attributions" and supporting more positive interpretations of performance results; "overconfidence" about faulty assumptions is also displaced by changing perceptions of team members.

Harvard researcher Amy Edmondson defines psychological safety as "a shared belief held by members of a team that the team is safe for interpersonal risk taking." She notes that this includes "a sense of confidence that the team will not embarrass, reject or punish someone for speaking up."[5] In diverse environments, which easily devolve into sub-groups of insiders and outsiders, competing factions, or even opposing tribes in larger organizations, team members who perceive themselves or are seen by others as relative "outsiders" are especially unlikely to speak out or to take risks. This phenomenon can be reversed as the sense of safety grows.

Google's Project Aristotle, which examined the factors correlated with success in a study of 180 internal teams, found that psychological safety was the single most important variable correlated with team effectiveness. Moreover, they discovered that although diversity alone was not a predictor of high team performance, **diverse teams *with* a high degree of psychological safety did perform at higher levels overall**. In other words, psychological safety is a vital ingredient of the "secret sauce" that enables diverse teams to realize their full potential.[7] Specific team behaviors associated with psychological safety include roughly equal air time for meeting participants and the readiness of team members to share incomplete ideas and their own personal vulnerabilities.

ABEER DUBEY
Director, People Analytics,
Google

- Objective: To identify what differentiates high performing teams from those that struggle.

- Analyzed 180 teams of tech and sales employees (over 200 interviews).

- Identified key features of successful teams, including psychological safety.

- *"Psychological safety allows teams to harness the power of diversity. That's because employees who have different points of view feel safe bringing their ideas to the table."*

Figure 7.2: Google's Project Aristotle[6]

2. Cultural Competence

Global team foundations must be built with an awareness of culture—otherwise team members may be unwittingly imposing their own preferred styles on others. Even the fundamental team building-block of trust is conveyed and interpreted in different ways that are culturally conditioned, so the actions required to create a foundation of psychological safety are not the same everywhere.

For instance, the statement, "Jump in any time with your questions and comments"—the expectation of the London-based team leader in the opening scenario—would be readily interpreted by colleagues from the same cultural background as an open, trust-building invitation to contribute to a discussion. However, others from a different cultural environment may perceive this same invitation to be risky and insincere, or they may lack the skills to participate in such a manner. Elsewhere we have covered various factors perceived as signs of trustworthiness through different cultural lenses.[8] The table below provides a list of sample trust-building actions by team leaders that are likely to be more or less effective depending on the cultural context:

Trust-Building: Cultural Comparisons	
Independent	**Interdependent**
Tell me what you think.	*I'd like for you to meet as a small group and then share your thoughts.*
Egalitarianism	**Status**
We need to find a solution, and you will have an important role.	*The boss has asked us all to come up with the best possible solution together, and expects us to have this by next Monday.*
Risk	**Certainty**
Jump in any time with your questions and comments. We're all just brainstorming here, and any ideas are good.	*I am sending you the agenda in advance so that you have time to prepare.*
Direct	**Indirect**
I disagree with your last comment.	*Please tell me more about your last comment.*
Task	**Relationship**
We have a full day of work ahead of us, and then those of us who still have the energy can go out to dinner together.	*We'll have dinner together the evening before our meeting so that those who haven't yet met in person can get to know each other.*

Figure 7.3: Trust-Building: Cultural Comparisons

Cultural competence in a global team environment means moving beyond cultural self-awareness to apply the three-part formula outlined in Chapter 3: know yourself, know others, bridge differences. The team profile here portrays culturally-based work-style preferences of the global team members in London and Singapore.

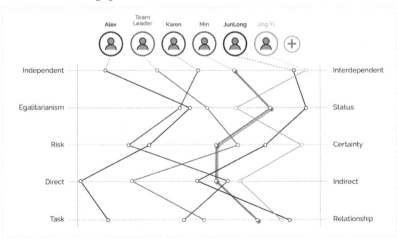

Figure 7.4: GlobeSmart Team Profile

The London-based team leader (second from left) has a personal profile that is more "Independent," for example, than the profiles of most other team members. Awareness of this contrast could prompt the leader to set aside a personal preference for more individualistic forms of expression—"Just speak up if you have something to say"—and modify the team meeting format to incorporate more group-oriented processes such as turn-taking, pausing the meeting to request comments in a virtual chat box, or allowing side discussions for small groups to solve problems. It might be necessary to take these steps on multiple occasions in order to set a new tone, to familiarize team members with the format, and to confirm the sincerity of the request.[9] This may require one-on-one conversations with Singaporean team members to build stronger relationships and to ask for guidance: "What could we do to get the other team members more involved? They've been pretty quiet during our meetings."

The bridge-building formula through which cultural competence is applied further counteracts each of the forms of unconscious bias outlined previously: "Confirmation" of mutually-held negative expectations is challenged with a new process that encourages wider contributions. Factional lines on the team favoring headquarters-based "Insiders" are at least partially dissolved, as all team members are invited to become more active participants. Mistaken "attributions" are replaced with more real-time profiles that also reflect team members' culturally-based tendencies, helping to explain the "why behind the behavior" of each person. And "overconfident" misjudgments are supplanted by active inquiry. These actions will make the outward manifestations of psychological safety, including roughly equal air time among team members and readiness to share ideas, far more likely to flourish.

3. Mutual Learning

Another characteristic of diverse high-performing teams, confirmed by Google's Project Aristotle, is constant mutual learning among team members. A team foundation of trust and psychological safety, fostered through culturally competent bridge-building, surmounts the barriers of unconscious bias and provides the launch point for a positive cycle of shared discovery and learning. For example, the director of Google X, Astro Teller, has helped teams achieve superior results by holding "pre-mortem" sessions during which team members are asked to highlight possible reasons that a team project could fail.[10] By seeking out flaws in new ventures, in spite of the perils commonly associated with criticizing executive pet projects or simply being wrong about anticipated problems, Teller's teams are able to address potential failure points at an early stage. Team members clearly need to feel free to take risks, speak up, admit personal failings, and learn from each other in such an environment.

In contrast to the negative cycle displayed earlier, inclusive global teams set in motion a positive spiral of trust, cultural competence, mutual learning, and high performance, with each of these steps further disconfirming lingering forms of bias and replacing them with realistic aspirations and heightened trust.

Figure 7.5: The Upward Spiral: Bias Unraveled

Those who have been in a strong mutual learning environment on a diverse team report that this is an unforgettable personal and professional experience. The team is "on fire" (in a good way) with ideas, energy, and creativity. Team members receive positive feedback not only from each other but also from internal and external customers, and the results that they achieve can turn them into the corporate version of rock stars.

A significant, intrinsically motivating side to this high-performing team equation is the almost daily insights that team members gain in their work together and the inspirational way that these insights are shaped into innovative products, services, and processes. Here are some comments from members of such teams about their experiences:

COMMENTS FROM GLOBAL TEAM MEMBERS

- *At first we actively disliked each other and there was very little trust, but after we realized that we were serving different stakeholders and were able to better align our goals, we actually began to develop real friendships and to get things done.*

- *We accomplished more in the past two days meeting together face-to-face than in the entire previous six months because now we know each other better and have a real foundation of trust.*

- *At some point, people stopped advocating for their own preconceived ideas and started listening to each other. That's when we really got creative.*

- *I can't even remember where this idea came from—it seems like we all contributed.*

- *Sometimes we end up with a completely different solution than what I was expecting because we listen to all players.*

- *If I see that people have been marginalized in a situation, I will specifically bring them into the circle, inviting them to participate in making decisions whenever they can contribute.*

- *The client insight came from our local salesperson, who knows the client better than anyone. The technical solution came from a client visit he made together with one of our corporate R&D experts—the conversation they had with the client led to a whole new package of products and services that our team has now rolled out to other markets.*

- *My headquarters-based team member helped me to find the contact person I was looking for. She told me in five minutes what it would have taken me five hours to find on my own.*

- *I had no idea about the realities of that market—the regulatory hurdles, the competition, the challenges in finding and keeping good talent. Thanks to our local colleagues we now have a much better go-to-market strategy.*

GLOBAL TEAMS: RETAINING A PERFORMANCE EDGE

A high-performing team needs to stay on its toes, and the application of inclusive behaviors should be a constant discipline. Ironically, as team members get to know each other and become more aligned, they have to be on guard against a stealthily accumulating "group-think" of the kind that produces blind spots for more homogeneous teams. Increased mutual comfort among an expanded group of "insiders" may lead to the formation of habits that contain resurgent biases against yet another group of perceived "outsiders": new team members, related project teams, or different functions.[11]

In other words, for a team to retain its positive momentum and to avoid slipping back into destructive habits, inclusive actions and the team characteristics that they support must continue. Behaviors such as "Learning About Bias" and "Working Across Boundaries" cannot be simply checked off a list but should be revisited as circumstances evolve.

Team members need to keep expanding their sphere of inquiry and insight by questioning established processes and incorporating fresh ideas and sources of information. The practice of "continuous learning" was taught long ago by the quality guru William Edwards Deming, and some of its underlying principles have applications far beyond factory floors when they are coupled with real inclusiveness in diverse team environments.

There are a number of best practices that are particularly conducive to ongoing mutual learning in an inclusive team setting. Here is a summary list:

INCLUSIVE GLOBAL TEAMS

- **Team Foundations**: Pay special attention to establishing and revisiting shared goals, roles and responsibilities, stakeholder interests, and trust.

- **High Context Kickoff**: Whenever possible, kick off the team's work by meeting face-to-face or at least using the most "high context" communication methods available (e.g., web meeting with cameras plus chat function rather than video or voice-only).

- **Meeting Process**: Set up a regular meeting process with clear expectations for when and how team members will be expected to contribute; provide opportunities to prepare in advance.

- **Tag Teams**: Establish "tag teams," or pairs of individuals based in different locations (e.g., headquarters and subsidiary) who work well together and can integrate contrasting perspectives.

- **Window Persons**: Exchange individual team members on a long-term or short-term basis so that there is a person in each key location who knows the people and the issues faced at other sites.

- **Show and Tell**: Dedicate a portion of the team's meeting time to have team members describe unique aspects of their markets that the rest of the team might not know about.

- **First-Hand Observation**: At least the team leader and ideally all team members should visit each other's work sites to increase shared understanding through joint meetings and conversations with local stakeholders and customers.

- **Check-ins**: Plan for one-on-one check-ins with key team counterparts before and after meetings to ensure that agendas include key issues and vital information is exchanged.

- **Information Sources**: Incorporate additional types of information into the team's review process that reflect unfamiliar market realities, sources of competition, or emerging opportunities.

- **Catalyst Role**: The team leader or meeting facilitator takes the role of "catalyst," seeking to identify and integrate good ideas regardless of their source, building joint solutions rather than being an advocate for a particular point of view.

- **Risk-Taking**: Recognize and reward team members willing to take measured risks to reinforce the value of learning from both success and failure.

- **Expand the Circle**: Invite members of other groups to join the team's discussions where relevant to expand team member awareness, broaden networks, and contribute different perspectives and ideas.

- **"Winner" Identity**: Take note of and celebrate team successes— even initial quick wins—that stem from mutual learning to underline its value and further inspire team members to take part.

08.
Regional Inclusion Challenges

Social ideals, terminology, business processes, and communication styles taken for granted at headquarters are not necessarily shared by employees around the world.

Are inclusion challenges the same everywhere, or are there differences across regions such as Asia-Pacific, EMEA, or North America?

Leaders who encounter employees or customers behaving in unfamiliar ways need to understand what drives their behavior. Such understanding is essential to begin to motivate, to sell, and to shrink the common gap between what we intend and the effects that our actions have. For leaders who interact with a diverse range of employees, globally or domestically, it is important to understand the differences among and even within countries.

For example, **women** are underrepresented in leadership positions worldwide, but this is particularly true in Asia-Pacific. A McKinsey study notes.

 Worldwide, slightly less than four women hold leadership positions for every ten men in business and politics. In Asia-Pacific, there is only one woman in leadership positions for every four men. In some countries in East Asia, there are only 12 to 20 women leaders for every 100 men.[1]

Women across Asia face a daunting combination of obstacles depending on the location: educational discrimination; threats to physical safety; social norms regarding work after childbirth and the role of men in child-rearing; limited childcare options and the perception that children are better cared for by family members. They also encounter workplace stereotypes that women are best suited to particular industries such as consumer goods, retail, or hospitality; lack of female executive role models; business entertainment settings that may exclude women; and invisible ceilings in many organizations that limit women's advancement to higher roles.

In Europe, although gender issues are also common, **ageism** is an increasingly critical theme and is likely to become more important due to demographic trends. In a comprehensive survey of 55,000 people from 28 European countries, more than a third of respondents representing all age groups reported seeing unfair treatment based on age. The rapidly aging workforce across most of Europe ensures that heightened sensitivity to age-based issues will continue for some time. The current ratio of four people of working age to each person over 65 is projected to change to a ratio of just two to one by 2050, portending a growing burden on social services. In Europe, age discrimination is reportedly experienced even more often than other forms of discrimination based on gender or race and is a frequent source of workplace disputes. "Older people are likely to be stereotyped as warm but incompetent, feeding low expectations and lack of inclusion."[2]

Sub-Saharan Africa is a huge region comprising 46 of the continent's 54 countries and over a billion people. In spite of vast changes as cities expand and economies modernize, the legacy of colonialism lives on in many places. **Ethnic differences** formerly aggravated by colonial masters attempting to extend and maintain control have made it difficult for many countries to unify their citizens and to ensure orderly transitions of power.[3] In addition to armed conflicts and genocide in places like Sudan and Rwanda, or election-related violence in Kenya, for example, ethnic rivalries influence conduct in some contemporary workplaces in less lethal but nonetheless significant forms. An employee may be afforded a position of prestige or looked down upon—even threatened—depending on ethnic or tribal affiliation. As one expatriate living outside of his native Somalia reports, "It was a relief for me to move to another country because at home people looked at what I did based on the tribe I came from, and when I made a decision that went against the interests of another group, I felt that both me and my family were threatened."

THREE COUNTRY EXAMPLES

Each country around the world faces its own unique constellation of inclusion challenges at the same time that it shares common themes with other locations. Here are a few examples that help to illustrate country-specific patterns and their implications for corporate inclusion initiatives:

Ghana

This West African nation of approximately 30 million people is well-known for its relative prosperity and democratic governance. It shares characteristics with its near neighbors but is distinguished from them in other ways—for example, Ghana is an anglophone country, with English as its official language and spoken by more than two-thirds of the population, surrounded by francophone neighbors: the Ivory Coast, Togo, and Burkina Faso.

Like its neighbors, Ghana contains a mix of ethnic groups, with over one hundred along with many languages, including 11 that are government-sponsored. The country's main ethnic groups are the Akan, representing almost half of the population, the Mole-Dagbon, Ewe, Ga-Dangme, and Gurma. Employees in the workplace are often aware of the ethnic backgrounds of their co-workers, and tribal references are common. The majority ethnic group, the Akans, and especially the Ashantis, their largest subgroup—with their numbers and the proud history of the Ashanti kingdom—can be perceived as feeling superior. However, such ethnic divides are comparatively less significant than in other locations on the continent such as nearby Nigeria, often taking the form of casual banter instead of dangerous tension.

Social distinctions that are still quite clear in Ghana are usually based on **education and socioeconomic class**. English language fluency is viewed as an indicator of educational background, and in spite of Ghana's overall literacy rate of 85 percent,

> **Social distinctions that are still quite clear in Ghana are usually based on education and socioeconomic class.**

levels of education vary widely from the elite with advanced technical degrees to members of less wealthy socioeconomic classes who may have the equivalent of a middle school education. The striking gap between rich and poor can be seen on the same city block, with high tea served on the finest china to nattily attired guests on the upper floor of an office building, while vendors with dubious hygiene and wearing makeshift clothing sell products on the street below.

Workplace opportunities are influenced by political, familial, or religious ties. Even extended family connections—including distant cousins or in-laws—carry considerable weight, as do school networks. Nepotism and cronyism are widespread and sometimes even expected by members of the same group. The majority of Ghana's population is Christian, with a Muslim minority of less than 20 percent. Church elders, clergy, and other leaders are generally held in high esteem. Although it might appear incongruous or inappropriate to employees of Western organizations accustomed to separating religion from the workplace, successful social and corporate initiatives sometimes involve partnerships with religious groups and incorporate religious values.

In white-collar workplace settings in Ghana, the people with whom local employees may feel the greatest tension are foreign expatriates whose hefty pay packages are seen as exceeding the value of their contribution. However, Ghana also has a relatively large number of economic migrants and illegal immigrants living within its borders. Estimates range widely, with the Ghana Immigration Service stating that immigrants number 14.6 percent of the total population, and are generally higher than the percentage of immigrants in European countries where this topic has been the source of controversy and political upheaval. Among other groups, an estimated one million Nigerians have immigrated to Ghana, and they are often accused of criminal activity, including internet-based fraud. Both Ghana and Nigeria have previously engaged in mass deportations of each other's citizens, depending on the economic climate of the times. Many Nigerians in Ghana complain that they are unfairly treated, being forced to close their shops and experiencing everyday discrimination in workplaces or on the streets.[4] The size and growth rate of Nigeria's population, which is now estimated to be approximately 200 million, or more than six times the number of Ghanaians, suggests that the interactions between the citizens of the two countries will only become more frequent.[5]

Men in Ghana generally have greater social privileges than women country-wide, with women confronting an array of barriers stemming from their social context. Women in the workplace are often called upon to carry out domestic-type chores such as fetching food or drinks, and may not be included or heeded in strategic meetings. Ambitious, competitive women are maligned and accused of having risen through providing sexual favors. There are relatively low numbers of women in executive or management roles. Sexual harassment in the form of *quid pro quo*, or the demand for sexual favors in exchange even for overseeing apprenticeships or administering standard functions such as tests, has been in Ghana's public eye based on a recent high-profile incident.[6] Harassment also takes place in more pervasive, everyday forms such as lewd remarks made to women by men who might actually be surprised to find that these are considered objectionable.

Inclusion in Ghana: Implications

Initiatives that address socioeconomic differences and the roles of women in the workplace are likely to have the most immediate relevance in addressing common sources of exclusion. Companies may want to consider providing supplementary education and training for those who have not benefited from elite higher education opportunities.

Efforts to extend Western sexual harassment standards will appear relevant if they make connections with local examples; *quid pro quo* harassment can be readily explained, but comments and conduct defined elsewhere as creating a "climate of harassment" might not be regarded in the same way by men or even by some women, so the starting point for training efforts may need to be different.

WHAT DOES IT MEAN TO BE AFRICAN?

Beginning in 2035, the number of young people reaching working age in Africa will exceed that of the rest of the world combined, and this trend will continue every year for the rest of the century. By 2050, one in every four humans will be African, and at the end of the century, Africans will comprise 40 percent of the world's total population.[7]

Five of the world's fastest-growing countries in terms of population range from west to east and north to south on the continent and include Nigeria, Ethiopia, Tanzania, Uganda, and the Democratic Republic of the Congo. Growth like this, along with its economic and humanitarian implications, makes it essential to reexamine previous images and stereotypes.

Cultural differences among Africans include religion, with adherents of Christianity—Protestant and Catholic—and Islam, as well as a variety of indigenous religions. There are also well-known differences between anglophone and francophone regions based on the legacy of colonialism, but differences among Africans go far deeper.

The African continent has over 3,000 ethnic groups, and its people speak two thousand languages. The incredible variety of African geography— mountains, desert, jungle, savannah—has shaped a genetic diversity among people within Africa that is said to be greater than the genetic differences between Europeans and Chinese. Because humans originated in Africa, human beings have had more time to adapt there than anywhere else in the world.[8] There are Africans from every major racial group, with hundreds of millions of Arab North Africans from Morocco to Egypt, and even roughly one million Chinese who have arrived as expatriates, laborers, or immigrants.

At least 180 million members of the African diaspora, including first generation African emigrants, live around the world in North America, the Caribbean, Central and South America, Europe, and Asia. People of African heritage living abroad have taken on other genetic and cultural characteristics. Black Africans in the U.S. reportedly have an average of 25 percent white genetic makeup, reflecting in part centuries of exploitation through the institution of slavery. Skin pigmentation among African-Americans with this genetic mix is largely a matter of random variation—among children from the same set of parents, one may appear "white" and the other "black."

Self-concept and identity across Africans of all backgrounds vary considerably as well: African-Americans traveling to Africa sometimes report being surprised that at the same time they may have looked down on their African counterparts as residents of less developed countries, those same counterparts saw them as less than fully African.

In the broadest sense, all of humanity originated in Africa—we are all Africans—and Africa's burgeoning population will exert an increasingly large influence worldwide through economic growth, migration, conflict, consumption, culture, and the sheer vitality of the most youthful population on earth.

Germany

Germany is the largest member country of the European Union, with a population of 82 million. It has the world's fourth largest economy in terms of GDP, and a highly skilled workforce. The country also has an **aging population**—with a median age of 47, Germany is the third oldest nation in the world, behind only Monaco and Japan (compared, for instance, with median ages of 38 for the U.S., 37 for China, 28 for India, and 18 for Nigeria).[9] Germany's population was previously predicted to decline to 68 million because of its low birth rate and had actually begun to decrease year over year. Now, due to higher immigration levels and a slight birth-rate increase, the population could remain relatively stable going forward.[10]

A long-term **demographic transformation** has been taking place in Germany which had its roots in the labor shortage of the post-WWII years. Guest worker programs were put in place to address this shortfall, and many immigrant laborers later became permanent residents. Since West Germany's reunification with East Germany in 1990 and the dissolution of the Soviet Union in 1991, several

> **More than one quarter of Germany's population are foreign-born or have a parent who immigrated to the country**

million ethnic Germans from other former Eastern Bloc countries have also exercised their right to return to Germany. The establishment of the European Union in 1993 allowed citizens from any EU country to work in other member states, causing additional economic migrants from EU nations to seek work in relatively prosperous nations like Germany, where job opportunities are available.

At this point, Germany has the highest ever number of residents who are either foreign-born or have a parent who was born in another country. Approximately 21 million people, or more than a quarter of the total population, are classified as having a "migration background." Two-thirds of these are from EU states, and the others are from elsewhere.[11] Most recently, over 1.6 million asylum-seeking refugees, primarily from the Middle East and Africa, have entered the country just since 2014.[12] Germany now contains a wide array of ethnic minorities, including more than 2.8 million Turks along with large numbers of Poles, Russians, Italians, Syrians, and Africans from various nations. The recent spike in immigration has led to increased political tension, with nationalist, anti-immigration candidates garnering more votes and representation in the German federal parliament.

The combination of a high-tech economy, an aging workforce, and large numbers of recent immigrants makes the transfer of knowledge and skills a crucial issue in German enterprises. As in other parts of Europe, the issue of age discrimination has received growing attention as well. The physical demands of manufacturing jobs, in particular, become more stressful and difficult for those advancing in age. This is sometimes seen as an intractable problem and a reason to lower expectations for worker output, slow down manufacturing lines, or even close down some facilities with aging workforces. Here is an example of how one leadership team attempted to address its workforce challenges by utilizing the unique capabilities of its older workers.

SILVER TO GOLD

The executives running a factory based near Munich, in German's southern state of Bavaria, were proud of their site's reputation for high quality and an extremely productive workforce. However, with many experienced older workers now retiring or approaching retirement age, they faced a two-fold onboarding problem.

First, the learning curve of newly appointed team leaders in the factory had proved to be time-consuming and inefficient. Because of the inexperience of these new leaders, for example, they would typically follow a very rigid, by-the-book process whenever non-planned events such as a minor quality glitch or mechanical issue would emerge. The procedures for addressing these events were complex and time-consuming, resulting in lengthy, detailed reports, some of which were unnecessary.

In addition, the factory had just voluntarily accepted a contingent of Middle Eastern refugees into its vocational training program. This was a highly visible project, and the initial interactions between these refugees and the workers assigned to train them had been more difficult than expected. After a short initial honeymoon period, poor communication and misunderstandings had led to increasing tensions, and the new employees were falling behind on their training milestones.

Based on extensive consultation with its works council, the factory's leadership instituted a new "Turning Silver into Gold" policy that paired experienced senior coaches/mentors with younger team leaders and with small groups of refugees. The experienced workers, who had no direct reporting line to either group, were able to help their younger team leader colleagues to better prioritize their activities. Rather than blindly implementing standard procedures, the team leaders learned to implement quality control measures more selectively and efficiently. As these junior leaders began to appreciate the expertise and experience that the senior workers brought to them, they became eager to reach out and ask for their input.

Likewise, with more focused, hands-on attention, the refugee trainees' pace of learning began to accelerate as well. The older coaches/mentors were sufficiently enthusiastic that they collaborated to create an accelerated onboarding process for workers who often brought skills of their own but lacked previous vocational training in manufacturing. They also made an effort to get to know each of the new arrivals on a personal level to better understand their backgrounds and interests, and implemented meeting best practices to ensure that the trainees, none of whom were fluent in German, were able to understand detailed technical explanations and to ask questions.

The positive energy generated by this initiative during its implementation was enormous, with visible relief for overburdened team leaders and for refugees trying hard to succeed in their new roles. Factory leaders realized that they were in the midst of a large-scale knowledge transfer to younger team leaders and to their newest employees only made possible through valuing senior expertise. They had underestimated the subtle "tacit" knowledge and judgment that older factory workers had acquired through long hands-on experience. Greater inclusion of senior workers and their expertise in turn made the factory more inclusive of its newest entrants. This effort was so successful that even the local factory vice president requested a personal coach/mentor.

Ironically, a major challenge that those running this initiative faced in expanding it to other parts of the company was to advocate for its importance in comparison with other company inclusion measures already in place related to gender and disabilities. Eventually, a regional inclusion initiative leveraging senior worker experience was launched, building on the positive energy and the precedent established within this plant.

Inclusion in Germany: Implications

Inclusion of senior workers may need to be weighed as a corporate priority in addition to other important goals. Experienced workers have both knowledge and the capacity for judgment that will likely need to be conveyed in a hands-on manner rather than solely through documentation.

Certain types of initiatives can be undertaken only through extensive consultation with enterprise-based work councils, but those entities may also be helpful in getting workers on board. Framing the contribution of older workers as "knowledge transfer" and/or "mentoring" could serve as one way to position such an effort positively for everyone involved.

The United States

The U.S. continues to struggle with its historical legacies of slavery and immigration. **Race, gender, and illegal immigration** are all sensitive, hot-button topics that must be handled with care. Tragic killings of black citizens and the Black Lives Matter movement have again brought issues of racial discrimination and social justice vividly into public awareness.

Federal law—in many cases augmented by state laws—prohibits discrimination against a broad list of "protected classes," or groups of people who are protected from employment discrimination based on race, color, religion, sex, age, disability, national origin, or veteran status. Alleged violations can result in major lawsuits against employers, incurring substantial legal costs and sometimes much larger expenses for settlements or penalties.

In addition to these legally protected categories, there has been a renewed recognition that **income and social class** matter as well. Income distribution, drug addiction rates, voting patterns, and levels of access to medical care all appear to diverge along class lines. These trends affect educational opportunities, too. Children from economically disadvantaged backgrounds attend top universities at strikingly low rates: "At 38 colleges in America, including five in the Ivy League—Dartmouth, Princeton, Yale, Penn, and Brown—more students came from the top 1 percent of the income scale than from the entire bottom 60 percent."[13] Companies seeking to recruit a diverse workforce must deliberately look to schools that are most effective in enrolling students from lower-income families.

Many people in the U.S. decline to identify themselves in narrow racial, socioeconomic, or cultural terms, and emphasize that they represent a mixture. The term, **"intersectionality,"** now often used within the field of inclusion and diversity, underlines the fact that a person can experience interdependent, overlapping forms of discrimination based on categorizations such as race, gender, social class, or sexual orientation. This term was coined by Columbia University Professor Kimberlé Crenshaw to explain how black women could experience prejudice both for being black and for being female.[14]

Others have raised the banner of intersectionality to describe different kinds of hyphenated identities. Understanding how exclusion occurs in various ways that impact a single individual surely enables a more accurate and customized approach to analyzing problems and identifying solutions. This also opens up avenues for individual expression by people who may have been previously uncomfortable describing important aspects of their life experience (e.g., military service, immigrant status, religious beliefs, sexual orientation). In addition to black women, other groups face multi-faceted challenges that are perpetuated by institutionalized discrimination and political disenfranchisement.

Critics, on the other hand, particularly those with a socially conservative perspective, claim that the concept of intersectionality sometimes reinforces a heightened sense of victimhood and a new type of "us" versus "them" mentality—the person or group facing the most disadvantages is the most abused, long-suffering, and deserving of special treatment.[15] Whether the outcome in any particular instance is progress toward greater inclusiveness or wrangling based on so-called identity politics likely depends upon the approach and attitudes of everyone involved: litigation or mutual outreach, demonization or dialogue, violent clashes or systemic change.

Multicultural identity is another U.S. trend that shares characteristics with intersectionality. It was punctuated by the election of former President Obama,

There is a substantial literature on the subject of "third culture kids" that describes children raised with multiple cultural identities.

the son of a white mother from the state of Kansas and a black father from Kenya. Kamala Harris, the current vice president, has Afro-Jamaican and Indian roots. Increasing numbers of citizens identify themselves as members of more than one race. There is a substantial literature on the subject of "third culture kids" that describes how children raised with multiple cultural identities—for example, through emigration or living part of their childhood abroad—come to terms with their personal backgrounds.[16]

Concepts such as "marginality" capture a common self-perception voiced by many with a multicultural background: "I don't really feel that I belong anywhere." Sadly, some never manage to turn this background into an advantage, living instead with a perpetual sense of being an outsider. Yet others leverage their multi-faceted cultural and linguistic fluency to achieve extraordinary levels of competence as business or government leaders, becoming serial bridge-builders between different worlds. Companies now frequently turn to multi- cultural individuals when establishing diverse teams or expanding subsidiaries abroad.

Inclusion in U.S.: Implications

Inclusion efforts need to address deep-rooted issues such as interpersonal and institutionalized racism. Minority employees want to have a "seat at the table," a real voice in discussions and decision making, and changes in organizational processes and systems to ensure greater workplace equity.

Some people, particularly those within the millennial workplace generation, may not consider themselves to be members of a single racial, ethnic, or cultural group (including the millennial category), but want to be understood on their own terms. Others regard themselves as disadvantaged based on their economic background or other factors, even though they do not fall into any group that is legally defined as a "protected class."

Organizational reforms and program designs should take such perspectives into account; simultaneously, change leaders must be prepared to encounter pushback against "identity politics," disparaged by critics as fostering hypersensitivity and a sense of victimhood.

INCLUSION INITIATIVES: QUESTIONING BASIC ASSUMPTIONS

Attention to regional and local variations around the world can lead to insights that require adjustments to inclusion initiatives. Social ideals, terminology, business processes, and communication styles taken for granted at headquarters are not necessarily shared by employees around the world who have been living in very different environments. Efforts to establish common organizational goals, principles, and standards of conduct are often still feasible, however, if they are adapted to local learning styles and current issues.

For example, here are discoveries made by a Western facilitator during a leadership development program held in Kenya with participants from across sub-Saharan Africa who had been identified as high-potential future leaders. At first she found that her attempts to spark discussion did not seem to work.

LEADERSHIP DEVELOPMENT IN KENYA

The initial atmosphere was one of suspicion and mutual distrust among the multinational hodgepodge of local employees and expatriates who made up the audience. There were too many inappropriate side remarks and put-downs, sighs, and rolled eyeballs. The non-Africans in the group had received previous training of sorts at their past companies and in schools—they clearly had an advantage and were dominating the discussions while being subtly condescending toward, and ridiculing, the Africans. This did little for the willingness of participants to work and learn together.

Everyone seemed to be distracted with the business of establishing a pecking order within their own subgroup. During the breaks, they would form separate clusters divided by nationality and rank. There was an odd dynamic even among the Kenyans themselves—several appeared to be a bit aloof from the others, who deferred very cautiously to them. It turned out that three individuals who stood apart were members of elite and powerful family groups. The others not only treated them with respect, but appeared to be intimidated by them and went out of their way to avoid disagreement.

Recognizing the divisive atmosphere in the room and evidence that some people were fearful about participating freely, the facilitator made adjustments to arrange for shorter days with everyone together in a large group format, creating separate time slots for one-on- one meetings with participants plus more small-group discussion. These changes led to further insights and unexpected challenges to standard Western assumptions about inclusive leadership, particularly related to the constructive application of power:

- **Empowerment**

  A common line of skeptical questioning was directed at the description of management's role in delegating tasks and "empowering" employees to carry them out. Delegation was fine in the participants' view, but they would ask,

  Who is really going to give away power? If you trust such people, they may pretend to represent you and support you, but then they will misuse the information you provide them or turn against you to serve their own agenda. When you make a fine show of empowering others, then it is easier to blame them when things go wrong!

- **Terminology**

  The materials brought from headquarters were seen as having too much unhelpful jargon.

  This is the company's clever way of manipulating us. They try to tell us that this is a common global language, but it's one that only they can speak. They're not fooling anybody.

- **Strategic Planning**

  The program segment on strategic planning met with a deflating response from some participants that seemed to be a reflection of socioeconomic gaps and attitudes toward time.

I'm just happy to be alive today. If you're a privileged person, you can think about planning. If you're not, you must deal with whatever God gives you

- **Insiders and Outsiders**

  Participants struggled with the idea of inclusion, noting that one's inner circle, as they defined it, was of course treated in a very different way from how those on the outside were treated. However, when urged to reframe the way they saw themselves within the company and to add new and expanded groups of insiders, this was a challenge they took quite seriously and which visibly impacted ways in which group members related to one another.

With persistence and adjustment, key inclusion principles began to take hold. These were expressed in forms that were unexpected and yet strikingly effective, and inclusion began to take on its own distinctively local tone.

LEADERSHIP DEVELOPMENT IN KENYA (CONTINUED)

At one point, a senior participant launched into a story. The facilitator considered interrupting this person as he headed off into what appeared to be unrelated subject matter, but then noticed that the rest of the audience was riveted by the vibrancy, the rhythm, and the colorful punctuation of his tale. The man recalled the tough times the subsidiary had faced during an economic downturn—how their company had almost pulled out of the country due to political interference and the lack of profits. After several more minutes of recounting this history, the storyteller turned to the way that the foreign subsidiary president at the time had consulted with others from various backgrounds, testing several alternatives before deciding on the proper course of action. The story culminated with a perfect illustration of inclusive leadership as the listeners nodded and murmured their assent.[17]

09.
Race and Ethnicity:
A Global Perspective

Leaders must tailor their plans for creating greater equity for all racial and ethnic groups in ways that are welcomed by local employees, delivering high performance along with real social impact.

Are race and ethnicity universal issues that employers should be addressing with a common approach?

A striking feature of the "Black Lives Matter" movement in the U.S. has been its reverberations around the globe. Demonstrations have occurred in every world region: Europe (e.g., in the UK, Spain, Germany, Italy), Asia (Japan, South Korea), South America (Brazil), Africa (Senegal), the Middle East (Turkey), and Australia.[1] The cross-border scope of this movement has caused many organizations to take a fresh look at how to address issues of race and ethnicity on a global basis. The previous chapter compared general inclusion issues in several world regions. Here we will focus on race and ethnicity, examining key factors that shape both similarities and differences between countries, along with specific country examples, and recommendations for companies that want to translate their values into specific actions and results. Although race and ethnicity are social constructs whose definitions change with the historical context, human perceptions of these constructs are nonetheless powerful and consequential.[2]

WHAT'S COMMON AND WHAT'S NOT

Racial and ethnic diversity, as well as issues of privilege, equity, and social justice, are built into most countries. At the same time, each place has its own unique background and constellation of social issues, and solutions that might be suited for one location could fall flat or be counterproductive in another. Key factors include:

Demographics

Commitment to Social Justice

Diversity and Intersectionality

1. Demographics

Some countries are more racially and ethnically diverse than others. China's vast population of 1.4 billion is predominantly Han Chinese, with an estimated 92% of citizens in this category. The more than 50 other Chinese ethnic groups —e.g., Zhuang, Manchu, Uighur, Tibetan, Mongolian— comprise a relatively small part of the overall population, and are primarily located in regions that are outside of the developed urban areas in China's eastern half.

Japan is even more ethnically homogenous, although not to the extent that its nationalist ideologues have proclaimed. The 2% of its population classified as ethnic minorities include the Ainu living in the northern island of Hokkaido, people of Korean ancestry forced to come to the country as laborers during World War II, and the so-called *burakumin*, formerly regarded as an "untouchable" social caste that worked in trades such as butchery or leather tanning considered unclean according to traditional religious standards.

In contrast with countries such as China and Japan, the United States is well on its way to becoming a majority-minority nation by around 2045, when the total number of racial minorities will outnumber members of the population classified as white.[3] Five states, including California and Texas, the nation's two largest by population, already have more minority residents than whites. Latinos are the largest and fastest-growing minority in the U.S., currently making up 18% of the national population, while African-Americans comprise 13%, Asian-Americans 6%, Native Americans or Pacific Islanders about 1.5%, and those who identify themselves as multiracial 2.6%.[4] The millennial generation, commonly defined as the age group born between 1981 and 1996, embodies future trends—its 44% minority population makes it the most diverse generation in U.S. history.[5] It is not surprising, given the sizable percentage of minorities among them, that millennials have taken a prominent role in the Black Lives Matter movement; they are likely to feel most keenly the importance of being able to live and work in an inclusive social context.

2. Commitment to Social Justice

Social justice has been defined in a number of ways based on different political perspectives and life experiences.[6] Common elements of most definitions include commitments to human rights, equal opportunity, and the rule of law for all, regardless of race or ethnicity. Yet even such bedrock ethical principles are not at all universally accepted, let alone put into practice.

At least a third of the world's population lives under dictatorships, with ruling classes focused on benefiting themselves and perpetuating their own rule. Many countries have deeply ingrained social hierarchies regarded by those in power as natural and unlikely to change,

Companies seeking to extend their commitment to social justice across borders are likely to face resistance from local elites invested in a socioeconomic status quo that favors those in power, and rulers who are resistant to outside influence unless it furthers their own agendas.

and the emphasis is often on maintaining central control while keeping rival groups out of power. Meanwhile, social justice is viewed skeptically as a nice idea that even the most fervent advocates have not been able to achieve in their own countries. Companies seeking to extend their commitment to social justice across borders are likely to face resistance from local elites invested in a socioeconomic status quo that favors those in power, and rulers who are resistant to outside influence unless it furthers their own agendas.

Autocratic political leaders tend to view the extension of equal rights to all citizens as a potentially dangerous way of empowering breakaway independence movements or minority groups that might seize power themselves. Rather than "celebrating" diversity—racial, ethnic, religious, or linguistic, for example—rulers often actively seek to suppress the claims of marginalized groups as potential sources of chaos and division rather than as an asset. Minority populations are routinely persecuted, expelled, or exterminated on the grounds that they are troublemakers (one example is Myanmar's lethal treatment of its Rohingya minority) and threats to "law and order."

A more superficially benevolent tactic is to endorse and publicize indigenous costumes and folk dances, while at the same time ruthlessly crushing any sign of actual resistance to those in power and smothering the charming locals with administrators, immigrants, and police supervision. Forced assimilation and the denial of basic human rights such as freedom of speech or religious expression are not just relics of unenlightened past eras, but a present-day reality in many places where leaders prefer to deny, dilute, or erase differences rather than to embrace them.

Foreign companies and NGOs have to choose their initiatives carefully in such environments. Yet they can offer welcome jobs with fair wages and opportunities to advance, bring in training and technology that enhance local capabilities, and support public health and literacy education.

3. Diversity and Intersectionality

Race and ethnicity come in various forms and are linked with other diversity factors in myriad ways. In many parts of Asia, it is more common to refer to ethnicity and national identity rather than to race, although paradoxically, lighter skin color is often regarded as more desirable.[7] India, for instance, has a staggering number of ethnic groups—more than 2,000—that are deeply interwoven with religious, linguistic, and regional differences. A Kannada-speaking Hindu adherent in the southern state of Karnataka may have very different career prospects and opportunities in life than a Punjabi-speaking Sikh in India's northwest or an Urdu-speaking Muslim in the huge northern state of Uttar Pradesh. The intersection of such factors frequently shapes an individual's access to education, employment, and political influence.

In other countries, racial and ethnic issues may be most closely linked with factors other than language, location, or religion. Supporters of the Black Lives Matter movement in the U.S. largely share a common native language, with the exception of native Spanish speakers. Their demonstrations, fanned by ubiquitous social media, have occurred across the country. This movement has also been predominantly driven by young secular participants who focus on addressing systemic institutional racism, with religious leaders having a less visible role than in the earlier Civil Rights movement of the 1960s. Political allies of Black Lives Matter have included other identity groups and political movements that lay claim to similar experiences of disenfranchisement and discrimination: e.g., Native Americans, Asian-Americans, Latinos, members of the LGBT+ community, and women advocating "equal pay for equal work" as well as an end to workplace sexual harassment through the "Me Too" movement.

COUNTRY EXAMPLES

To have a more concrete sense of how to take a locally relevant approach to issues of race and ethnicity, it is useful to examine several specific country examples along with their practical implications for companies seeking to roll out cross-border initiatives.

1. The United Kingdom: Multiracial Immigrants

Colonial History

Understanding the topic of race and ethnicity for major Western European nations requires knowledge of their prior colonial empires and subsequent legacy. The empire of the former Great Britain, for example, once spanned the globe ("The sun never sets on the British empire") and comprised more than a quarter of the world's population. Britain's colonial possessions included India, Pakistan, Bangladesh, South Africa, Nigeria, Uganda, Kenya, Botswana, New Guinea, Hong Kong, Jamaica, Canada, Australia, and so on—the post-colonial Commonwealth alliance still contains more than fifty countries.

For centuries, Great Britain, following the examples of Portugal and Spain, was also one of the world's largest contributors to the spread of slavery through its trading activities. British ships brought Africans into its American colonies on the Eastern seaboard and in the Caribbean for forced labor starting in the 1600s, and its East India Company held as many as 10 million people in bondage on the Indian subcontinent. Slavery continued on a large scale in Britain's colonies abroad until the 1800s, although the number of enslaved Africans or Asians in the British Isles was relatively small. Anti-slavery movements resulted in a series of laws in the first half of the 1800s that began to curb this practice, even though it continued in various locations through illicit means. The Royal Navy actually created a West Africa Squadron that became a significant force in curbing trans-Atlantic traffic in slavery, capturing large numbers of ships and freeing their prisoners. Great Britain was thus both a major contributor to the institution of slavery and an early supporter of its abolition.

Immigration

In the contemporary United Kingdom (encompassing England, Northern Ireland, Wales, and Scotland), a major hot-button issue tied to the country's history is immigration. This issue involves racial and ethnic differences but is not primarily focused on inequities between blacks and whites, although these are now being more openly acknowledged.[8] In the wake of World War II, labor shortages led to policies that encouraged immigration from former British colonies. Immigrants arrived in large numbers from countries such as India, Pakistan, and later Bangladesh; others came from African nations, including South Africa and Nigeria. The entry of the U.K. into the European Communities (later the European Union) in 1973 also meant that job seekers could arrive freely from other parts of Europe. Many Eastern Europeans, most notably from Poland, began to arrive as well, along with political refugees from the Middle East and elsewhere. Foreign-born residents now comprise approximately 14% of the U.K.'s population, the highest number in the country's history. The largest minority immigrant groups are Asian (8%) and blacks (3%) from Africa or the Caribbean.

Current social issues such as "Brexit," or withdrawal from the European Union, have been driven in part by anti-immigrant sentiment. Generational differences have also come into play with the U.K.'s aging population, along with cultural gaps between the cosmopolitan metropolis of London and more conservative rural areas.

Those favoring curbs on immigration express the view that new arrivals compete with native-born citizens for jobs while diluting traditional customs. A response from some immigrants themselves that points to the country's colonial legacy has been, "We are here because you were there."[9]

Generational differences have also come into play with the U.K.'s aging population, along with cultural gaps between the cosmopolitan metropolis of London and more conservative rural areas.

Practical Implications

Companies that seek to address race and ethnicity in the U.K. will need to take into account the *multiracial, multiethnic issue of immigration*, considering how to both ensure that foreign nationals and their descendants from any background are treated fairly, while other members of the workforce are not alienated or left behind.

Policies suited to an aging workforce and gaps in opportunities and income between rural and urban residents will also likely be welcomed.

Example

Roche, the Switzerland-based pharmaceutical firm, has won recognition as a top local employer through its focus on inclusion and its impact on long-term employee development and retention.

It employs workers from 42 different nationalities in the U.K., with more than 50% female leadership, and four generations in the workforce. It has also made progress in employing both veterans and people with disabilities.[10]

2. Brazil: Mixed-Race Diversity

Brazil, with nearly half of the land mass and population of South America, plus 40% of the continent's economy, is a trend-setter for the region in many ways. Its Portuguese language and colonial heritage set it apart from other South American countries, which are primarily Spanish-speaking, but there is much else that is shared. Brazil borders on ten of the continent's twelve other nations (Ecuador and Chile are the only exceptions) and is engaged in economic and cultural exchanges with all of them.

White, Black, and Brown

One of Brazil's most striking demographic characteristics is its large mixed-race population, similar to the population of nations in the Caribbean such as Cuba or the Dominican Republic. The country's official census has a mixed-race category (pardo, or "brown") that comprises 43% of the population. Brazil's other citizens also include not only whites (48%) and blacks (7.6%), but also people of Asian ancestry (1%) such as the descendants of Japanese immigrants, and its indigenous population (0.4%). The country's racial and ethnic diversity differs substantially by region as well—the southern third of the country, home to major cities such as Sao Paulo, Curitiba, and Porto Alegre, is predominantly white due to patterns of European immigration and settlement, while the majority population elsewhere is multiracial.

Rich vs. Poor

Brazilians today still face stark socioeconomic differences with deep historical roots. The country was slow to abolish slavery, only ending it in 1888 after 350 years, and the influence of this institution remains.[11] Across Brazil's diverse population, there is a wide gap between rich and poor that is reflected in income, employment, upward mobility, access to health care, and incarceration rates. Brazil ranks as one of the world's five countries with the largest wealth gap, with a relatively high unemployment rate and one-fifth of its population living in poverty, including the residents of its huge urban shanty-towns known as favelas.[12] Brazil's struggling educational system contributes to ongoing inequality; it is rated in the bottom ten of seventy countries in science, math, and reading, and a third of citizens over the age of 25 have not completed elementary school.[13]

Brazil's government has long championed the cause of a "racial democracy," contrasting this favorably with discriminatory practices of other countries such as the U.S. or South Africa that enforced segregation and forbid racial intermarriage. However, the citizens belonging to its elite and middle class are primarily white, and darker skin color is closely linked with social disparities: "The widespread acceptance of multiracial identities in Brazil coexists with steep racial inequality."

A distinctively Brazilian conundrum is that policy solutions such as affirmative action quickly collide with mixed race backgrounds; residents reportedly use more than 136 categories of skin colors to identify themselves, making binary classifications problematic. Some universities have resorted to phenotypes, or physical characteristics, to determine who should be eligible for preferential treatment, regardless of ancestry.[14] Brazil's anti-racism laws have not been effective in preventing workplace discrimination and more subtle racial slights against either black or multiracial employees. Employers seeking to provide equal opportunities for all must overcome informal barriers along with more systemic ones.[15]

Practical Implications

Foreign companies in Brazil need to consider *socioeconomic differences across its mixed-race* spectrum. Organizations will be particularly welcomed if they can provide jobs in areas with high unemployment, education and training for workers in need of supplementary skill-building, and other benefits such as quality health care—all while contributing to local community development.

Example

Mercado Libre, the Argentina-based e-commerce company growing rapidly throughout Latin America, has successfully expanded to neighboring Brazil. Mercado Livre, as it is called in Brazil, is now the company's largest operation. It has appealed to consumers with limited financial means—including those without credit cards—with its Mercado Pago payment system, while also extending numerous loans to small and medium-sized businesses. Unlike many other multinationals that have made cutbacks, the company has been hiring aggressively in a variety of skill categories and expanding its presence across Brazil; employees report a comparatively high rate of satisfaction with their working conditions. Mercado Livre has also been building out its own logistics infrastructure to address delivery issues that affect other multinational companies in this huge country, including a large new logistics center in Brazil's less prosperous northeast.[16]

3. Nigeria: Ethnicity, Religion, and Region

Nigeria, Africa's largest national economy, is an economic powerhouse with a complex history and a fractured present. People with similar skin color share control of the government and yet are separated by a host of different factors, including ethnicity, religion, and political interests. Many of the country's residents pride themselves on their entrepreneurial ingenuity, their skills as problem-solvers, and their freedom of speech and expression.[17] Nigeria's cultural vibrancy, including a large "Nollywood" film industry, renowned musicians, and a diaspora of 15 million citizens living abroad (major destinations include the U.S. and the U.K.), have given the country a soft power that extends well beyond its economic influence.

The tensions and the opportunities that exist within Nigeria today merit particularly close scrutiny, as they are one key to grasping the fast-growing human potential across the massive African continent, which is larger than China, the U.S., and Brazil combined.

SARS Protests

Nigeria has been in the global spotlight for public demonstrations against the country's Special Anti-Robbery Squad (SARS). This branch of the national police force has been accused of abuse of power, police brutality, unfair profiling of law-abiding citizens, and other charges that will sound familiar to those who have followed the Black Lives Matter protests in the United States and elsewhere. Nigerian demonstrators have made explicit references to Black Lives Matter themselves while appealing to global celebrities for support, and have even succeeded in persuading Jack Dorsey, CEO of Twitter, to endorse their cause, putting him in an alliance with the rap musician Kanye West.

However, those accustomed to seeing the issues cataloged by anti-SARS protestors through the black vs. white racial lens that is such an integral part of U.S. history would likely find Nigeria puzzling. There are few whites in the country, citizenship is reserved primarily for people with indigenous ancestry, and influential positions in national, state, and local governments are held almost exclusively by blacks.

So what does diversity in Nigeria mean, and what are the most important issues regarding race and ethnicity?

Historical Context

Many Nigerians are quick to cite their country's colonial history with Great Britain as one source of its current challenges. In the early 1900s, the British brought together different administrative regions and tribal groups to form the Colony and Protectorate of Nigeria, which finally gained its independence in 1960. **Nigeria today combines more than 300 ethnic groupings and 500 languages**—the four largest ethnic groups are the Hausa, Yoruba, Igbo (or Ibo), and Ijaw. The country's major political fault lines are both ethnic and religious. The Hausa or Hausa-Fulani groups in the north are primarily Muslim, and were formerly part of the Sokoto Caliphate conquered by the British in the early 1900s. The Yoruba, Igbo, and Ijaw in the south are predominantly Christian.

British government and commercial interests encouraged the export of natural resources and agricultural cash crops. This policy shaped Nigeria's developing economy, which now relies on oil exports as a primary source of government income and must import manufactured goods and food supplies due to its own lack of economic diversification. Nigeria's oil industry was nationalized in 1971, but relationships with multinational enterprises continue through joint ventures; approximately half of the country's crude oil production comes from a joint venture with the Anglo-Dutch enterprise Royal Dutch Shell.

Ethno-Religious Conflict

More than a century after colonial Nigeria was assembled, the country still regularly faces internal tension and conflict—with its citizens separated by a host of factors, including ethnicity and religion. Unlike other nations with a clear majority/minority split in terms of religious affiliation, the numbers of Muslims and Christians in Nigeria are roughly equal. The Muslim-dominated north holds a slight edge in terms of population, and has generally been Nigeria's preeminent political force, although government control rotates by informal agreement between leaders from the Muslim north and the Christian south. The country's regional differences have come to be reflected within its major cities as well through internal migration:

Cities remain largely segregated along ethno-religious lines, and confrontation between ethnic groups is common. Often, ethnic clashes in one part of the country can set off a chain of reprisal riots and attacks in other parts of the country. All major ethnic groups have formed militias to protect their own interests and perpetrate violence on other groups. While illegal, these vigilante groups continue to act with impunity for lack of stringent law enforcement.[18]

In this environment, conflicts that might otherwise be seen as primarily political or economic—e.g., disputes regarding government appointments or conflicts over land or cattle—are viewed through a religious lens, with Muslims and Christians taking sides against each other. Thousands of Nigerians have died in riots and through other forms of violence at their fellow citizens' hands, with accompanying destruction of property and forced internal migration of displaced communities. While Nigeria's leaders have been democratically elected since 1999, a prior series of coups and attempted coups, decades of military rule, and recurring charges of election fraud mean that the country's democratic institutions are tenuous.

Regional Differences

There are clear distinctions between Nigeria's regions in terms of economic development and access to education. The north, with fewer natural resources and less industry, also has some of the world's highest rates of illiteracy. "Nigeria has 13 million out-of-school children, the highest in the world, according to UNICEF, and more than 69% of them are in the north. As a result, the region has Nigeria's lowest literacy rates, with some states recording just 8%."[19]

Many political leaders in the north have resisted what they see as the negative social impacts of Westernization, countering these suspect influences through actions such as the imposition of Sharia, or Islamic law, in areas under their control. Boko Haram, the extremist Muslim group based in Nigeria's northeast, attacked a girls' school and kidnapped hundreds of students, many of whom are still missing, citing religious justification for opposing the education of girls. Other attacks on schools have continued.

Ethnic Elites

Rather than having a single established majority population that controls the lion's share of the economy, in Nigeria, a relatively small number of elite members of each major ethnic group have monopolized and exploited the nation's resources at the expense of other citizens. Nigeria is the largest oil and gas producer in Africa, and vast wealth has been generated from its rich oil reserves centered in the Niger Delta. However, predictions that the country's economy would undergo a sustained boom thanks to these resources have not been realized as kleptocratic elites, sometimes in league with their multinational partners, have siphoned off the nation's wealth for their private benefit while struggling with each other for control. Endemic corruption is abetted by Nigeria's lack of an effective social safety net and a tradition of mutual support among family members, which mean that individuals who attain positions of power are likely to receive constant appeals for assistance from members of their extended family.

Meanwhile, national and state governments run by corrupt elites have often failed to provide even basic services such as quality education, medical care, access to clean drinking water, or a steady supply of electricity to the wider population. Chronic inflation, especially in the price of basic food staples, has created food insecurity for much of the population[20]— the unemployment rate is currently over 25%, and 40% of Nigerians, or almost 83 million people, live below the country's poverty line of $382 (U.S. dollars) in annual income.[21] Such shortcomings often lead to mutual finger-pointing that exacerbates ethnic and religious tensions:

> Mismanagement of national resources and misrule by multi-ethnic and multi-religious coalitions of successive rulers since independence have impoverished and denied opportunities to the majority of Nigerians. As a result, religious rhetoric blaming members of other religious communities and proposals for religious reform as a solution to society's ills have found purchase among the masses.[22]

Governance issues in many parts of Nigeria are also affected by the "federal character" principle, originally designed to ensure the balanced representation of diverse ethnic groups within public service institutions. In practice, this has become a quota system based on states of origin. Unfortunately, the wide gap in educational levels across the country has meant that some appointees are unqualified to carry out their roles, focusing instead on personal gain for themselves and their allies. Likewise, admissions to top government-run secondary schools are regulated to ensure broad representation in a way that has produced major gaps in qualifications:

> Almost every year, livid social media posts, newspaper columns and parliamentary debates follow the publication of cut-off marks for the exams... Students from some states in northern Nigeria sometimes require scores as low as two out of 200 to be admitted, compared to students from states in the south who need scores of at least 139.[23]

Marginalized Groups

Although the most striking demarcation lines in Nigerian society are between north and south, Muslims and Christians, the country's daunting complexity is reflected in its total of 63 different political parties, representing a wide array of interests. There are many smaller ethnic groups, such as the Kanuri or the Nupe, and each region contains minority groups of its own. These minorities include Muslim residents in the south, Christians in the north, minority Shia Muslims, Protestants and Catholics, farmers and herders—each with their own priorities and grievances. Among the country's various marginalized groups, two that deserve particular mention are victims of slavery and human trafficking, as well as the urban "Yahoo Boys."

Slavery & Human Trafficking

Slavery as an institution in Nigeria reportedly both pre-dated the transatlantic slave trade and survived long after it was abolished. The Sokoto Caliphate in the north had an estimated 1 to 2.5 million enslaved non-Muslims, primarily used as plantation workers, as late as 1900. Most were acquired through a rapid series of conquests in the early 1800s.[24]

Among the Igbo tribe in the country's southeast, there were traditional forms of slavery originally tied to indigenous customs and religious beliefs. These practices expanded in the sixteenth and seventeenth centuries as European colonies were established in the Caribbean and North and South America. Later, when the British abolished their own slavery trade in the nineteenth century, an unintended result was a glut of enslaved people in Igbo markets.

Slavery persisted in Nigeria until it was officially abolished in the early twentieth century, continuing in some places until the 1940s. The vestiges of this form of human bondage persist, as the descendants of formerly subjugated people face various forms of discrimination in Nigeria today. Estimates of the number affected range up to 10% of the country's 42 million Igbo, for example, or several million people. Contemporary forms of discrimination include prohibitions against intermarriage with partners from other caste backgrounds, restrictions on attaining certain social positions or titles, and even limitations on free speech.

While the negative impacts of slavery in Nigeria may sound familiar, it is also different from slavery elsewhere in that it has been based on factors such as ancestry, religion, point of origin, or personal conduct—one major group was either taken as captives from faraway communities or enslaved to compensate for debts or crimes.

Westerners trying to understand the Igbo system often reach for its similarities with the oppression of black Americans. This analogy is helpful but imperfect. Igbo discrimination is not based on race, and there are no visual markers to differentiate slave descendants from freeborn. Instead, it trades on cultural beliefs about lineage and spirituality.[25]

Another type of slavery that continues to flourish throughout much of Nigeria is human trafficking. The scale of such trafficking is staggering— estimates indicate that Nigeria has almost 1.4 million citizens who have been enslaved in this way, with an average age of fifteen.[26] Desperately poor parents, particularly those with large families to support, sometimes make the wrenching decision to sell or give away their own children in order to make ends meet. These children may be taken in by their new owners ostensibly as domestic servants, but then frequently become subject to economic exploitation and physical abuse while being denied access to education.

A still more heinous practice is luring young women or girls into prostitution. Criminal groups make false promises of paid housekeeping and other jobs, domestically or abroad, and then coerce women into forced servitude. A smaller number of these people are exported to North Africa and even to Europe for prostitution and other forms of exploitation; Nigerian victims have been identified in 34 different countries and four world regions. Meanwhile, human traffickers also import enslaved persons from nearby countries into Nigeria.[27]

Yahoo Boys

The protests against the Special Anti-Robbery Squad that have attracted global attention encapsulate another set of tensions in Nigeria, with entrenched establishment forces receiving pushback from primarily youthful protesters. The SARS police branch initially established to combat violent crime is accused of becoming a rogue criminal organization itself, extorting blameless civilians for the gain of its own members.

Amnesty International claims it has documented "at least 82 cases of torture, ill-treatment and extra-judicial execution by SARS" over the last three years.[28] Among the most serious charges leveled against members of SARS are that they have stopped individuals driving attractive vehicles for unfounded reasons and either extorted money from the owners or left them dead on the side of the road while taking possession of the vehicles themselves.

SARS members seem to target younger Nigerians who are profiled as being prosperous and/or non-traditional due to their career, lifestyle, or appearance. A nice car, tattoos, dreadlocks, dyed hair, or even just possessing a laptop can become grounds for police to stop and arrest them without reasonable cause. The targeting of this particular set of people is tied to a negative social stereotype of so-called "Yahoo Boys," a pejorative term for internet scammers, whether or not those detained by the police have anything to do with such activities. Nosy traditionalist citizens have aided such discriminatory profiling by reporting to the police young neighbors who happen to be working from home, an uncommon practice in urban Nigeria until quite recently.

As Nigeria marks the 60th anniversary of its independence, protesters against SARS have called for a fairer justice system and greater social equity, and are expressing their general frustration with poor governance and corruption.

The majority of them are between 18 and 24 years old, have never experienced steady electricity in their lifetime, did not enjoy free education in the country and had their years at university punctuated and elongated by lecturers going on strike. The frustration with the police is a reflection of the frustration with the state in general.[29]

Although the anti-SARS protests have encountered a violent police response and only half-hearted promises of reform, youthful demonstrators have garnered visibility and assistance through their own internet-savvy forms of media outreach. Nigerian IT and fintech firms, high-profile entertainers, sports figures, and international celebrities have all expressed their support.[30]

The organizing abilities and passionate exercise of free speech on the part of protestors were reinforced by a groundswell of popular sympathy that took government authorities by surprise. The protests leveraged not only technical skills but also artistic flair, playing songs such as "This is Nigeria" (a counterpoint to Childish Gambino's song "This is America"), "Black on Black," and the classic protest song "Jaga Jaga" (meaning chaos or disarray). As one commentator notes, "these songs convey protesters' swirl of anger, frustration, melancholy and hope while buoying up their fight against police brutality, bad governance and call for accountability."[31]

In spite of subsequent threats against protest leaders, the appeal for a better future from this energetic segment of Nigeria's population is a hopeful sign in a country with a turbulent past and uncertain prospects as an emerging global giant.[32]

Practical Implications

Ethnic traditions and social obligations may appear today as paternalistic politics or favoritism within Nigerian organizations. Local managers who reach a position of power often use that power to surround themselves with team members from their own ethnic group or sub-group. They tend to use their authority to promote or favor employees from their community while excluding others. Such acts are seen as a source of security for both leader and allies, shoring up loyal factions of mutual protection.

Such actions can have further consequences. If a person is promoted based on merit, others may complain that the promotion occurred due to an ethnic or regional affiliation with the boss. Conversely, a well-qualified candidate may not be promoted for fear of the appearance of nepotism.

Multinational companies committed to merit-based talent development need to understand local social dynamics fueled by ethnic loyalties while putting measures in place to ensure greater objectivity such as blind hiring and promotion practices, utilizing diverse teams to conduct talent reviews and succession planning, and job rotation to broaden employee perspectives and discourage factionalism. They must also engage in careful due diligence of supply chains and government relations to avoid risky ties with political corruption or organized crime.

Example:

Google Nigeria is rated as one of the country's top employers, based on criteria that include "transparent performance management," or systems designed to favor merit and counter cronyism.[33] It has also introduced a number of products designed to serve local consumers in an ethnically diverse country where many people have scant access to resources.

A dedicated motorcycle travel mode in Google Maps assists riders of Nigeria's 10 million motorcycles in finding their way through crowded streets; a product named Google Go enables internet access even on low-RAM smartphones or with unstable network connections; an application of machine learning helps farmers to detect and prevent crop diseases, thereby boosting their harvests; and a version of Google Lens allows users to point their camera at a sign and hear the words translated, with support for the Hausa, Yoruba, and Igbo languages.[34]

MARGINALIZATION: THE COMMON THREAD

Worldwide social unrest has presented a compelling opportunity for organizations to reassess their policies on race and ethnicity. Global companies are being challenged to recognize and respond to the unique circumstances of their employees and customers to promote greater social justice and to better serve growing markets.

Supporters of the Black Lives Matter movement in the U.S., with its focus on racial equity, are likely to find familiar themes as well as unexpected variations in the three country examples discussed above. In the U.K., Brazil, and Nigeria, **there are insider/outsider dynamics, the use and abuse of power and privilege, popular stereotypes and biases against "others," and the resulting marginalization of large segments of**

the population. These social dynamics contribute to unequal access to education, job opportunities, housing, and health care, along with a lack of economic and sometimes even physical security. Institutional systems, grounded in each country's history, fortify an inequitable status quo that must be addressed to bring about meaningful change.

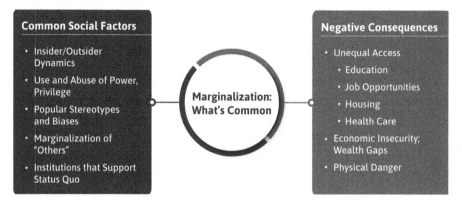

Figure 9.1: Marginalization: What's Common

On the other hand, race may not be the most critical diversity factor from a local perspective —there are other factors contributing to marginalization that are sometimes more important. Moreover, the racial and ethnic profile of a country or region can take many forms, depending on its social context and history. Each country's challenges linked to race and ethnicity must also be seen in the context of locally prominent issues such as immigration, socioeconomic inequality, rural/urban differences, religious strife, and political affiliation. **In the U.K., immigration is foremost in the public perception, and the immigrants themselves are multiracial; Brazil faces a stark socioeconomic gap across its mixed-race spectrum; in Nigeria ethnicity and religion are far more important factors than skin color in the distribution of political and economic power.**

Figure 9.2: Race & Ethnicity: Global Diversity

Multinational organizations seeking to globalize their inclusion efforts related to race and ethnicity can find validation and common cause in the presence of shared cross-border challenges. Well-intentioned organizational leaders may also want to push for common worldwide action steps to address inequities and achieve greater social justice. Unfortunately, an approach that ignores variations in the ways that similar issues are manifested on a global basis could shape initiatives that fail to produce the desired results, with employees who are confused about how to apply foreign principles and solutions to their local environment. They may even encounter unforeseen legal or reputational hazards due to perceived violations of local laws and taboos.

Leaders must tailor their plans for creating greater equity for all racial and ethnic groups in ways that are welcomed by local employees, delivering high performance along with real social impact. The most effective organizations do not push for actions that look the same everywhere, although their approach can uphold common values and be part of an integrated talent and business strategy.

PART FOUR: DEVELOPING INCLUSIVE LEADERS

Brain-Based Leadership:
What's Missing?

Inclusive Leadership Development

Five Organizational Levers

10.
Brain-Based Leadership: What's Missing?

The core problem with the current applications of neuroscience to leadership is not that they are wrong but that they are incomplete, unbalanced, and potentially misleading.

What are the value and limits of current neuroscience-based approaches to inclusion and diversity?

Approaches to leadership based on neuroscience are alluring. Advances in functional magnetic resonance imaging (fMRI) have provided an exciting new window into the everyday workings of the brain. Consultants and coaches eagerly cite the latest neuroscience research as the basis for their leadership advice, focusing on how it can be applied to vital tasks such as driving a successful change initiative.

And what could be a more common human asset than the brain, with its magnificent synapses and plasticity as well as its flaws? Brain-based leadership development seems sensible, scientific, and compelling, with the potential for global applications that bridge pesky nuances, paradoxes, and differences.

WHAT COULD POSSIBLY BE MISSING?

Before jumping on this popular bandwagon, let's explore factors that comprise a full human being and contribute to successful leadership. Here's an example:

AN EXPATRIATE IN HONG KONG

Albert Farnsworth was a fast-rising leader from the UK assigned to run a firm in Hong Kong that his company had recently acquired. Confident in his prior leadership track record, primarily from his work in northern Europe, and armed with the advice of a U.K.-based coach informed by neuroscience research, he developed a plan for integrating the new acquisition.

Albert sought to reduce status threats related to the acquisition by demonstrating respect for the status of the firm's previous leaders. He preserved their titles, assigning to himself the newly-coined title of managing director. In his usual egalitarian style, he frequently asked local managers and employees for their input on key decisions, with brainstorming sessions designed to draw out their ideas. He sought to preserve employees' sense of autonomy and certainty by establishing broad goals for the organization and then giving them room to create their own solutions—this was a leadership style that had worked well for him in the past and had been a key part of his own success story to date. He also began to introduce them to their new matrix counterparts around the world, stressing how the new parent company's relatively flat hierarchy enabled the best ideas to move quickly between regions.

Unfortunately, the plan did not generate the results that Albert had anticipated. Both sales and morale began to drop, his team brainstorming sessions seemed to go nowhere, and soon key junior employees began leaving the firm, hired away by local companies. When Albert asked his local HR manager for results from employee exit interviews, he was unpleasantly surprised by the criticisms of his own leadership, expressed in comments such as the following:

- *"We don't know who the boss is anymore. Our previous leaders didn't perform well, and that is why they had to sell the company. Now they are stuck in the middle between us and Albert and don't know what to do."*

- *"Albert is always asking for our opinions, which makes us think that he doesn't know what he is doing and is a weak leader."*

- *"He seems to delegate and disappear. We want someone we can bring problems to and then solve them together."*

- *"We want more change and faster. The market is moving very rapidly here, and the new boss should fire older managers who can't keep up."*

Albert's primary failing and one that almost derailed his career was his attempt to replicate his prior success by using the same leadership style in a different cultural environment. In this case, his application of neuroscience to address the importance of status issues during the ownership transition contributed to overconfidence in his plan and actually reinforced his cultural ignorance rather than providing him with contextually appropriate leadership strategies.

BRAIN-BASED LEADERSHIP: THE MISSING HEMISPHERE

There have been various critiques of neuroscience-based leadership approaches and their skillful branding, which includes the display of colorful brain models and fMRI images at training events to highlight their scientific aura. Warren Bennis, a well-known pioneer in the field of leadership development, noted that much of this new movement repackages prior insights, especially those of Daniel Goleman on emotional intelligence. He states, "What worries me is people being taken in by the language of it and ending up with stuff we've known all along."[1]

Although such comments raise concerns, there is arguably a deeper problem with neuroscience-based leadership approaches that has not received sufficient attention. Their universal claims and attractive packaging can reinforce a convenient "one size fits all" solution for leadership development across global organizations. Such standardized solutions are usually ethnocentric, reinforcing the impulse to evaluate others based on our own standards and to make "them" more like "us"; this becomes even easier to justify with a seemingly invincible scientific rationale to back it up.

The core problem with the current applications of neuroscience to leadership is not that they are wrong but that they are incomplete, unbalanced, and potentially misleading. It turns out that there is a lot more evidence available, including research from additional branches of neuroscience, that can help provide a fuller picture of humanity with vital implications for leadership.

NATURE AND NURTURE

Anyone who studied Psychology 101 in college during the past fifty years was likely introduced to the nature vs. nurture debate. Simply put, research indicates that **human beings are products of both their genetic makeup (nature) and their physical and cultural environments (nurture).**

In fact, a key differentiator of humans from other species is that they are less genetically pre-programmed (nature) and more responsive to novel or changing environmental factors (nurture). Humans develop from childhood based on cultural influences such as how they are held, whom they live with, where they sleep, what they eat, the sounds they hear, the stories they are told, the ways in which they are praised or scolded, and so on. One definition of culture is that it is a way of addressing common human challenges in a particular environment. Each culture passes on the successful survival methods of its elders that fit a distinctive time and place, and these learnings shape the way that each brain is configured.

To date, neuroscience-based leadership approaches have focused primarily on the "nature" side of the nature/nurture equation, highlighting common features of human physiology and cognitive functioning, while generally ignoring the "nurture" or environmental component, which plays an equally powerful role in shaping human development. **Culture is too often treated cheerfully as an organizational feature to be "built" or "redefined"** based on scientific insights into the brain, **rather than as a pervasive developmental influence that shapes the very functioning of the brain itself** in different ways, depending upon our upbringing.

CULTURE AND THE BRAIN: RESEARCH EXAMPLES

There are a number of studies commonly neglected by current neuroscience leadership gurus that provide fascinating and important evidence for how human brains can be wired differently based on cultural influences.

Study #1: Does Self Refer to "Me" or "We"?

The prefrontal cortex region of the brain is believed to represent our idea of the self. One research study found that this area became active when U.S. study participants thought of their own personal identities and traits. For Chinese study participants, on the other hand, this region was activated by adjectives describing both themselves and their mothers.[2] In other words, the very **definition of self is shaped by culture**. Different definitions of "me" or "we" can and do lead to very different leadership styles.

Study #2: Attention to Objects vs. Context

Another study revealed distinctly different attentional bias based on culture. This study showed sample images to both Western and East Asian participants. Westerners, whose cultures place a high value on independence and individuality, tended to focus their attention on particular foreground objects, with less regard for context and relationships among items.

In contrast, East Asian participants, whose cultures emphasize interdependent relationships and awareness of context, focused their attention on the context of the image and demonstrated relational processing of information.[3]

So not only our self-definition but also **what we pay attention to is culturally influenced.** Leaders from varied cultural backgrounds may notice quite different things, with some focusing on the action items in the foreground and others examining the broader context.

Study #3: Valuing "Modesty" or "Assertiveness"

A third study found that the area of the brain that produces dopamine, or the "feel-good hormone," responds differently based on cultural conditioning. The study showed volunteers from the U.S. and Japan drawings of a person standing in a relatively submissive pose, with head down and shoulders hunched, and of another person standing in a more dominant pose, with arms crossed and face forward.

Respondents interpreted the same pictures differently based on their cultural values. Japanese participants produced dopamine when viewing the first drawing, as they interpreted the submissive posture positively, seeing it as a demonstration of modesty and respect. U.S. participants produced dopamine when viewing the second drawing, as they saw the dominant pose as an indication of confidence and strength.[4]

IMPLICATIONS FOR LEADERS

These three studies and others like them from the emerging field of "cultural neuroscience" have enormous implications for the development of leaders on a global scale. To avoid becoming the latest form of ethnocentrism, dressed up this time in white lab coats, brain-based leadership approaches must embrace both nature and nurture to help leaders work effectively around the world.

> **How we define ourselves, what we perceive, and the judgments we make are all shaped by our cultural environments...**

If how we define ourselves, what we perceive, and the judgments we make are all shaped by our cultural environments, leaders need to understand both what makes them similar to *and* what makes them different from their global colleagues. They must also cultivate skills for adapting to each other in integrated global workplaces that could involve virtual meetings, travel to distant locations, or interacting with a diverse mix of colleagues in the same building.

Approaches to leadership informed by neuroscience are incomplete if they fail to take into account not only how the brain functions but also the cultural influences that shape it. What are the implications of a more holistic view of the brain, encompassing both "nature" and "nurture," for leadership development?

CULTURE AND LEADERSHIP: THE MISSING HEMISPHERE

Consider the SCARF model described by David Rock, head of the NeuroLeadership Institute and author of Your Brain at Work. Although the five elements of this model—Status, Certainty, Autonomy, Relatedness, and Fairness—are convincingly linked with research into fundamental brain functions such as our "fight or flight" impulses, all of these elements are also subject to culturally based indoctrination and interpretation. It would be a mistake to assume that each SCARF element manifests itself similarly everywhere or that the model can applied to promote **"culture change" without cultural understanding**.

For example, while it is true that Status, the "S" in SCARF, is important everywhere, this aspect of human behavior is expressed and interpreted quite differently based on particular environmental contexts. Some cultures are far more hierarchical than others, and hierarchy is also manifested in different ways. In China, for instance, it is relatively common to have a person who is clearly in the role of the **"boss"** issuing orders in a directive style, while many U.S. and northern European organizations attempt to distribute significant authority to other leadership team members and throughout the organization, endorsing **"leadership at all levels."**

In one cultural environment the greatest perceived threat could be having a leader who is overly directive, violating others' sense of status, while in another, it might be having no boss or unclear lines of authority. In the case of Albert Farnsworth, by attempting to drive change in his new environment using his own culturally conditioned approach to status—delegating authority to local leaders, engaging in regular brainstorming sessions, and introducing local employees to their global matrix counterparts—the result was confusion and disengagement rather than effective "culture change."

As generations of expatriates have discovered at great cost, culture change is possible within an organization or team with sustained focus over time, but only based on deep knowledge of the broader national cultural environment—and woe to those who embark on a mission to change the whole country. Through the mental lens of Albert's relatively hierarchical, group-oriented local employees in Hong Kong, and in contrast to his self-image as a skillful facilitator and change agent, Albert appeared instead to be a weak and uncertain leader who failed to make decisive changes while preferring to delegate without sufficient follow-up.

Status can even take on different, complex forms based on national and organizational cultures that frequently harbor contradictions. Many companies in the U.S. pride themselves on their egalitarian cultures and informal styles, while still taking for granted executive compensation that may be as much as 900 times the median employee salary. Major differences can also exist among generations, regions, functions, genders, and socioeconomic classes within the same country.

In Albert's new Hong Kong-based acquisition, it turned out that generational differences were critically important. The most senior managers whose own parents had known great hardship and social chaos (many were refugees from China's civil war and the Cultural Revolution) valued the respect for their status offered by an unchanged job title as well as continuity with previous policies. Meanwhile, employees in the same workplace from a younger millennial generation were more accustomed to prosperity and constant opportunities for growth. Many of these employees were far less attached to the status quo and more ready to embrace change, expressing impatience at Albert's slow pace in moving conservative senior leaders out of the way. ("After all, they are the ones who failed and had to sell the company.") For these younger employees, his demonstration of respect for the status of senior local managers was misplaced, and quickly became a source of frustration and disengagement.

What is true for Status also holds for any other aspect of the SCARF model—universal human traits are molded by one's physical environment and cultural upbringing and are expressed in workplaces around the world in ways that are both similar and different. The SCARF model highlights what we need to pay attention to, but not necessarily how to adapt our approach to fit different global environments. **Leaders ignore culture at their peril, including the nuances and differences within cultures as well as among them**. Numerous costly failures, including cross-border acquisitions, change initiatives, and rollouts of well-intended inclusion and diversity efforts ("Gender issues are the same everywhere, right?") can be traced to lack of cultural knowledge.

CULTURAL DIFFERENCES: FIVE DIMENSIONS

Each of the cultural dimensions depicted in Figure 10.1 below represents a spectrum of behavior that varies based on cultural context.

These dimensions of culture overlap with four out of five elements of the SCARF model:

- *Status:* Egalitarianism/Status

- *Certainty:* Risk/Certainty

- *Autonomy:* Independent/Interdependent

- *Relatedness:* Task/Relationship

Such dimensions highlight contrasts among national cultures that have been borne out by decades of research, including data from hundreds of thousands of survey respondents. National cultures may change over time, but the process is generally slow and uneven, and can result in either convergence or divergence in comparison with other national norms. The ways in which people actually behave along each of these dimensions are influenced by their own dynamic cultural settings just as they are by the structure of the brain—in fact, these two pervasive influences on human behavior are closely intertwined.

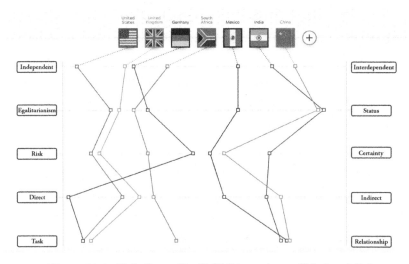

Figure 10.1: GlobeSmart Profile^{SM} Dimensions of National Culture

LEADERSHIP DEVELOPMENT: IMPLICATIONS

So what are the implications of the "nurture" side of the nature/nurture equation for leadership development? There is, of course, value to current neuroscience-based approaches if they are used wisely, based on the knowledge that they address one part of the leadership development picture and are not a panacea. When used exclusively, however, particularly in a global leadership context, they can be readily classified as fitting either the "Denial" or "Minimization" phases of the intercultural development scale that charts movement from a monocultural, or ethnocentric, mindset, to an intercultural mindset.[5]

The stages in this scale, themselves derived from extensive research, are Denial, Polarization, Minimization, Acceptance, and Adaptation. Leadership approaches that focus on human similarities while consistently underestimating differences cannot support progress toward the more advanced stages of this intercultural developmental spectrum. Approaches grounded in the brain's physiology often tell us that our brains perceive "difference" as a potential threat, but give us inadequate guidance for how to adapt. **Full understanding of the power of culture requires a pragmatic embrace of both similarities and differences**.

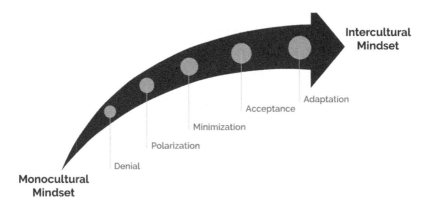

Figure 10.2: Intercultural Development Continuum[6]

Holistic approaches to neuroscience and leadership development will incorporate both nature and nurture, or brain physiology and culture. Current and future global leaders need to cultivate knowledge and skills that include:

- Personality *and* cultural self-awareness—personal characteristics as well as culturally based assumptions

- Psychological *and* cultural neuroscience—common features of the human brain as well as the developmental effects of different cultural contexts that also influence how humans behave

- Culture change *and* cultural influence—how to change culture in comparatively small-scale settings (particularly organizational and team cultures) while at the same time recognizing the pervasive influence of national cultures (transmitted via families, schools, and workplaces) on our behavior

A balanced approach to leadership development includes deliberately paradoxical terms such as "adaptive authenticity," acknowledging the need to work with both what we are given and who we can become.

Leaders must draw upon their own upbringing and core values while being deliberately open to "mind-blowing" experiences with colleagues from different backgrounds that could change them forever. This approach is flexible and open-ended, acknowledging that **successful leaders can and do accomplish tasks very differently,** and that there are various ways to inspire colleagues and to solve problems effectively in different environments.

One-size-fits-all approaches to leadership development in any form are alluring but ultimately bound to run squarely into their own limitations. Even attractive and modern-sounding packages such as neuroscience-based leadership can prove lopsided and therefore circumscribed in their usefulness unless they embrace how human beings are both fundamentally similar and profoundly different.

11.
Inclusive Leadership Development

Leaders must constantly have their antennae up to anticipate and respond to inevitable change, and one vital way to do this is through fully embracing inclusivity.

How can inclusive leadership be incorporated into leadership development programs?

Global organizations' efforts at leadership development often lag behind the rapidly evolving business landscape. Many programs are still designed from a headquarters perspective and calibrated for a relatively narrow group of participants, neglecting markets and groups of employees critical to the company's future. Large-scale demographic trends and shifts in economic momentum have been gathering strength for decades. In addition, it is quite likely that leaders will have to respond to future events that are unanticipated and unprecedented.

Futurists warn that it is a mistake to assume that the years to come will unfold in a logical extension of present trends. Non-linear events have always shaped human affairs as well, and their magnitude along with the rate of change seems to be increasing. Geopolitical upheavals, natural disasters, the impact of disruptive technologies—we can predict that such events will occur, but with only limited specificity. Over the past twenty years, the world has experienced terrorist attacks, armed conflicts, pandemics, and extreme weather events linked with global warming. Meanwhile, technologies have emerged that once seemed remote or implausible such as social media, smartphones, artificial intelligence, autonomous vehicles, and genetic modification.[1]

People in leadership roles will need to respond both to visible trend lines and to the unknowns that lie ahead. "The future is already here. It's just not very evenly distributed." This quote, sometimes attributed to the science fiction writer William Gibson,[2] suggests that we are surrounded by clues and incipient trends, but these are hard to ferret out and often frustratingly opaque. **Leaders must constantly have their antennae up to anticipate and respond to inevitable change, and one vital way to do this is through fully embracing inclusivity**.

LEADERSHIP DEVELOPMENT: FATAL FLAWS

So how is the practice of leadership development handling the massive tectonic shifts in demographics and global economic growth, or cultivating leaders who can respond flexibly to future events? Although leadership programs utilized by major multinationals typically incorporate a polite nod to the value of inclusion and perhaps even a trendy keynote address, many also share characteristics that can easily reinforce and perpetuate a dangerous corporate myopia. Here are a few common characteristics of both corporate leadership centers and renowned executive education programs that may lead participants to underestimate the significance and the challenges of key growth markets and demographic changes, as well as the need for more inclusive approaches.

Luxury Learning

People who design leadership development programs often have great affection for high-tech learning centers. The audio-visual equipment is sharp and reliable, there are comfortable accommodations nearby, travel arrangements are straightforward, it is feasible to invite top executives, and a location near headquarters provides access to strategy gurus and leading-edge R&D technology. A program held at this type of center is likely to be safe, predictable, and enjoyable for participants.

The problem with such venues is that they are almost completely unlike major emerging markets in which the organization must learn to win against aggressive competitors, nor do they reflect the conditions in slums and factory districts that often remain unseen in the same urban areas where headquarters employees live and work.

Our evolving world is messy and unpredictable. Some locations have a dynamism and speed of change that is difficult to grasp unless you witness it in person; others are mired in conflict and chaos, with disenfranchised citizens longing for change. Corporate learning centers provide a view from the top of the corporate mountain, but not a visceral sense of the gap between rich and poor, squalid living conditions, traffic congestion, power outages, corruption, youthful consumer preferences, or fast-moving new market forces. Statistics, trends, and case examples from distant lands seldom convey real vividness or urgency. Likewise, poverty and prejudice at home, along with calls for social justice, may seem distant even when they come from next door.

The Parade of Professors

Academic experts can provide deep insights and relevant special expertise, whether the topic is finance, marketing, strategy, or innovation. For leadership program organizers, there is also a level of security and reassurance in inviting an expert with a reputation as a polished speaker. However, the net result is seldom linked to a real "crucible" experience.

Professors accustomed to Western business school examples and learning styles tend to neglect the interests and potential contributions of minorities or participants from other countries. Reward systems also matter, and these can affect the contributions of most professional educators. Faculty members at top universities are rewarded for prolific publishing in their areas of specialization, not for learning about the strategic priorities and unique business circumstances of their corporate clients (unless of course these serve their research purposes). They are normally happy to fill a slot in a leadership program and pocket a nice paycheck, but then they want to get back to their own work.

Academics with an ambitious publication agenda are also seldom inclined to expend extra effort customizing learning solutions to meet an organization's specific needs or spending a lot of time getting to know program participants. Nor are they motivated to collaborate with other program faculty by exchanging information, reinforcing common themes, and creating a seamless participant experience. The outcome can be a series of disconnected lectures that are informative but fail to draw out less strident voices or to have a transformational impact on participants.

Expert Executives

The concept of "leaders teaching leaders" has become a part of numerous leadership development programs, and was established as a regular practice in the latter part of the previous century at General Electric's Crotonville and other major corporate learning centers. Leadership program participants typically look forward to the chance to rub shoulders with top executives, and many executives themselves relish the chance to share their own stories and accumulated organizational wisdom.

A potential issue with such executive involvement is that it might reinforce concepts and methods from the slow-growth center of the enterprise while undervaluing opportunities in non-traditional markets. A "leaders teaching leaders" approach generally relies on head- quarters-based leaders to do the teaching. Some of these executives are akin to generals who were victorious in a previous war and are still trying to apply the same tactics to the next one, even though the technology and the field of battle have altered radically.

Leaders who have never actually lived in a high-growth market may have a cognitive understanding of the business, but are unable to provide relevant practical advice about how to lead effectively in places where logistical challenges, ambiguous market data, employee turnover, nimble local competitors, and government meddling are commonplace. They sometimes also assume that models and systems that have worked in one setting can be readily imported to a new location, even when this is highly problematic.

Canned Culture

There is increasing recognition that culture—whether national or organizational—is a crucial factor in activities such as building effective virtual teams, integrating new acquisitions, or rolling out new organization-wide systems. Yet culture is usually an afterthought in leadership development programs. When it is introduced, culture is frequently

> **Culture is usually an afterthought in leadership development programs.**

presented in a "canned" format that presents country profiles, tidy distinctions, well-rehearsed stories about cross-border protocol snafus, and hackneyed dos and don'ts, while neglecting to tie this to significant business or mindset challenges.

"The keenest irony in this form of "canned culture" presentation, and in leadership programs in general, is that the actual diversity of program participants may be underutilized or ignored. Participants from minority backgrounds or from other parts of the world are often quiet due to language differences, deference toward senior executives, a lack of confidence in the face of executive peers, or a reluctance to put forward personal viewpoints with which others may disagree. Given a real forum for expression, such participants would be able to share their own valuable perceptions of employee engagement issues, local cultural variations and contradictions, and changes affecting consumer tastes and buyer preferences. They could provide timely, relevant cultural knowledge for dealing with unfamiliar environments at home and abroad, and for organization development.

However, the culturally-embedded design of most leadership programs—which assumes, among other things, that participants will actively speak up, challenge, ask questions, and voice opinions with which others may disagree—normally ensures that those who are most comfortable with the dominant culture play leading roles in discussions and team projects, while others hold back.

Unintended Consequences

In short, **existing leadership programs tend to reinforce mature market perspectives while unintentionally blocking or trivializing diverse viewpoints**—especially from people or locations that may provide the greatest future growth opportunities and competitive threats. Program participants who have relevant experience are regularly marginalized and judged negatively based on their hesitation to express their views according to current executive standards for assertive discourse and polished presentation skills; sometimes, these standards are even codified in the form of allegedly "global" leadership competencies. At their seductive worst, such programs can instill a sense of overconfidence in headquarters-based participants that they have mastered global leadership skills by going through an elite experience and hearing from relevant experts, when instead they have been insulated from voices that could better help them to face present and future market realities. Meanwhile, participants from other backgrounds may go away shaking their heads in disappointment at their own performance and with the disinclination of others to seek out their points of view, much less heed their advice.

How can leadership development break out of this damaging set of design flaws and the insular patterns of behavior that they support, particularly if the organization's long-term survival depends on success in unfamiliar environments?

THE CRUX OF LEADERSHIP DEVELOPMENT: DIVERSIFYING EXPERIENCES

An interesting line of recent psychological research focuses on so-called "diversifying experiences," which are defined as "unusual and unexpected events that… violate normality, break cognitive schemas, and promote a thinking style characterized by cognitive flexibility."[3] Such experiences are linked with the crucible experiences cited in Chapter 3, along with research on the correlation between overseas assignments and higher levels of creativity. Diversifying experiences, by transgressing the usual rules and boundaries that exist in our minds, stimulate individuals to examine challenges from a different standpoint and to adopt new problem-solving strategies. The increased cognitive flexibility fostered through this mental adjustment process is described as "the ability to break old cognitive patterns, overcome functional fixedness, and thus, make novel (creative) associations between concepts."[4]

This type of flexibility is essential not only for creativity, but also for effective leadership in a changing business environment. Studies of successful global leaders have produced similar terms—frame-shifting, agility, dexterity—that have become common features of the global leadership lexicon.[5] **Cognitive flexibility provides a missing link between multicultural environments and diverse domestic settings because both require the ability to step back from fixed mental patterns and to form new ones in order to function effectively**. This cognitive capability appears to be associated with emotional flexibility in the form of heightened empathy and personal resilience as well.

> **Diversifying experiences, by transgressing the usual rules and boundaries that exist in our minds, stimulate individuals to examine challenges from a different standpoint and to adopt new problem-solving strategies.**

Diversifying experiences that build cognitive and emotional flexibility are also vital for countering insular leadership development patterns. A particularly valuable finding of the research on this topic is that these experiences come in many forms, ranging from extreme to mild: early loss of a parent, living abroad, the experience of prejudice, or even perceived violations of the laws of physics. Profound life experiences such as personal tragedies or large-scale business crises cannot be readily timed or pre-planned, and expatriate assignments are time-consuming and expensive, but there are other learning opportunities that are more readily available, although usually less transformative.

For instance, exposure to the customs and ideas of immigrants, who are currently the topic of much controversy, may be a source of diversifying experiences, as there is a historical link between periods of increased immigration and exceptional creative achievement. Even virtual reality experiments have produced statistically significant results. One study found that subjects in a virtual reality environment who actively experienced unexpected events such as a suitcase on a table that increased or decreased in size depending on their proximity, or who were instructed to prepare a sandwich in an unorthodox manner, scored higher than control group participants on subsequent measurements of cognitive flexibility.[6]

It still appears to be true that the more acute and long-lasting the experience of pattern-defying incongruity a person encounters, the more profound the developmental impact, affirming Nancy Adler's observation that the deeper the culture shock, the greater the learning.[7] Nevertheless, fresh possibilities for leadership development emerge from the evidence that particular violations of established common sense are also conducive to meaningful learning. **A range of more or less structured and life-changing experiences can be leveraged for their developmental value.** Here is a list of options, starting with relatively simple examples, along with comments suggesting related assumptions that could be challenged.

Diversifying Experiences

- Virtual reality game ("Physical objects are not moving in the way they are supposed to.")

- Conversation with an immigrant work colleague ("I had no idea about what she went through to get here, the struggles she has experienced, or her impressions of me.")

- Attending an employee resource group meeting ("I thought that everyone in our company felt that they were being treated equally.")

- Stretch goals ("I'm not going to get there with the old methods. I have to find a new path.")

- Demanding boss ("What I had thought was a solid performance turned out to be mediocre in the eyes of my manager.")

- Action learning project ("People from other functions brought perspectives that were very different from mine.")

- Design thinking project ("Customers reacted very differently to our prototype model than we had anticipated.")

- Disruptive technology development ("This technology will change the basis of competition in our industry.")

- Leading a global team ("I learned that I need to do a lot more to draw out the opinions of all team members.")

- Assignment to a new function ("I am going to have to develop a new skill set to be successful in this role.")

- Expatriate assignment ("Most of my team members quit, and I was not going to meet my objectives; I had to hire new team members and find a different way to manage people in this country.")

- Encountering prejudice ("I thought that I was a valued member of this organization, but it seems I'm being regarded as a second-class citizen with limited possibilities for getting ahead.")

- Crisis management ("This event wasn't supposed to happen and is not in my job description; I'm not prepared for such a huge, high stakes role.")

- Personal loss ("Losing a parent turned my whole world upside down.")

Leadership Program Design

Although the items listed above are very different, each entails a struggle with circumstances that were unanticipated and inconsistent with the person's prior experience and assumptions, while offering the possibility for an active response. Leadership development programs can both create and tap into such experiences, and without this feature, miss a precious opportunity for maximum impact.

Inclusion in its broadest form integrates people from diverse backgrounds—along with the ideas and information that they bring—to benefit employees, the organization, and customers. Two methods for creating diversifying experiences in the context of a formal leadership development program are to either take participants to new markets or to incorporate diverse perspectives at headquarters.

FIRST-HAND EXPERIENCE

At least one segment of many executive leadership programs can be productively dedicated to direct, first-hand experience of fast-growth markets at home or abroad. While leaders may have seen numerous reports about countries such as India, China, Indonesia, or Nigeria, there is no substitute for going to a place to fully grasp its significance. Increasingly advanced virtual communication media can provide a taste of other locations through live video feeds, face-to-face virtual conversations, and other curated materials, but they are still less immersive or compelling than actually being there. Most of the world's growth markets are dynamic environments where thousands of citizens are entering the middle class each day, and millions move each year from the countryside to the city. These are incredibly rich learning environments where people new to such settings meet with surprises just walking down the street.

It is, of course, possible to go to a new location and spend a safe and comfortable week in hotel meeting rooms, with little outside contact. We recommend instead an intensively inclusive agenda that includes direct contact with:

- Local employees
- Expatriates
- Customers
- Competitors
- Suppliers
- Distributors
- Joint venture partners
- Government officials

Systematic daily debriefings and group discussions regarding each of these encounters help to surface outmoded assumptions and to consolidate new learnings. They also provoke wider questioning about risks and growth opportunities, unanticipated customer demands, disruptive forms of innovation that are occurring outside of a company's home market, new sources of competition, government initiatives, regulatory hurdles, and supply chain challenges.

Leadership program coordinators might shudder at all the things that can go wrong with schedules and logistics in emerging market environments. But this inherent messiness and unpredictability can be seen either as horrifying or as part of the learning experience. Delayed flights, power outages, choked traffic on bumpy, dusty roads, animals in the street, and motorcycles carrying families of six or seven all provide unforgettable messages about the nature of the local marketplace.

Leaders from tidy developed countries also experience a vivid sense of their own limitations and/or potential for personal growth. Some revel in the market dynamism and opportunities, while others recoil at the sights, sounds, and smells—even the sheer press of humanity in crowded urban settings. Testing one's dietary limitations or willingness to try new foods offers non-trivial learnings about flexibility and resilience. "Agility," a term habitually bandied about in leadership programs, is not merely cognitive but also a gut-level response to witnessing urban poverty, experiencing the effects of polluted air and water, feeling violations of personal space, eating unfamiliar foods, and sweating or freezing in an unfamiliar climate.

Over the years, we have witnessed many "aha" moments from program participants that occurred on the spot. Each of the quotes below shows evidence for how diversifying experiences can stimulate fresh cognitive flexibility and non-habitual responses:

> - *I have a new respect for one of our local competitors. I had thought they were a couple of product cycles behind us, but now I know that they are much closer to our level of quality, with a price point that is thirty percent lower.*
>
> - *I sat through a virtual meeting with my local colleagues here late at night and watched how they were verbally run over by my team members back at headquarters. Now I am much more deliberate in inviting them into team meetings and ensuring that they have their say— they have begun to share important market insights.*
>
> - *The workers in the factory here are so young! I can't believe the product quality is near the top of our global system with an average worker age of twenty-six!*
>
> - *Our brand is positioned completely differently in this market in a mode that allows us access to a different type of customer.*
>
> - *The experience I have in a slow-growth market in Europe could be very useful to my colleagues here who have not yet had to live through a market slowdown.*

> - *Our China operation can supply product to our markets in Africa at a competitive price point that we couldn't achieve elsewhere.*
>
> - *We will need to bring more sourcing and production here to India in order to meet local pricing expectations.*
>
> - *We have employees based in this region who could really benefit from a short-term assignment abroad—it would be a big motivator to them, a useful retention tool, and a means to help them interface more effectively with their global colleagues. I've already started to make arrangements for this to happen.*
>
> - *Our joint venture partners in this country are actually very different from each other, and it is a mistake to think of them in the same way. We have to deal with them differently based on their internal politics and government ties.*
>
> - *We are looking to this country as a key growth market, and yet we have only a handful of local executives at the top levels. We need to accelerate talent development here in a major way.*

Another rather miraculous outcome of leadership programs focused on first-hand experience in fast-growth markets is that participants who reside in these locations are suddenly front and center. A leader from India or China, for instance, who might have stayed quietly in the background during a program held at headquarters, deferring to more vocal participants, is suddenly an authority to whom all participants turn. Local leaders earn fresh recognition for their market knowledge, multilingual skills, customer and employee contacts, and business results.

Expatriates, too, who may have long felt that their perspective was neglected and their many labors ignored, now find themselves frequently tapped for insights about their current home. **A geographical shift**

in program location tends to produce a comprehensive re-sorting among participants: levels of participation, prestige, and respect all shift toward a new orientation focused on requirements for growth in expanding markets. This, too, can be a revelation and an exercise in cognitive and emotional flexibility for participants who now have a new perspective regarding their own level of knowledge and the contributions that others could make.

HEADQUARTERS-BASED PROGRAMS: INSIDE-OUT TO OUTSIDE-IN

It is possible for leadership programs based at headquarters to bring the "outside in," both in terms of content and process, and to avoid viewing the world from an "inside-out" perspective that excludes and imposes ideas on others. Embedding inclusive perspectives and practices requires a comprehensive approach that, instead of treating "canned culture" as a tidy module replete with other people's examples, regards **the entire program as an opportunity for live, real-time discovery and joint culture-building**.

Executive Experts

In contrast to one of the common program flaws mentioned previously, expert executive speakers who describe their own diversifying experiences—how they had their assumptions about people or markets tested and in response developed new, more flexible leadership patterns—can validate the importance of such experiences and serve as a role model. When program participants know that a person above them in the hierarchy whom they respect and admire has struggled to become more inclusive, this gives them permission to open up and talk about their own difficulties and questions.

360 Feedback

Feedback comes in various forms, and there are myriad delivery instruments, some better than others. The key function that any instrument should serve is to make inclusive leadership a challenge that is personal rather than abstract. One of the most vital aspects of any assessment exercise is to know the gaps between self-perception and the perceptions of others: "I thought I was a pretty inclusive leader, but some of the people I'm working with don't seem to agree!"

Participants also learn how they are or are not unique. Most people are relieved to discover that others are struggling with similar issues. It is just as crucial for leaders to recognize their own unique characteristics and styles, which enable them to balance authenticity with a willingness to experiment with new patterns of behavior.[8] "Openness to experience" is one of the so-called Big Five personality traits most often associated with success living abroad—leaders who have a realistic sense of their profile in this area may choose to leap into a larger or smaller crucible for their next assignment.

Program Content

Participants are more likely to build inclusive leadership skills if they are introduced to a few basic models, techniques, and examples. Leadership behaviors such as self-awareness, invite the unexpected, and frame-shifting provide the basis for inclusivity, as does the related three-step process for bridge-building (see Chapter 3). It is also important to understand how inclusion is defined, one's own current stage on the path to greater inclusivity, and what practical next steps are possible. Inclusive leadership examples and best practices should incorporate a diverse array of subject matter in terms of geography, functions, culture, race and ethnicity, etc., so that participants from various backgrounds will feel that the material speaks to them.

Context and frameworks must be tied quickly to participants' direct experiences, either from their own past or sometimes even what is happening among them on the spot. If prompted, nearly everyone will be able to recall a time when they caused or experienced exclusion themselves, and were forced to question basic assumptions. Providing a format to describe these events helps each person to reinforce and build on prior lessons, to learn from others, and to expand their leadership repertoire. Leaders learn most readily from their peers, and they often find it quite exciting to share their own experiences with others using a simple format such as:

- *Here's what I assumed*

- *Here's what I experienced*

- *Here's what I learned to do differently*

Program Process

Psychological safety is a feature not only of high-performing teams (see Chapter 7) but also of leadership development programs that are firing on all cylinders. The same outward manifestations—roughly equal air time, a willingness to take risks and offer up untested ideas, and a rapid pace of mutual learning—hold true as well. Program facilitators may need to use every technique they know in order to establish this kind of climate as quickly as possible: setting ground rules, asking well-targeted questions, drawing out some participants, requesting others to hold back, using small groups of various sizes, conducting pair exercises, providing structured opportunities to contribute, holding panel discussions, asking for alternative points of view, pushing back against one-sided opinions, and blending different modalities such as short presentations, experiential learning, games, debate, poetry, or humor.

The most powerful facilitation techniques bring attention to real-time interactions in the room—for instance, a previously silent participant who has just offered a valuable perspective based on another's invitation—yet must be used with caution because they can either take the discussion to a whole new level or shut it down if someone feels embarrassed or criticized. At its best, active facilitation of live interactions reveals the complexity behind cultural generalizations (e.g., "Germans are very direct"; "Japanese nod their heads even when they disagree"; "Hispanics are family-oriented") by cheerfully exploring possible explanations that may confirm, contradict, elaborate, or qualify standard wisdom. Participants may also bring with them charged emotional baggage based on polarizing views in their environment, and facilitators need to act in a deft, neutral manner to turn this into a listening and learning opportunity rather than rhetorical combat.

In addition to keeping participants busy and challenged, leadership development should provide chances for reflection, both personal and strategic. Diversifying experiences are more readily digested and installed as lasting behavior patterns or traits when people are given structured opportunities to recall the event, to enrich it with greater detail, and to absorb it more fully, reinforcing new neural pathways in the process.[9] Diaries, guided reflection, and silence all make reflection easier, and serve to balance the contributions of extroverts and introverts—the latter may offer up startling insights once they've had time to think carefully about a topic.

Coaching

Coaching enables leaders to dig in and apply what they are learning. Skillful coaches build trust quickly and clarify objectives, meanwhile holding up a mirror that a leader may or may not be eager to see. They ask great questions, know when to push and when to hold back, work with coachees to build and explore options, and ask for realistic commitments—always circling back to see if these have been met. They are thoughtful, unselfish, honest, persistent, challenging, and sometimes irritating.

Another key role that a coach can play is to identify narratives that a leader offers, whether these are positive or self-defeating, and to question their accuracy and utility.[10] As a veteran psychologist was fond of noting, "If you observe carefully, you'll see that nine out of ten people walking down the street are talking to themselves."[11] Leaders are no exception to this regular internal story-telling activity, and deeply entrenched stories (some possibly inherited from parents or colleagues) may be the most tenacious obstacles to increased cognitive and emotional flexibility.

A leadership program participant could have a terrific new insight thanks to a diversifying experience, but that precious step toward a more inclusive mindset is soon erased by several laps around a familiar mental story track that confirms old biases and precludes new and more effective action. The shockingly low rate of retained learning and application from some programs is probably due as much to this narrative hamster wheel as to urgent job demands that absorb the energy of participants upon their return to work. Good coaches will break this news gently and suggest that we can do better.

Inclusive Narratives

Mental flexibility is reinforced and expanded through narrative flexibility. When the previous story no longer fits, it is time for a different one. **Just as a strong organizational culture that is no longer suited to a changing business environment becomes a critical weakness, outmoded story lines—silent or voiced—do not serve leaders well**. Because current events are perceived through an aged and cracking lens, such stories instigate misinterpretations and make the narrator look out of touch.

When dated narratives about prior successes or failures are shared among groups of executives at home or expatriates abroad, they may foster cliquish conduct and "shoot the messenger" responses to those who dare to offer more current views, or "not invented here" rejections of employees with better ideas. Leaders who are not fully engaged with present realities or emerging possibilities will probably find that their employees, too, become disengaged. Yesterday's heroes and their patterns of behavior can also crowd out and ultimately exclude potential future leaders.

Story-telling is typically taught in a leadership context as an instrument for more effective persuasion or for exerting wider influence—by touching people's heartstrings or appealing to their values, leaders are more likely to gain support and to win that big investment in their project. But fresh stories that feature genuine examples of inclusive leadership are perhaps even more valuable.

Some cultures feature master story-tellers who have spent a lifetime learning their craft and are hard to imitate. However, people without such a cultural pedigree learn to tell effective stories as well. **By capturing a practical example of how a diversifying experience led them to question their assumptions and to change, leaders can reinforce inclusive patterns in their own minds, within their team, and throughout the organization.** Simple narratives have the advantage of being short and credible:

Narratives of this kind highlight individual uniqueness, foster a wider sense of in-group belonging, and build a climate of greater inclusion. But there is more to the art of narration than story-telling. **Leaders must also learn to balance "story-telling" with "story-asking."** This means tactfully inviting others to share narratives of their own about their backgrounds and experiences, while taking care to avoid being intrusive or reopening old wounds. Narratives that emerge in this way can serve as another means to bridge differences among team members, conveying a fuller picture of each person's complex identity and accelerating mutual learning.

SAMPLE STORY: "WRONG ABOUT ANGELA"

What I assumed:

Angela was new to the team. At first I had her pegged as an average contributor with limited future potential because she struggled to get up to speed on the project. I had already started to exclude her from discussions of complex technical issues.

What I experienced:

When I started working with Angela more closely, I realized that she is incredibly bright and committed, and she responded to my feedback by learning quickly and volunteering to take on more responsibility. She also has a positive attitude and a sense of humor that have brightened the atmosphere of the whole team. Now, after a year of working together, she is going to step into my role as team leader when I move to the next job. I never would have imagined this at first. Was I ever wrong about her!

What I learned:

I misjudged Angela's potential because she had come from a totally different line of business and was new to the company. From working with her, I've learned to postpone judgment a bit, to work with team members more closely to figure out what their background is and what they are capable of doing, and then to start raising the bar while offering additional coaching to those who want it. This is what I'm doing with everyone on my new team, and it seems to be working.

EVERYDAY INCLUSION

Leadership development programs commonly provide useful ideas and tools along with an impetus to change. But they are also just one aspect of a growth process that spans a whole career and are part of a much larger inclusion challenge. Organizations have an imperative and an opportunity to build inclusion at every level, taking a comprehensive approach to each phase of the global talent cycle.

At the same time, inclusion is a personal responsibility. It is up to each leader to assess where they are on their own inclusion journey and to consider the value to themselves, to others, and to the business of taking further steps. The vital next step that any leader can take is to identify and engage in everyday acts of inclusion that widen the circle of "us," while seeking out experiences that will further expand hearts and minds.

12.
Five Organizational Levers

Leaders who embrace new ideas, colleagues, and ways of serving customers can make their institutions uniquely sustainable.

What kinds of organizational changes are most essential to support inclusion? Is it possible to measure progress toward a more inclusive work environment?

Inclusive actions flourish most readily in a supportive environment. Many leaders want to increase inclusion organization-wide but are uncertain about where to start or what changes to prioritize in order to achieve their goals. A comprehensive approach to the inclusive leadership journey usually produces the best results, with a special focus on five key levers of organizational support:

1. Recruitment

2. Executive Engagement

3. Coaching/Mentoring/Sponsorship

4. Key Performance Indicators

5. Policy and Process

This chapter combines our own experience with a sampling of recent research. Although many of the studies in this area are U.S.-centric, findings based on broader samples and international data are referenced where feasible, along with data from our own *Inclusive Behaviors Inventory*.

LEVER #1: RECRUITMENT

Competing successfully for talent means hiring the most capable recruits to grow markets and serve customers wherever a company has operations. In sought-after fields such as engineering or computer science, mid-career hires come at a premium price, and college students may have multiple internships under their belts and job offers in hand well before they graduate. What makes one firm's recruitment efforts more effective than another's?

Shifting technologies and global demographics mean that new employees are often different from their predecessors in many ways: technical training, native language, nationality, racial and ethnic background, communication styles, and so on. A core dilemma that most recruitment efforts face is *"How can we ensure a 'cultural fit' with our new recruits while opening our organizational culture to change at the same time?"* This dilemma overlaps with a common challenge that most leaders face when they are elevated to new and more complex roles: "What got you here won't get you there."[1] In other words, the very work patterns that have been the foundation for success thus far, either for an individual or for an organization, may become obstacles as the environment changes. Industries rarely stand still, and there is a constant imperative to preserve essential cultural elements and competencies that continue to be relevant—values, expertise, relationships—while injecting new ideas, perspectives, and energy.

Managers in charge of recruitment in larger organizations usually have a keen awareness of this dilemma, yet they are under pressure to meet targets and fill open job slots. Moreover, they must work with an extended network of employees who conduct job interviews or travel to job fairs and college campuses. This network sometimes includes people who are happy to return to their alma mater, to revitalize their prior connections, and to seek out others who fit with their own implicit success criteria. These key players in the recruiting process, however, may not be deliberately seeking to identify others who could be successful but are unlike them.

How can managers ensure that their entire extended team is working in an inclusive way? Here are some characteristics of successful recruiting teams:

CHARACTERISTICS OF SUCCESSFUL RECRUITING

- The entire recruiting team shares **common goals** for finding candidates who are both well-qualified and diverse, with special attention to areas in which the company needs to expand its representation in order to grow and serve the communities where it operates.

- **Job descriptions** are scrutinized for language that might cause qualified candidates to exclude themselves based on gender, race, or other characteristics (see Figure 12.1).

- Use **non-traditional methods** such as Boolean search (a method of using key words and modifiers to search, for example, for particular types of colleges, associations, or names) to locate underrepresented candidates and create a more diverse hiring pool.

- Interviewers use a **common set of questions** and a common process for recording responses and impressions to reduce the effects of subjectivity.

- Recruiting teams incorporate a **diverse set of perspectives** through steps such as two-person interview teams for high-priority candidates, with interviewers comparing their impressions afterward. (This does not necessarily mean that members of every interview team must fully reflect the diversity of the candidates under consideration, which may be unfeasible for some organizations and exhausting for underrepresented minority members.)

- Teams consider establishing a **minimum number of minority candidates to interview** to ensure that they start with a sufficiently broad candidate pool. It is best to have multiple candidates rather than just one.[3]

- Recruitment team members volunteer to take on different roles such as contrarian or **devil's advocate** to ensure that various viewpoints are considered. ("How much of a change agent will this person be? Is there another candidate who would challenge us more?")

- Teams consider establishing a **"blind audit" qualification process** focused on task performance, analogous to the practice of blind orchestra audits which has resulted in the selection of more female orchestra members than in the past. (See Figure 12.2)

- Recruiting team members build the skills needed to **recognize and counteract unconscious bias** in interviews and selection. For example, each aspect of unconscious bias outlined in Chapter 4 can apply to the recruiting process. Here are simple examples using the CIAO model:

  - **Confirmation Bias**: This candidate is like me, and therefore she is more likely to be successful in my company than other candidates.

  - **Insider Bias**: This person participated in many of the same groups and activities that I did during my university years, so I am confident that he will fit in well.

  - **Attribution Bias**: Candidate A did well based on hard work and persistence; Candidate B received special treatment.

  - **Overconfidence**: I know what my company needs and which qualifications are most essential for a successful career here.

Kieran Snyder
Cofounder and CEO,
Textio

- Created software to provide clients with feedback on the likelihood that a job description will attract diverse candidates.

- Looks for patterns in data related to job descriptions in postings (how many applied, how long the job was posted, the demographic groups it attracted).

- The tool highlights words based on how well they do or do not work to attract a diverse audience.

- Mozilla reports the software has helped them fill positions 17% more quickly.

Figure 12.1: Modifying Job Descriptions[2]

Cultural competence is relevant to recruiting team member preparation as well. Knowledge of culture-based behavior patterns can be important not only for dealing with international candidates but also for making accurate judgments about diverse styles of work and communication within the same country. **"Intuition" is often misleading in an environment where people are assessing cues based on different cultural styles and behavior**.

For instance, an interviewer who is a very "Direct" communicator may underestimate candidates whose "Indirect" style leads them to be modest about prior achievements. Likewise, an "Independent," "Task-focused" interviewer may be put off by a candidate who gives a more "Interdependent" or "Relationship-oriented" response, even when that candidate has a strong track record of achievements. All team members should be prepared to recognize instances in which their own cultural profiles could cause them to misjudge candidates who are otherwise well-qualified and could be successful within their organization.

Kedar Iyer
Cofounder and CEO,
GapJumpers

• Created an online blind audition process where potential applicants are given a job to complete (e.g., web developers are asked to create a webpage). Hiring managers assess the completed task without any personal identifiers, including name, gender, work experience or educational background.

• Clients have seen a 60% jump in applicants from underrepresented groups compared to traditional screening.

• Reduces time to fill a position by almost 40%.

Figure 12.2: Blind Audition Process[4]

LEVER #2: EXECUTIVE ENGAGEMENT

Nearly every set of criteria for an organization-wide inclusion initiative underlines the importance of getting key executives on board. There are countless pitfalls when executives are not committed or are half-hearted supporters. Initiatives that begin with fanfare sputter out due to sporadic investment of time or money; decisions are made that ironically neglect the input of true inclusion champions; and employees observe that the actions of executives themselves are undermining basic inclusion principles. In the absence of sustained executive commitment, other priorities ultimately take precedence and the focus on inclusion fades, leaving a deep layer of skepticism throughout the employee population. On the positive side, there is increasing empirical evidence that support for diversity on the part of top management is linked with favorable business outcomes such as higher revenue from innovation.[5]

Executives are under relentless pressure to perform. These leaders need to hit their growth targets, limit expenses in the face of rising costs, keep customers happy, retain vital employees, and invest in the next generation of technology. They are normally pleased to be able to celebrate success, to raise compensation, and to hire more people; yet even in the midst of good times they have to keep the potential for harder days in their minds as well. In organizational life there are few things more painful than having to lay off employees when the market turns downward or, worse yet, to declare bankruptcy when expenditures exceed revenue and the banks refuse to extend further credit. Executive roles are normally quite visible, and failure could permanently damage reputations that have been built up over years of hard work.

Executives are naturally most responsive to initiatives that are tied to growth, cost optimization, or acquiring superior talent. They want to win, and have also been trained to probe investment proposals for strengths and weaknesses. "How exactly is your initiative going to help us?" they are likely to ask. There is no substitute for a rational, company-specific business case that ties a proposal, for example, to organizational goals for expansion in a promising market, reduced legal costs related to alleged discrimination, or being able to lure key talent away from rivals. If an objective is to hire and retain high-potential employees from all backgrounds, they will want to track progress and revisit this at regular intervals, just like their other goals.

Senior leaders who are most dedicated to inclusion also tend to have some prior experience that made it significant and personally poignant for them: a difficult stint living abroad; minority status or a close friend who is a minority group member; a family member with a disability; understanding of the consequences of gender bias and sexual assault; a spouse who is an immigrant; a personal brush with illness or death. Parenthood has an impact as well: "Research on male CEOs, politicians, and judges shows that fathers of daughters care more about gender equality than men without children or with only sons."[6]

Those without such a background can still deepen their insight and commitment through the kinds of diversifying experiences described in Chapter 11. Peer feedback helps them to consider how they are perceived by the people around them, and corporate training efforts can feature exercises such as personal "story-telling" that enable them to see into others' lives. Such events need to be facilitated with sensitivity to ensure that the result is insight and inspiration rather than perceived blaming and shaming.

PERSONAL HISTORIES

At an offsite retreat, executive team members were asked to describe aspects of their personal history others might not know about. Several of the stories that emerged were surprising to everyone. One leader, whom everyone assumed had come from a wealthy family setting, described his childhood being raised on a farm, the scholarship that was his only chance to attend college, and the opportunity a former manager who believed in his potential had given him to move into a challenging new role that was a career game-changer.

> *Another participant, who was one of the last to speak, said quietly that she was the only person from her small town in China to have passed the entrance exam for a university in Beijing and to have attended business school abroad, and that she was now sponsoring a program to enhance educational opportunities for girls back in her home province.*
>
> *The team members came away from the event with a much deeper appreciation for each other, and one summed up the shared spirit that emerged from their conversation by saying to the others, "I'm going to help you in every way that I can, and I am committed to supporting every single one of our future leaders regardless of what their backgrounds are."*

There are potential downsides to executive enthusiasm, too. These include proposals for large-scale, monolithic solutions. Some corporate directors of inclusion and diversity have found themselves coping with sudden directives from leaders who have become true believers: "Women clearly face problems everywhere in the world. I've seen this with my own eyes. You have one goal this year, which is to raise the number of women managers company-wide!" Such directives may or may not constitute a reasonable next step, and they are sometimes not based on a broad and balanced inclusion strategy.

Another issue can be translating a single executive's enthusiasm to the rest of the leadership team and to mid-level managers who aren't yet on board in the same way. Given the competitive and peer-conscious nature of people who have climbed the career ladder, a way to entice greater commitment is to establish project teams with specific goals: sell products to members of a growing minority population; preserve vital talent from a recent acquisition; build a more diverse pipeline of future leaders. Working together and even competing to make the biggest contribution on behalf of a common cause is frequently a more compelling invitation for senior leaders to get on board than is mandatory training.

Engaged executives normally also want to go beyond projects and task forces, and will look for a way to institutionalize inclusion efforts. Potential structures for sustaining inclusion over time include appointing a direct report to the CEO with a title such as Chief Diversity Officer (CDO), adding inclusion to the portfolio of the human resources department, or making this a responsibility of business units or divisions. There are potential pros and cons with each approach, and as a result, many organizations create their own hybrid structures.

Chief Diversity Officer

Pros: This structure brings visibility to the topic of inclusion and diversity, and creates a clear line of accountability. It brings the CDO to the table with other members of the executive team, reinforcing their awareness of inclusion priorities.

Cons: Especially when there is little actual budget and few direct reports to this position, it can become more of a "movie star" role that enables line managers to avoid taking responsibility themselves. (One veteran of this role referred to it as having "alligator arms"—in other words, a short reach for actually getting things done.)

Human Resources

Pros: The human resources (HR) function has the personnel, both at headquarters and embedded within business units and regions, to follow through on initiatives. HR professionals can also ensure that inclusion initiatives are aligned and integrated with other policies and processes related to talent development, succession planning, and so on.

Cons: HR often has a long list of objectives, and a new addition to this list might be regarded as a low priority in the absence of explicit directives and a dedicated budget. The link with HR could imply ties with legal compliance measures in some organizations. Inclusion may not be seen as a business imperative by other departments; it will be associated with the image of the HR department, whether positive or negative.

Business Units

Pros: When line managers take responsibility for inclusion, there can be considerable grass roots interest and energy, with specific applications to each part of the business. Many employees look to business leaders as role models, and real commitment by line managers transmits a clear message: "We are serious about this!"

Cons: If line manager adoption is uneven and uncoordinated, there are likely to be mixed signals and mixed results. Different managers may adopt their own homemade models and approaches, and, if this is the case, it will become difficult to track progress or disseminate best practices in a coordinated fashion.

LEVER #3: COACHING, MENTORING, & SPONSORSHIP

Research suggests that providing focused support has a strongly positive effect on the advancement of minority employees.[7] This support can take a variety of forms, depending on career stage and corporate culture.

Coaching

New recruits from backgrounds outside of the corporate mainstream often find themselves a step or two behind from their first day in the organization. While others seem to dress appropriately, know the right things to say, and are off and running quickly, it may take longer for minority employees to learn their way around. The initial culture shock for them is greater, and they also frequently encounter subtle or not so subtle messages indicating that less is expected of them or that they are expected to perform in a niche role with limited upside prospects. As a result, compared to members of the majority culture, it is common for this population to experience lower job satisfaction, negative performance evaluations, and higher attrition.

Coaching that is targeted at individuals or groups of early career employees can be useful in countering trends that, over time, tend to transform a diverse recruiting class into a homogeneous set of leaders. Although coaches are usually not positioned to call for organizational change, in their one-on-one conversations they can shed objective light on the internal narratives of employees that sometimes lead to conclusions such as, "My opportunities are limited," or "I just don't belong here." Women and minority employees, in particular, may have questions, beliefs, or doubts about themselves that foster a lack of self-confidence or willingness to take on risks for the sake of career advancement.

The examples in Figure 12.3 were gathered from a large pool of Asian women managers who attended a recent conference in Singapore, and reflect, in part, social expectations in the region that still place the main responsibility for family care and child-rearing on women while regarding men as the primary breadwinners.

Figure 12.3: Self-Limiting Questions & Beliefs: Examples

Coaching provides individuals with the chance to clarify and test their own beliefs, while exploring which of those beliefs are based on real obstacles and which are unfounded. When this type of coaching is conducted in a small group context, it also allows participants to share their fears and concerns with each other and to learn that they are not alone in having doubts about their ability to succeed. Coachees are able to discuss possible solutions together and build a network of supportive contacts in the process. As self-limiting doubts are addressed, coaching conversations can move on to identifying key areas for knowledge acquisition and skill-building, as well as discussing how to move forward with professional and personal development while addressing obstacles.

Mentoring and Sponsorship

For employees who are candidates for management roles, mentors or sponsors serve several purposes. First, they can offer information, contacts, visibility, and candid feedback that candidates would otherwise miss out on, limiting their career opportunities and areas for professional growth. Choice leadership assignments are normally offered to insiders with whom top executives are already comfortable, and **effective mentors or sponsors help promising candidates step over the threshold from outsider to insider.**

Second, mentors or sponsors may provide encouragement and support for taking on responsibilities that candidates are capable of handling but hesitate to assume. Extensive interviews with women in one large organization produced a troubling set of findings for those committed to equal developmental opportunities. Many women observed that men are considered for, and accept, a role or promotion where they may not have all the qualifications or experience required. The trend for women, however, is that they are not considered for, nor will they accept, a role for which they do not feel completely qualified.

Other research suggests that a lack of confidence or hesitancy to take risks, both of which are sometimes attributed to gender differences, could actually be natural responses to organizational realities: "Because women operate under a higher-resolution microscope than their male counterparts do, their mistakes and failures are scrutinized more carefully and punished more severely. People who are scrutinized more carefully will, in turn, be less likely to speak up in meetings, particularly if they feel no one has their back. However, when women fail to speak up, it is commonly assumed that they lack confidence in their ideas."[8] Encouragement—"You can do this!"—plus the knowledge that one has a supporter who is willing to provide both guidance and a safety net in case things go wrong, could be just enough for women or minority candidates to contribute more innovative ideas or to accept a challenging role they would otherwise decline. **An employee's image of what a new role or course of action entails could be a barrier** even when there are ways to prepare for or to avert potential problems.

Sponsors typically have the mandate to ensure that their protégé stays with the organization and is able to advance. Along the way, many become personally invested in their candidate's progress. Personnel decisions about recruiting or next-level positions tend to fall into a gray zone where biases easily take hold; under these kinds of circumstances minorities and women are more frequently evaluated critically and eliminated from the candidate pool, while men from the majority culture are given the benefit of the doubt.[9] Such decisions can be swayed by a credible advocate who is able to make a pitch on a candidate's behalf, both highlighting objective qualifications and conveying an emotional undertone of personal conviction. **A powerful and enthusiastic sponsor may go beyond encouragement and advocacy to take on the role of a "snowplow"** who helps to smooth the way for protégés, assuring that they will have opportunities commensurate with their abilities and be judged fairly for their performance. Some companies prefer to avoid putting an official sponsorship program in place—appointing only mentors instead— because this might be seen as a form of favoritism toward certain employees; other firms are sufficiently alarmed by lower retention or promotion rates for targeted groups that they regard sponsorship as an indispensable method for leveling the playing field.

Benefits accrue to mentors or sponsors as well as to the candidates they are supporting. Each individual who takes on such a role should keep in mind potential pitfalls.

COMMON PITFALLS FOR MENTORS OR SPONSORS

- Rushing to be "helpful" without thoroughly understanding a protégé's circumstances; providing guidance that fits the mentor's own experience and background but not those of the mentee

- Letting bias or stereotypes—e.g., "Women lack confidence," or "Minority candidates have advanced through affirmative action"— get in the way of a clear assessment of individual capabilities

- Trying to solve problems without sufficiently enabling mentees to figure things out and take action themselves where needed

- Letting mentees' self-doubts prevent them from taking on roles that they could handle

- Pushing protégés too hard to jump into roles they are not ready for; failing to understand what they can or cannot change in their own social context

- Failing to provide ongoing support to those who have taken on new challenges but are now struggling

- Allowing enthusiasm for their protégés and sense of competition with other sponsors lead them to create a new set of unfair advantages or disadvantages

LEVER #4:
KEY PERFORMANCE INDICATORS (KPIs)

The metrics used to gauge progress in inclusion tend to be relatively blunt instruments. It is easy to measure numbers of women, minorities, or people of various nationalities in management roles, for example, and there is value in establishing a baseline for comparison with external benchmarks and for setting future targets. What an organization chooses to prioritize and track will naturally depend on the legal framework that governs its headquarters operations, the locations in which it has a presence, its business priorities and plans for growth, and its corporate mission and values.[10]

Several cautionary notes apply to the use of inclusion metrics, however. The first is that the mere presence of a diverse range of employees in different roles or at various levels does not guarantee positive business outcomes. Moreover, although for statistical purposes it is preferable to have clear and straightforward ways of categorizing people, the reality is usually more complex: "No one is just female, or just black, or just Muslim. Each person is 'a whole package of interlocking attributes.'"[11] Employees with multicultural backgrounds may be reluctant to identify with any single nationality—this would force them to choose between parents, or between their current homes and their countries of origin. LGBTQ+ employees in some countries may push for non-binary gender categories, while in other places these categories are illegal. Racial classifications such as "white," "black," or "Asian" may fail to take into account differences in socioeconomic backgrounds or educational opportunities.

There is also research pointing to the value of "deep-level diversity"[12]— personality, values, and abilities—that is not immediately apparent or easy to track. Differences in cognitive styles, too, fall into this category of less readily visible features. The leadership team attributes most closely linked to innovation, according to one recent study, are diversity in career path, industry background, national origin, and gender.[13] At the same time, employees who belong to racial minorities may feel that excessive focus on personalities or cognitive styles fosters neglect of the difficult work of addressing social inequities with deep historical roots, unequal distribution of power and privilege, and limited opportunities for advancement.

The presence of employees who straddle multiple categories can be regarded either as an obstacle or as a source of opportunities for deeper and more fine-tuned analysis. Organizations with data for large numbers of employees could be asking questions that might lead to effective follow-up measures:

- Is there a difference in the functional backgrounds of women who advance in our organization versus those who do not?

- Are some nationalities more successful than others?

- Are Hispanics with an international background promoted at the same rate as those with a domestic background?

- When individuals join as mid-career hires from similar or different industry backgrounds, how do they progress in comparison with other employees?

Follow the Talent Cycle

The diversity of executive teams or board members receives considerable attention due to media scrutiny, but the entire talent cycle merits careful examination. To track the progress of a particular group or groups of people over time—most commonly based on gender, race, or nationality—it is valuable to establish measurements for each phase of the employee life cycle. Leaders confronted with a lack of diversity in their ranks are tempted to say, "The main problem is our recruitment pipeline. We have to hire more qualified recruits to increase our pool of talent!" This helps to kick the can down the road while avoiding the need for close scrutiny of day-to-day organizational patterns, especially when ownership for metrics is delegated to a staff function such as the chief diversity officer or human resources rather than being owned by each line of business. However, the value of inclusive practices comes from their application to the full path from fresh recruit to executive, and from holding line management as well as staff functions accountable. Here are common examples of common metrics that can be applied to successive stages of the employee talent cycle.

- *Recruitment*: Is the company hiring qualified employees from priority institutions or industry backgrounds in the targeted categories?

- *Representation*: Does the demographic profile of employees reflect the general population and/or the available pool of technical specialists?

- *Workplace Climate*: How do the satisfaction rates for different groups of employees compare with each other based on race, gender, age, rank, or nationality?

- *Compensation*: Are employees in the same job categories being paid at equal rates regardless of their backgrounds?

- *Retention*: Is the organization successful in retaining employees of all categories at the same rate, and if not, which groups tend to have higher or lower rates of attrition?

- *Promotion*: Are all groups promoted at the same rate at each level of advancement? If not, which groups tend to move ahead or fall behind, and at what point in their careers?

- *Succession*: Is there a robust, diverse pipeline of future executives with the right experience to step into top jobs?

Figure 12.4: Talent Cycle Metrics[14]

Other metrics that some firms examine include participation in skill-building programs and costs related to prevention, investigation, and legal defense of employee discrimination claims. On an optimistic note, some organizations have targeted specific initiatives based on skill requirements and a sense of social mission. SAP, for instance, is in the midst of a multiyear recruiting and onboarding effort that will increase the number of "neurodiverse" employees to 1% of its total workforce—a number chosen because it corresponds roughly to the percentage of people in the general population with a diagnosis of autism.[15] For companies with international operations, tracking whether they have sufficient local national talent with the requisite skills to drive future plans for growth and market penetration becomes another vital metric.

Measuring Inclusive Actions

The five dimensions that comprise the Inclusive Behaviors Inventory provide a model for building individual self-awareness and commitment to inclusive actions. This framework can also be useful for measuring inclusion on the organizational level in order to identify and address common challenges.[16]

Combined survey results from a large database and a variety of companies and industries indicate that, among the five dimensions discussed throughout this book, respondent self-ratings for several items for the "Getting Results" dimension, for example, are near the bottom of the scale.[17] Such evidence is not surprising, as even people who endorse the general principle of inclusion and who are doing their best to apply it still struggle with complex, nitty-gritty applications such as decision-making or meeting customer needs.[18]

For an organization that mirrors such overall results, targeting selected development opportunities related to this particular survey dimension or items within it could be components of an effective strategy.

Learning About Bias	Building Key Skills	Working Across Boundaries	Becoming a Champion	Getting Results

Figure 12.5: Inclusive Behaviors Inventory

LEVER #5: POLICY & PROCESS

Experience with well-meaning initiatives to foster greater inclusion has demonstrated that some methods work better than others. Ineffective methods can even have unintended negative consequences. For example, mandatory diversity training may produce a backlash among employees who continue to discriminate in subtle ways; testing designed to promote fairness is sometimes applied unfairly to screen out minorities but not others; and grievance systems tend to spark retaliation. Each of these methods is actually correlated with declines in the number of women and minorities in management roles.

Meanwhile, alternative methods such as voluntary training, mentoring, task forces, and dedicated diversity managers are correlated with relatively positive outcomes.[19] Other research points to the need for a foundation of inclusive organizational practices in order to reap the potential benefits of diversity; these include participative leadership, equal pay for equal work, and a strategic emphasis on diversity and inclusion led by the CEO.[20]

Psychological Leverage

Such positive or negative results appear to be influenced by basic psychological principles, including aspects of unconscious bias that were presented in Chapter 4. Humans value the capacity for autonomous action—which is linked with one's basic sense of control over environmental circumstances and ability to handle stress—and tend to react negatively when their autonomy is threatened by directives issued without consultation.[21] A form of confirmation bias known as anchoring influences managers who read employee self-evaluations before writing their assessments, leading them to unintentionally reward self-promotion and punish modesty.[22] "Insider" versus "outsider" dynamics shape whether a candidate for employment or promotion is subjected to rigorous testing. Having a grievance filed against you or your department could produce an instinctive "fight" response, possibly due in part to overconfidence that your own department is blameless.

Those who shape policies and processes designed to promote inclusion are well advised to not only take these aspects of the human psyche into account, but to turn them to their advantage. **Voluntary training or task force participation enables participants to preserve their own sense of autonomy while shaping an updated concept of themselves as supporters or champions of inclusion**. When managers view employee self-assessments after they have formulated their own evaluations rather than before, this enables them to judge more objectively and to better coach those with inflated self-images as well as those who lack confidence.[23] Structured recruiting interviews and involvement of minority team members can counter insider bias and produce a sense of teamwork in service of a common cause. Leaders who convincingly describe their own inclusion journey, perhaps through transformative personal experiences or encounters with workplace colleagues, encourage employees to drop their "fight" response to perceived threats, responding instead with empathy rather than overconfident denial of responsibility.

Informal organizational practices may be more powerful and pervasive than formal ones, and are reinforced by social values that shape role expectations. Analysis of how office "housework" assignments—taking notes, handling meeting logistics, ordering food, planning parties, keeping lists of tasks, and so on—are made in comparison with the process for assigning coveted growth opportunities indicates that the less prestigious roles are assigned disproportionally to women and minorities, including employees hired for professional roles.[24] Similarly, many organizations send informal signals through office space allocations, forms of recognition, or even pictures displayed on the walls. **It is worth scrutinizing these kinds of informal aspects of office life for the signals they send about fairness and equal access to opportunities**. Seemingly small adjustments can have a surprisingly large symbolic effect.

Work-life flexibility is another area where both informal and formal policies come into play. Although organizations normally have formal policies related to childbirth, for example, actual practices vary widely according to national laws, health issues, family situation, and individual preferences. Conducting a personalized check-in with each individual before, during, and after maternity or paternity leave helps employees to feel that they are valued and will be able to continue their careers in ways that fit their own aspirations; adopting a child holds its own distinctive set of challenges for which employees may need understanding and support.[25]

Policy & Process Overview

- Executive sponsorship and role modeling
- Participative leadership practices
- Task force participation
- Voluntary training
- Structured recruiting interviews
- Equal pay for equal work
- Coaching and mentoring
- Peer group support; prevention of "onliness"
- Performance assessment prior to viewing self-evaluations
- Fair distribution of office housework; development opportunities
- Informal signals: office space; recognition; pictures on the wall
- Work-life flexibility
- Dedicated inclusion and diversity function

Figure 12.6: Key Policies & Processes

Career Crossroads

Beyond formal and informal measures to increase organization-wide inclusion, intensive efforts targeted at specific career points are also very useful. Our experience with a variety of organizations in different industries suggests that there are three particularly crucial inflection points, or career crossroads:

- **Onboarding**: If the starting point for a career is compared with a marathon run, not everyone is toeing the same starting line on the first day of work. Some are suited up and ready to go, having practiced for years and ready to take off at a sprint, eyeing fellow racers who are equally well-prepared. Others are still getting dressed for the race, wondering what a marathon is, or are delayed on the subway trying to get to the starting point. If you are the first person in your family to have a professional career, are self-conscious about how you stand out as a racial minority, are working in a white-collar workplace environment for the first time, and/or are unsure that your prior education and training have prepared you adequately for this new job, you are likely to start out at a different pace.

  A structured onboarding program for all employees addresses this unequal starting point issue in several ways. It provides everyone with a shared basis of knowledge about the organization, a common introduction to organizational values and strategy, and insider tips that may otherwise filter through to some new employees but not to others. Such onboarding can also include teambuilding exercises that encourage a sense of camaraderie, self-awareness, shared purpose, and mutual inquiry rather than rivalry and unexamined bias.

- **First Promotion**: The KPIs favored by many organizations regularly provide findings that are both startling and disappointing. **In spite of extensive recruiting efforts targeting women and minorities, for example, such groups often fall behind the overall performance curve in their early career stages**, receiving low assessments on average and thus fewer chances for advancement. This marked difference in performance ratings usually begins with the first assessment and extends through initial promotion decisions at the two- to five-year mark (depending on the industry). Employees who see themselves already falling behind their peers at this stage are less likely to be fully engaged at work or to sign up for the next stage of training or testing.

They are also more likely to leave, and the organization's talent pipeline suddenly begins to sprout leaks.

Rather than blaming recruiters for not finding the right talent and then repeating this pattern with another crop of new hires, it is better to apply more systemic solutions to the causal factors that appear most salient. Targeted internship programs prior to full-time employment, for instance, are commonly linked with better performance results for minority hires than for those without an internship experience—this makes sense because employees who have been interns take on full-time jobs with a good understanding of the corporate culture and a fairly clear sense of performance expectations.

A related area of research focuses on the positive effect of having more than one woman or minority member on a team, rather than just one such individual who generally experiences greater isolation and more biased interactions. Whether on executive teams or within an everyday workplace context, the implication is that it is better to assign two or more employees in one location rather than to spread women or minorities so thin that they all experience the negative effects of "onliness."[26] Peer relationships created through group coaching are another way to build a network among individuals who might otherwise feel isolated.

> **Whether on executive teams or within an everyday workplace context, the implication is that it is better to assign two or more employees in one location rather than to spread women or minorities so thin that they all experience the negative effects of "onliness."[26]**

The first-line manager or supervisor also plays a critical role. It is most effective to apply a three-legged stool of support for employees facing a crucial career inflection point that is linked with frequent, unwanted turnover. Two of the three legs are coaching that promotes self-reflection and resilience, plus a mentor/sponsor who offers insider insights, encouragement, and opportunities to take on a more responsible role when this is warranted. The third (and most often neglected) leg of the stool is the direct manager or supervisor. Research has long identified the relationship with one's immediate manager as being the single most important factor linked with overall employee turnover.[27] First-line managers are frequently new to formal leadership roles, having previously been individual contributors themselves, and are preoccupied with learning to oversee a broad set of technical responsibilities in addition to managing people.

Under pressure to perform, managers may revert to the set of "go-to" people with whom they are most familiar, shying away from proactively managing the diversity on their teams. This tendency can be unintentionally reinforced by a human resource department that provides a scary list of "don'ts" regarding protected classes of employees, sexual harassment, and/or discriminatory acts that could embarrass the organization and instantly derail a manager's career. Providing managers or supervisors with information and skill-building opportunities to leverage the diversity on their teams can get these junior leaders pointed in a more inclusive direction while tapping their energy and ambition. They may also need to know that someone is paying attention in order to keep the task of countering natural sources of bias front of mind. The presence of a dedicated inclusion and diversity function keeping track of targeted KPIs is correlated with higher promotion rates for women and minorities.[28]

Most first-line managers welcome a list of "dos" that they can safely engage in while avoiding the "don'ts," yet many have to generate this list on their own, if ever, through lengthy trial and error. Here is a set of recommendations for supervisors to begin to comprehend and tap the full capabilities of their team members. The list of acceptable areas of conversation varies considerably according to cultural and legal norms; we have kept it focused on professional topics.

Dos for First-Line Managers or Supervisors

Relationship-Building: Make an effort to get to know each team member. Ask about:

- Professional interests: *Please tell me about what you're most interested in doing or learning.*

- Prior experience: *What kind of prior work experience do you have that would help me to understand your background?*

- Strengths and areas for improvement: *What would you identify as your own greatest strengths and/or developmental areas?*

- Current challenges or concerns: *Do you see any particular challenges or have any concerns about your current tasks?*

- Motivation: *What kind of work do you find most exciting? What do you like most about your current role, and what do you want to do more or less of if we can arrange it?*

- Career plans, aspirations: *Do you have any thoughts about the next steps in your career? Is there anything you would like to learn about?*

- Requests for support: *How can I best support you? What can I do to be a better manager?*

- Open-ended: *What else would you like me to know about you? Is there anything else you would like to discuss?*

  Note: Questions about personal subjects—hobbies, health, family, etc.— are expected in some cultures, especially in informal settings, and are regarded as prying or even illegal in others.

Opportunities: Provide all team members with equal opportunities to engage in activities and take on tasks that fit their capabilities, including meeting participation, technical training, and project assignments.

Informal Contacts: Include all team members in informal conversations and events—water-cooler conversations, company updates, social occasions, andso on.

Feedback: Ensure that all team members receive performance feedback on a timely, even-handed basis. Make comments that are constructive, objective, concrete, and conducive to action.

Assessment: Focus assessment on job performance relative to key objectives; be careful to check for possible forms of bias when giving ratings or stating observations.

Figure 12.7: Dos for First-Line Managers or Supervisors

- **Transition to Executive**: The challenges that occur at the upper end of the talent pipeline come in a variety of forms, and many of these are cultural. Leaders who have performed well within the confines of a particular function, business unit, or country operation may one day find themselves being assessed for or placed in executive roles with a different, less familiar set of norms. The two examples that follow illustrate how the assessment process itself may require cultural calibration and show sample adjustments that individuals need to make.

WHAT'S WRONG WITH THE BRAZILIANS?

The director of leadership development for a major organization was surprised by the failure rate of high-potential Brazilian candidates going through the firm's "assessment center" evaluation process for the next level of leadership. The candidates from Brazil, even those with otherwise stellar credentials, were only passing the battery of assessment center tests at a 20% rate, far lower than the 50% rate of their North American peers. Upon further investigation, it turned out that Brazilian candidates were receiving very low scores for critical competencies such as "clear and direct communication" and "results orientation."

Still mystified by these outcomes, the head of leadership development decided to sit in on some of the assessments. She realized that the core problem was primarily cultural: "When the candidates from Brazil were asked a question, they would usually respond first with a story, and only later with an answer. It turned out that they felt this was a better way to get their point across that was also quite common in their country, but it earned them consistently low grades from our North American assessors. When we coached them to flip their communication around and start with the answer before telling the story, the assessment results changed in a hurry. Our candidates soon even started to coach North Americans coming to Brazil on how to alter their own communication styles to become more effective."

EXECUTIVE PRESENCE

Henry, an Asian manager in a Western company voiced his despair over the feedback he had received. "They're telling me I don't have executive presence. What does this mean? I've worked here for twenty years and have always received great performance reviews. Now I've finally worked my way up almost to the top and they're telling me that something is missing. Is it the clothes that I'm wearing?" he asked, pointing to his shirt and shoes that conveyed a flawless business-casual appearance suited to his industry. "Or is it the fact that I'm originally from Hong Kong and don't speak perfect English?"

Upon further examination, it turned out that a key point was the way Henry was communicating information. "Henry is too much in the weeds," was a common remark from the top executive team members. "He needs to be able to step back and give us the picture at the 30,000-foot level and then dive into the details if we need that level of analysis." What Henry had thought was a reasonable and important level of detail for others on the team turned out to be too much information.

> *They wanted to hear his big picture summary and then to be able to drill down as needed. Once Henry began to adjust his style and provide the right doses of information at the right times, switching nimbly between his strategic summary and a "deeper dive" set of numbers when requested, he was soon welcomed to the executive team. Several team members commented that they had misjudged his capabilities.*

In both of these cases, individuals who were at the cusp of taking on executive roles found ways to increase their self-awareness and to adjust their actions through frame-shifting or style-switching. These are key global leadership capabilities that help leaders deal with culturally conditioned approaches to areas such as communication or hierarchy, which are frequent sources of misunderstanding. Learning to serve as a "cultural guide" is also important, as this enables leaders to explain why things are done a particular way in a different cultural setting, thereby assisting others with frame-shifting as well.[29]

But new executive team members should not be the only ones who are adapting. Senior- level teams get the best results when all of their members have gone through diversifying experiences of their own—serving in various functions, businesses, and geographies, for example—and are prepared to adjust to each other. It is naturally important to have certain core operating procedures, but these should not be allowed to preclude consideration of different perspectives or prospects for doing business. Instead of expecting new members to simply assimilate themselves to a dominant monocultural style, leadership team members with an agile mindset will deliberately engage them as a source of possible insights into cultural norms, best practices, or untapped markets.

CONCLUSION

Individual initiative is the most powerful driver of inclusion. There is no substitute for leaders at all levels who are willing to take up the cause of inclusion because they believe in its value, both for the business and for everyone involved. Such initiative can also be inspired and its effects multiplied by the five organizational levers described above; the combination of individual initiative with supportive systems produces a productive whirl of creativity and enthusiasm. People shape the culture in which they live, and are in turn shaped by it.

Of course, there may be a degree of diversity or inclusiveness that is overwhelming to an organization, especially one that is unprepared. Diverse perspectives that are irreconcilable or poorly managed inhibit timely decision-making and fully aligned implementation; inclusion that is overly focused on satisfying every constituency and checking every box becomes detached from the business case. And providing equal access to challenging opportunities does not mean staffing projects with employees who are unqualified. There is no single, easy switch for turning on inclusion, or for adjusting the setting upward. Selecting which organizational levers to pull and when depends on the environment and the needs of the business.

Yet inclusive leadership ultimately molds the capacity of an organization to renew itself.[30] No business model or pattern of success lasts forever, and many once-mighty companies, not to mention empires, have been relegated to the dustbin of history or are now visibly in decline. Organizations need to be able to change and grow, to reinvent themselves in the face of shifting circumstances. The term sustainability has become overused, but inclusive leaders who embrace new ideas, colleagues, and ways of serving customers can make their institutions uniquely sustainable. Inclusion is the price of vitality, an essential ingredient for building open, self-renewing systems.

ENDNOTES

1. Introduction

[1] "Herodotus' Comment on Cambyses' Madness," *Livius.org*, October 26, 2018, https://www. livius. org/sources/content/herodotus/herodotus-comment-on-cambyses-madness/

[2] John P. Kotter and James L. Heskett, *Corporate Culture and Performance* (Free Press, 2011).

[3] The concept of "growth mindset" was coined by Carol Dweck of Stanford University based on her work with disadvantaged students. Although her studies have been criticized in academic circles as difficult to replicate, the growth mindset idea has subsequently been adopted by major corporations and consultancies. Dweck has published numerous works on this topic, including the book, *Mindset: How you can fulfill your potential*. Constable & Robinson Limited, 2012. For her TED Talk summary, "The Power of Believing That You Can Improve," see: https://www.ted.com/talks/carol_dweck_the_ power_of_believing_that_you_can_improve

An irony of the growth mindset approach is that it overlaps with the process orientation for which Japanese companies became famous in the 1980s, often under the rubric of "continuous improvement". At that time, many U.S. executives and academics were critical of this movement as insufficiently results-oriented, yet now it is embraced as a new path to achieving better results.

2. Inclusion Trends

[1] Behavioral therapies are based on the premise that changing one's actions can have lasting effects. The early, often-criticized behavior modification techniques of B.F. Skinner, which linked specific behaviors with positive or negative reinforcement, have since been supplanted with a variety of therapeutic methods that are now standard approaches for treating mental health disorders, marital problems, and substance abuse.

[2] See, for example, Lisa Kepinski and Tinna C. Nielsen, "*Inclusion Nudges Guidebook*" (CreateSpace Independent Publishing Platform; 2nd edition, 2016).

[3] "Emerging markets" is a problematic term, as the countries that fall under this rubric are at least as distinct from one another as they are similar. See, for example, "Why "emerging markets" is an outdated definition," *Financial Times*, August 4, 2015, https://www.weforum.org/agenda/2015/08/ why-emerging-markets-is-an-outdated-definition/

Another suggestion has been to use the term "high-growth" markets, but not all so-called emerging markets are growing rapidly, if at all. In general, it seems most accurate to refer to the characteristics of specific countries, so we will use the "emerging markets" label sparingly throughout this book.

[4] "The International Migration Report 2017," *United Nations Department of Economic and Social Affairs*, December 18, 2017, https://www.un.org/development/desa/publications/international-migration-report-2017.html. "The number of migrants as a fraction of the population residing in high-income countries rose from 9.6% in 2000 to 14% in 2017".

[5] Clifford Geertz, cited in, "Clifford Geertz: Work and Legacy," *Institute for Advanced Study*, https://www.ias.edu/clifford-geertz-work-and-legacy

[6] There were more than 70,000 workplace discrimination charges filed in the U.S. in 2019 alone, and a significant percentage of these result in costly penalties or settlements. "EEOC Releases Fiscal Year 2019 Enforcement and Litigation Data," *U.S. Equal Employment Opportunity Commission*, January 21, 2020, https://www.eeoc.gov/newsroom/eeoc-releases-fiscal-year-2019-enforcement-and-litigation-data

[7] Romain Dillet, "French data protection watchdog fines Google $57 million under the GDPR," *TechCrunch*, February 2019, https://techcrunch.com/2019/01/21/french-data-protection-watchdog-fines-google-57-million-under-the-gdpr/

[8] Robin J. Ely and David A. Thomas, "Getting Serious About Diversity: Enough Already with the Business Case," *Harvard Business Review*, November-December 2020, https://hbr.org/2020/11/getting-serious-about-diversity-enough-already-with-the-business-case

[9] Richard Dobbs, et al, "Urban world: The shifting global business landscape," *McKinsey Global Institute*, October 2013, https://www.mckinsey.com/featured-insights/urbanization/urban-world-the-shifting-global-business-landscape

[10] Rocío Lorenzo, Nicole Voigt, Miki Tsusaka, Matt Krentz, and Katie Abouzahr, "How Diverse Leadership Teams Boost Innovation," *Boston Consulting Group*, January 2018, https://www.bcg.com/publications/2018/how-diverse-leadership-teams-boost-innovation

[11] Sylvia Ann Hewlett, Melinda Marshall, and Laura Sherbin, "How Diversity Can Drive Innovation," *Harvard Business Review*, December 2013. The authors note the importance of both inherent diversity, defined as the characteristics people are born with (e.g. gender, ethnicity, sexual orientation), and acquired diversity, or traits gained through experience (e.g. working in another country, selling products to people of a different gender).

[12] Juliet Bourke, "The Diversity and Inclusion Revolution: Eight Powerful Truths," *Deloitte*, January 22, 2018, https://www2.deloitte.com/us/en/insights/deloitte-review/issue-22/diversity-and-inclusion-at-work-eight-powerful-truths.html

[13] "High-Impact and Inclusion: Diversity Models and Findings," *Bersin by Deloitte*, 2017; Juliet Bourke, "Which Two Heads are Better Than One? How Diverse Teams Create Breakthrough Ideas and Make Smarter Decisions," *Australian Institute of Company Directors*, 2016.

[14] Vivian Hunt, Sara Prince, Sundiatu Dixon-Fyle and Lareina Yee, "Delivering Through Diversity," *McKinsey & Company*, January 2018.

[15] *Glassdoor*, 2014.

[16] "Creating Competitive Advantage Through Workforce Diversity," *Corporate Leadership Council*, 2012.

[17] "SheForShield: Insure Women to better protect all," *IFC and AXA*, September 2015.

[18] "When the only legitimate conversation about diversity is one that links it to economic gains, we tend to discount the problem of inequality... Why should anyone need an economic rationale for affirming the agency and dignity of any group of human beings?". Robin J. Ely and David A. Thomas, "Getting Serious About Diversity: Enough Already with the Business Case," *Harvard Business Review*, November-December 2020, https://hbr.org/2020/11/getting-serious-about-diversity-enough-already-with-the-business-case

3. Inclusive Leadership: Dealing with Difference

[1] See, for example, Robin DiAngelo, *White Fragility: Why it's so hard for White People to Talk about Racism*, Chapter 1 (Beacon Press, 2018). DiAngelo uses the term "unearned advantages," and in her view "racial socialization" benefits anyone who is white, regardless of their other life circumstances. For a critique of DiAngelo's work see John McWhorter, "The Dehumanizing Condescension of 'White Fragility,'" *The Atlantic*, July 15, 2020, https://www.theatlantic.com/ideas/archive/2020/07/dehumanizing-condescension-white-fragility/614146/

[2] "The Global Leader," *Corporate Leadership Council (CLC) Human Resources*, Corporate Executive Board, Executive Briefing, February 2012.

[3] William Maddux is interviewed in the video, "How to Stimulate Creativity? Go Live Abroad," *INSEAD*, 2009, https://www.youtube.com/watch?v=aKcu_ztYCtk&t=358s

[4] Nancy J. Adler, *International Dimensions of Organizational Behavior*, 4th Edition (South-Western College, 2002), 263.

[5] Exodus 2:22 describes the birth of Gershom to Zipporah and Moses: "And she bore him a son, and he called his name Gershom: for he said, I have been a stranger in a strange land." (*The Bible*, American King James Version)

[6] Warren Bennis and Robert J. Thomas, "Crucibles of Leadership," *Harvard Business Review*, September 2002.

[7] From the *Fukanzazengi*, or meditation instructions, of Eihei Dogen, a 13th century Japanese Soto Zen master who spent five years studying in China, later returning to Japan.

[8] We prefer the term "cultural competence" over similar terms such as "cultural intelligence" because it strongly suggests not only awareness but also effective action.

[9] Ernest Gundling, Terry Hogan, and Karen Cvitkovich, *What is Global Leadership? 10 Key Behaviors that Define Successful Global Leaders* (Nicholas Brealey, 2011), 54–57.

[10] Ernest Gundling, Christie Caldwell, and Karen Cvitkovich, *Leading Across New Borders: How to Succeed as the Center Shifts* (Wiley & Sons, 2015), 85.

[11] Big Bill Broonzy (1903-1958), "Black, Brown, and White," *YouTube*, https://www.youtube.com/watch?v=k0c1c0ZsTLA

[12] Baldwin, James, *The Price of the Ticket: Collected Non-Fiction*, 1948-1985 (St. Martin's Press, 1985).

4. Inclusive Behavior: Learning About Bias

[1] Daniel Kahneman, *Thinking Fast and Slow* (Farrar, Straus and Giroux, 2013).

[2] Edward T. Hall, *The Silent Language* (Fawcett Publications, Inc., 1959), 39.

[3] See, for example, Daniel Goleman, *Emotional Intelligence: Why it Can Matter More than IQ* (Bantam Books, 1995); and "What Makes a Leader?," *Harvard Business Review*, 1998.

5. Inclusive Behaviors: Building Key Skills & Working Across Boundaries

[1] Adapted from Lee Gardenswartz and Anita Rowe, *Diverse Teams at Work: Capitalizing on the Power of Diversity* (Society for Human Resource Management, 2003). Used with permission.

[2] Many ancient societies distinguished, for instance, between warriors and farmers, and names like the English words "Smith" or "Miller" reflect craft-based identities such as blacksmithing or milling grain.

[3] Adapted from Ernest Gundling, Christie Caldwell, and Karen Cvitkovich, *Leading Across New Borders: How to Succeed as the Center Shifts* (Wiley & Sons, 2015), 92.

[4] See: https://www.globesmart.com/

[5] Ernest Gundling and Anita Zanchettin, *Global Diversity: Winning Customers and Engaging Employees Within World Markets* (Nicholas Brealey, 2008).

6. Inclusive Behaviors: Becoming a Champion & Getting Results

[1] See, for example, Karen Catlin, *Better Allies: Everyday Actions to Create Inclusive Engaging Workplaces* (Karen Catlin Consulting, 2019).

[2] Adapted from Ernest Gundling, Christie Caldwell, and Karen Cvitkovich, *Leading Across New Borders: How to Succeed as the Center Shifts* (Wiley & Sons, 2015), 132.

[3] Edward de Bono, *Six Thinking Hats: An Essential Approach to Business Management* (Little Brown and Company, 1985).

[4] See Ernest Gundling, *Working GlobeSmart* (Davies-Black, 2003), 223 - 225. Nancy Adler refers to these three steps of team interaction as scope, representation, and process.

[5] Amie Tsang, "Nivea Pulls 'White is Purity' Ad After Online Uproar," *The New York Times*, April 4, 2017, https://www.nytimes.com/2017/04/04/business/media/nivea-ad-online-uproar-racism.html

Amy Wang, "Nivea's 'White is Purity' ad campaign didn't end well," *The Washington Post*, April 5, 2017, https://www.washingtonpost.com/news/business/wp/2017/04/05/niveas-white-is-purity-ad-campaign-didnt-end-well/

Kirstie McCrum, "Tesco in Ramadan blunder after offering bacon Pringles to Muslims," *Mirror*, January 24, 2015, https://www.mirror.co.uk/news/uk-news/tesco-ramadan-blunder-after-offering-5939413

"Zara's 'Holocaust uniform' and other clothing errors," *BBC News*, August 27, 2014, https://www.bbc.com/news/blogs-magazine-monitor-28944516

"Racist Chinese Laundry Detergent Ad," *YouTube*, May 26, 2016, https://www.youtube.com/watch?v=X27dvuBSyXE

[6] Tom Kelley, *The Ten Faces of Innovation* (Doubleday, 2005).

[7] Ernest Gundling, Terry Hogan, and Karen Cvitkovich, *What is Global Leadership? 10 Key Behaviors that Define Successful Global Leaders* (Nicholas Brealey, 2011), 92.

[8] Ibid, 92–94.

7. Global Teams

[1] Nancy J. Adler, *International Dimensions of Organizational Behavior*, 4th Edition (South-Western College, 2002), 145-146.

[2] Jeffrey Young, "Most Professors Think They're Above-Average Teachers. And That's a Problem." *EdSurge*, May 24, 2018, https://www.edsurge.com/news/2018-05-24-most-professors-think-they-re-above-average-teachers-and-that-s-a-problem

[3] Global Team Assessment - https://www.globesmart.com/products/global-team-assessment/

[4] See Appendix A, Team Launch: Foundations, in *Leading Across New Borders*. Ernest Gundling, Christie Caldwell, and Karen Cvitkovich (Wiley & Sons, 2015), 187–189.

[5] Amy Edmondson, "Psychological Safety and Learning Behavior in Work Teams," *Administrative Science Quarterly*, 44(2), June 1, 1999.

[6] Abeer Dubey and Julia Rozovsky, People Analytics, Google, *YouTube*, Jun 23, 2016, https://www.youtube.com/watch?v=KZlSq_Hf08M&list=PLORfsVTCrTYL47i_E2CrroChUPJ2J2K-8&index=3

[7] Reference: Novid Parsi, *"5 Leaders Who Are Disrupting Diversity,"* SHRM, January 16, 2017.

[8] Factors related to how trust is perceived in a global team context are: qualifications, relationships, performance, expectations, and ethics. See Appendix A, Team Launch: Foundations, in *Leading Across New Borders*. Ernest Gundling, Christie Caldwell, and Karen Cvitkovich, (Wiley & Sons, 2015), 187–189.

[9] In the movie, "Crazy Rich Asians," which is based in Singapore, a Singaporean friend of the female protagonist must be asked three times to attend a party for the rich and famous before saying yes. She turns down the first two requests in proper ritual style so as to appear modest, and also to ascertain that the request was a real invitation rather than just a polite gesture, before immediately agreeing to the third request. It turns out she was actually so eager to attend that she already had the party attire in the trunk of her car! Colleagues steeped in an interdependent, hierarchical, indirect cultural context may need to be asked to contribute more than once because they want to blend in, and they prefer to confirm that such a request was made out of a genuine desire for input.

[10] Stanford Technology Ventures Program, "Astro Teller: Predict Failures before Beginning," *Youtube*, Apr 27, 2016, https://www.youtube.com/watch?v=mlVVlr0B0FA

[11] Ernest Gundling, Terry Hogan, and Karen Cvitkovich, *What is Global Leadership? 10 Key Behaviors that Define Successful Global Leaders* (Nicholas Brealey, 2011), Chapters 3–4.

[12] Unconscious bias is similar in some respects to the advanced "Terminator" model that reconstitutes itself all too quickly even after being cleaved or shattered.

8. Regional Inclusion Challenges

[1] Jonathan Woetzel, Anu Madgavkar, et al., "The power of parity: Advancing women's equality in Asia Pacific," *McKinsey & Company*, April 2018, https://www.mckinsey.com/featured-insights/gender-equality/the-power-of-parity-advancing-womens-equality-in-asia-pacific

[2] Dominic Abrams, et al., "Ageism in Europe and the UK," *European Research Group on Attitudes to Age (EURAGE)*, 2011, https://core.ac.uk/download/pdf/10635079.pdf

[3] There is considerable dispute about definitions of tribalism, its current influence in Africa, and the role of colonial powers in shaping it. See, for example, Christine Mungai, "Pundits who decry 'tribalism' know nothing about real tribes," *The Washington Post*, January 30, 2019, https://www.washingtonpost.com/outlook/pundits-who-decry-tribalism-know-nothing-about-real-tribes/2019/01/29/8d14eb44-232f-11e9-90cd-dedb0c92dc17_story.html

Mungai notes that traditional tribes shared culturally sanctioned forms of intergroup conflict resolution, and that women often married outside of their original ethnic groups. For a different point of view, see for example, Roger Cohen, "Tribalism Here, and There," *The New York Times*, March 10, 2008, https://www.nytimes.com/2008/03/10/opinion/10webcohen.html

[4] See, for example, "Ghana: Traders Association Protest Alleged Closure of 400 Nigerian-Owned Shops in Ghana," *Premium Times*, September 24, 2018, https://allafrica.com/stories/201809250016.html

[5] According to United Nations estimates, the population of Nigeria will exceed that of the U.S. by around mid-century.

[6] See, for example, "Probe rape claim against GBA boss—FIDA," *Ghana Web*, January 21, 2019, https://www.ghanaweb.com/GhanaHomePage/NewsArchive/Probe-rape-claim-againt-GBA-boss-FIDA-716832

[7] Salih Booker and Ari Rickman, "The Future is Africa, and the United States is Not Prepared," *The Washington Post*, June 9, 2018, https://www.washingtonpost.com/news/democracy-post/wp/2018/06/09/the-future-is-african-and-the-united-states-is-not-prepared/

[8] Randolph E. Schmid, "Africans have world's greatest genetic variation," *NBC News*, April 30, 2009, https://www.nbcnews.com/id/wbna30502963

Michael C. Campbell and Sarah A. Tishkoff, "African Genetic Diversity: Implications for Human Demographic History, Modern Human Origins, and Complex Disease Mapping," *U.S. National Library of Medicine, National Institutes of Health*, October 13, 2010, https://www.ncbi.nlm.nih.gov/pmc/articles/PMC2953791/

[9] *CIA World Factbook*, 2017.

[10] Richard Fuchs, "Germany is Not Shrinking," *Deutsche Welle*, February 4, 2017, https://www.dw.com/en/germany-is-not-shrinking/a-37415327

[11] "German population of migrant background rises to 21 million," *Deutsche Welle*, July 28, 2020, https://www.dw.com/en/german-population-of-migrant-background-rises-to-21-million/a-54356773

[12] Charley-Kai John, "Number of migrants in Germany hits record high," *Reuters World News*, April 12, 2018, https://www.reuters.com/article/instant-article/idAFKBN1HJ2BQ

[13] Gregor Aisch, et al., "Some Colleges Have More Students From the Top 1 Percent Than the Bottom 60. Find Yours," *The New York Times*, January 18, 2017, https://www.nytimes.com/interactive/2017/01/18/upshot/some-colleges-have-more-students-from-the-top-1-percent-than-the-bottom-60.html

[14] Kimberlé Crenshaw, "Why Intersectionality Can't Wait," *The Washington Post*, September 24, 2015, https://www.washingtonpost.com/news/in-theory/wp/2015/09/24/why-intersectionality-cant-wait/

"Intersectionality, then, was my attempt to make feminism, anti-racist activism, and anti-discrimination law do what I thought they should—highlight the multiple avenues through which racial and gender oppression were experienced so that the problems would be easier to discuss and understand."

Kimberlé Crenshaw, "Mapping the Margins: Intersectionality, Identity Politics, and Violence Against Women of Color," *Stanford Law Review*, Vol. 43, No. 6 (Jul., 1991), 1241–1299.

"Where systems of race, gender and class domination converge, as they do in the experiences of battered women of color, intervention strategies based solely on the experiences of women who do not share the same class or race backgrounds will be of limited help to women who because of race and class face different obstacles."

[15] For a summary of critiques of ways in which intersectionality has been applied, see Jane Coaston, "The intersectionality wars," *Vox*, May 28, 2019, https://www.vox.com/the-highlight/2019/5/20/18542843/intersectionality-conservatism-law-race-gender-discrimination

[16] David C. Pollock, Ruth E. Van Reken and Michael V. Pollock, *Third Culture Kids: Growing Up Among Worlds*, Third Edition (Nicholas Brealey, 2010).

[17] Based on experiences recorded by Julia Sloan.

9. Race and Ethnicity: A Global Perspective

[1] Elaine Godfrey, "The Enormous Scale of this Movement," *The Atlantic Monthly*, June 2020, https://www.theatlantic.com/politics/archive/2020/06/protest-dc-george-floyd-police-reform/612748/

[2] See, for example, Ta-Nehisi Coates, "What We Mean When We Say 'Race Is a Social Construct,'" *The Atlantic*, May 16, 2013, https://www.theatlantic.com/national/archive/2013/05/what-we-mean-when-we-say-race-is-a-social-construct/275872/

"Our notion of what constitutes 'white' and what constitutes 'black' is a product of social context."

[3] Valerie Wilson, "People of Color Will be a Majority of the American Working Class in 2032," *EPI.org*, June 9, 2016, https://www.epi.org/publication/the-changing-demographics-of-americas-working-class/

[4] Jonathan Vespa, David M. Armstrong and Lauren Medina, "Demographic Turning Points for the United States: Population Projections for 2020 to 2060," *U.S. Census Bureau*, February 2020, https://www.census.gov/library/publications/2020/demo/p25-1144.html

[5] William H. Frey, "The Millennial Generation: A Demographic Bridge to America's Diverse Future," *Brookings Institution*, January, 2018, https://www.brookings.edu/research/millennials/

[6] Marc Fleurbaey, "Survey: Social Justice Divides Americans," *The Conversation*, July 26 2018, https://theconversation.com/survey-social-justice-divides-americans-100398

Jonah Goldberg, "The Problem With 'Social Justice'," *Newsday*, February 9, 2019, https://www.newsday.com/opinion/commentary/social-justice-rothman-goldberg-1.27014335

[7] See, for example, "Asia reacts to Johnson & Johnson skin-whitening creams' withdrawal: 'pure racism … our rights are being infringed," *Reuters*, June 22, 2020, https://www.scmp.com/lifestyle/fashion-beauty/article/3090015/asia-reacts-skin-whitening-creams-withdrawal-pure-racism

[8] See, for example, Richard Allen Greene, "Britain's Big Race Divide," *CNN.com*, June 22, 2020, https://edition.cnn.com/interactive/2020/06/europe/britain-racism-cnn-poll-gbr-intl/

Ashley-John Baptiste, "Racism in the UK: 'I Feel Like an Alien'," *BBC News*, June 12, 2020, https://www.bbc.com/news/av/uk-53002818

Guy Faulconbridge, "UKIP in Chaos Over Racist Messages," *Reuters*, January 22, 2018, https://www.reuters.com/article/uk-britain-politics-ukip-idUKKBN1FB0SN

Laura Smith-Spark, Nima Elbagir and Barbara Arvanitidis, "The Greatest Trick Racism Ever Pulled Was Convincing England it Doesn't Exist: How Britain Failed to Deal With Systemic Racism," *CNN.com*, June 22, 2020, https://edition.cnn.com/2020/06/22/europe/black-britain-systemic-racism-cnn-poll-gbr-intl/index.html

[9] "'We are here because you were there': Immigrants' Responses to the Rise of Anti-Immigrant Discourses in Britain," *University of Leicester*, October 30, 2014, https://www2.le.ac.uk/departments/sociology/research/conferences-and-workshops/2018201cwe-are-here-because-you-were-there201d-immigrants2019-responses-to-the-rise-of-anti-immigrant-discourses-in-britain

[10] "Roche," *Best Companies*, July 2020, https://www.b.co.uk/company-profile/?roche-104350

Adria Harris, "Making the mix work: is your business diverse and inclusive?," *The Telegraph*, January 13, 2020, https://www.telegraph.co.uk/business/business-reporter/workplace-diversity/

[11] Terrence McCoy, "They Lost the Civil War and Fled to Brazil. Their Descendants Refuse to Take Down the Confederate Flag," *The Washington Post*, July 2020, https://www.washingtonpost.com/world/the_americas/brazil-confederate-flag-civil-war-americana-santa-barbara/2020/07/11/1e8a7c84-bec4-11ea-b4f6-cb39cd8940fb_story.html

[12] Grant Suneson and Samuel Stebbins, "These 15 Countries Have the Widest Gaps Between Rich and Poor," *USA Today*, May 28, 2019, https://www.usatoday.com/story/money/2019/05/28/countries-with-the-widest-gaps-between-rich-and-poor/39510157/

[13] "A Silver Lining in Brazil's Struggling Education System," *The Wilson Center*, June 25, 2019, https://www.wilsoncenter.org/blog-post/silver-lining-brazils-struggling-education-system

[14] Cleuci De Oliveira, "Brazil's New Problem With Blackness," *Foreign Policy*, April 5, 2017, https://foreignpolicy.com/2017/04/05/brazils-new-problem-with-blackness-affirmative-action/

[15] Edward Telles, "Racial Discrimination and Miscegenation: The Experience in Brazil," *UN.org*, July 2020, https://www.un.org/en/chronicle/article/racial-discrimination-and-miscegenation-experience-brazil

[16] Vinícius Andrade, "MercadoLibre to Invest Record $1.8 Billion in Brazil," *Bloomberg*, March 2, 2021, https://www.bloomberg.com/news/articles/2021-03-01/mercadolibre-to-invest-1-8-billion-in-brazil-as-volume-surges

William Barnett, Gary Mekikian and Christy Johnson, "The Rise of Mercado Libre," *Stanford Graduate School of Business*, January 8, 2020, https://www.gsb.stanford.edu/faculty-research/case-studies/rise-mercado-libre

[17] "The Best Thing about Nigeria is…," *BBC News*, March 27, 2015, https://www.bbc.com/news/world-africa-32036328

[18] "Ethnicity in Nigeria," *PBS News Hour*, April 5, 2007, https://www.pbs.org/newshour/arts/africa-jan-june07-ethnic_04-05

[19] "Nigeria turns 60: Can Africa's most populous nation remain united?," *BBC News*, October 1, 2020, https://www.bbc.com/news/world-africa-54357810

[20] Ruth Olurounbi, "Nigerians hungrier now, thanks to Buhari's policy on food imports," *The Africa Report*, October 18, 2020, "Nigerians spend nearly 60% of their earnings on food purchases, the highest in the world", https://www.theafricareport.com/46445/nigerians-hungrier-now-thanks-to-buharis-policy-on-food-imports/

See also, Ruth Olurounbi, "Nigeria: If you thought 2020 was bad, brace yourself for 2021," *The Africa Report*, November 6, 2020, https://www.theafricareport.com/48706/nigeria-if-you- thought-2020-was-bad-brace-yourself-for-2021/

[21] "Nigeria releases new report on poverty and inequality in country," *The World Bank*, May 28, 2020, https://www.worldbank.org/en/programs/lsms/brief/nigeria-releases-new-report-on-poverty-and-inequality-in-country

"Nigeria Economic Alert," *PricewaterhouseCoopers*, September 2020, https://www.pwc.com/ng/en/assets/pdf/economic-alert-september-2020.pdf

[22] Moses Ochonu, "The Roots of Nigeria's Religious and Ethnic Conflict, *Public Radio International, The World*, March 10, 2014, https://www.pri.org/stories/2014-03-10/roots-nigerias-religious-and-ethnic-conflict

[23] "Nigeria turns 60: Can Africa's most populous nation remain united?", *BBC News*, October 1, 2020, https://www.bbc.com/news/world-africa-54357810

[24] John P. McKay et al., *A History of World Societies, Volume 2: Since 1450*, (Bedford/St. Martin's, 2011), 755.

Mohammed Bashir Salau, *Plantation Slavery in the Sokoto Caliphate: A Historical and Comparative Study* (University of Rochester Press, 2018).

Sources indicate that Sokoto Caliphate slavery conditions may have been different than forms of slavery elsewhere, with accumulation of property and greater upward mobility possible for some enslaved individuals.

[25] Adaobi Tricia Nwaubani, "The Descendants of Slaves in Nigeria Fight for Equality," *The New Yorker*, July 11, 2019, https://www.newyorker.com/news/dispatch/the-descendants-of-slaves-in-nigeria-fight-for-equality

[26] "Global Slavery Index," *The Minderoo Foundation*, 2018, https://www.globalslaveryindex.org/2018/data/country-data/nigeria/

[27] "Nigeria: Human Trafficking Factsheet," *Pathfinders Justice Initiative*, September 10, 2020, https://pathfindersji.org/nigeria-human-trafficking-factsheet/#:~:text=Per%20the%20

[28] Suyin Haynes, "'We Are Able to Get Things Done.' Women Are at the Forefront of Nigeria's Police Brutality Protests," *Time*, October 21, 2020, https://time.com/5902123/nigeria-women-endsars-protest-movement/

[29] Nduka Orjinmo, "End Sars protests: The young Nigerians who forced the president to back down," *BBC News*, October 13, 2020, https://www.bbc.com/news/world-africa-54508781

[30] Sarah McGregor, ed., "Startups with an Unusual Fight," *Business Week*, November 8, 2020.

[31] Tochi Louis, "The Nigerian songs relevant to protesters during #EndSARS movement," *Pan-African Music*, November 6, 2020, https://pan-african-music.com/en/endsars-protesters-songs/

[32] Rick Gladstone and Megan Specia, "Nigeria's Police Brutality Crisis: What's Happening Now," *New York Times*, November 14, 2020, https://www.nytimes.com/article/sars-nigeria-police.html

"How the End SARS protests have changed Nigeria forever," *BBC News*, October 24, 2020, https://www.bbc.com/news/world-africa-54662986

[33] Benjamin Dada, "Top 10 companies to work for in Nigeria," *Dada Benjamin*, November 25, 2019, https://www.benjamindada.com/best-tech-companies-to-work-for-in-nigeria/

[34] "Google for Nigeria: making our products more helpful to more people," *Google in Africa*, Jul 24, 2019, https://www.blog.google/around-the-globe/google-africa/google-nigeria/

See also, "How Google is helping to solve local problems in Nigeria," *CNN Videos: Innovate Africa*, https://www.cnn.com/videos/tv/2019/11/19/innovate-africa-google-nigeria.cnn

10. Brain-Based Leadership: What's Missing?

[1] Jena McGregor, "The Business Brain in Close-up," *Bloomberg Businessweek*, July 23, 2007, https://www.bloomberg.com/news/articles/2007-07-22/the-business-brain-in-close-up

[2] Sharon Begley, "West Brain, East Brain: What a Difference Culture Makes," *Newsweek*, February 18, 2010. Begley is also the author of several books, including "The Emotional Life of Your Brain," and "Train Your Mind, Change Your Brain."

[3] Angela Gutchess, Robert Welsh, Aysecan Boduroğlu, and Denise Park, "Cultural differences in neural function associated with object processing," *Cognitive, Affective, & Behavioral Neuroscience*, 2006, 102–109.

[4] Study by Jonathan Freeman et al. originally published in *Neuroimage*, Vol. 47, No. 1, 2009; also summarized in an article by Beth Azar, "Your Brain on Culture," *American Psychological Association*, November 2010, Vol 41, No. 10, that cites numerous advances in the field of "cultural neuroscience." Nalini Ambady is quoted as stating, "We see that what the brain finds rewarding reflects the values of the dominant culture. People can see the same stimulus but have completely different neural responses." See also, for example, Heejung Kim and Joni Sasaki, "Cultural Neuroscience: Biology of the Mind in Cultural Contexts," *Annual Review of Psychology*, Vol.65:487-514, January 2014.

[5] "The first stage of ethnocentric thought is denial, in which people who are isolated from other cultures consciously ignore those other cultures' values. The final stage of ethnocentric orientations is minimization. People in the minimization stage focus only on personal similarities (e.g., physical, biological, philosophical), but do not legitimize other societies' broad cultural frameworks." Jingzhu Zhang, "Test Review: The Intercultural Development Inventory Manual," *Journal of Psychoeducational Assessment, Sage Publications*, February 20, 2014, http://journals. sagepub.com/doi/abs/10.1177/0734282913505075?journalCode=jpaa

[6] The Intercultural Development Continuum was originally developed by Mitchell Hammer and Milton Bennett. It is now owned by IDI, LLC, which is a division of Hammer Holdings, Inc. See, https://idiinventory.com/ publications/the-intercultural-development-continuum-idc.

11. Inclusive Leadership Development

[1] In contrast, a highly anticipated crisis was Y2K, which turned out to be a relatively minor event in part because companies planned ahead to blunt its impact (millennials may have to look this up).

[2] Pagan Kennedy, "William Gibson's Future is Now," *The New York Times*, January 13, 2012, https://www.nytimes.com/2012/01/15/books/review/distrust-that-particular-flavor-by-william-gibson-book-review.html

[3] Simone Ritter, Rodica Damian, Dean Simonton, et al., "Diversifying Experiences Enhance Cognitive Flexibility," *Journal of Experimental Social Psychology*, February 21, 2012.

[4] Ibid.

[5] See, for example, Ernest Gundling, Terry Hogan, and Karen Cvitkovich, *What is Global Leadership? 10 Key Behaviors that Define Successful Global Leaders* (Nicholas Brealey, 2011); Paula Caligiuri, *Cultural Agility: Building a Pipeline of Successful Global Professionals* (Jossey- Bass, 2014); Andy Molinsky, *Global Dexterity: How to Adapt Your Behavior Across Cultures without Losing Yourself in the Process* (Harvard Business Review Press, 2013).

[6] Ritter, Damian, and Simonton, Ibid.

[7] Nancy J. Adler, *International Dimensions of Organizational Behavior*, 4th Edition (South-Western College, 2002), 263.

[8] Herminia Ibarra, "The Authenticity Paradox," *Harvard Business Review*, January–February 2015.

[9] Rick Hanson describes this process in a personal development context using his HEAL model. Rick Hanson, *Hardwiring Happiness: The New Brain Science of Contentment, Calm, and Confidence.* (Harmony, 2016).

[10] See, for example, David Drake, *Narrative Coaching* (CNC Press, 2015).

[11] Lecture by Professor Albert Hastorf, Stanford University Department of Psychology.

12. Five Organizational Levers

[1] Marshall Goldsmith, *What Got You Here Won't Get You There* (Hachette Books, 2007).

[2] Excerpted and adapted from "5 Leaders Who Are Disrupting Diversity", by Novid Parsi, ©*Society for Human Resource Management*, January 16, 2017 (used with permission). Photo by Daniel Berman.

[3] In the U.S., this is commonly called the "Rooney Rule," a practice in professional football that requires interviewing at least one minority candidate for open coaching positions.

[4] Excerpted and adapted from "5 Leaders Who Are Disrupting Diversity", by Novid Parsi, ©*Society for Human Resource Management*, January 16, 2017 (used with permission). Photo by Jose Luis Stephens.

[5] Rocío Lorenzo, Nicole Voigt, Miki Tsusaka, Matt Krentz, and Katie Abouzahr, "How Diverse Leadership Teams Boost Innovation," *Boston Consulting Group*, January 2018, https://www.bcg.com/publications/2018/how-diverse-leadership-teams-boost-innovation

[6] An interview with Iris Bohnet by Gardiner Morse, "Designing a Bias-Free Organization," *Harvard Business Review*, July–August 2016.

[7] Frank Dobbin and Alexandra Kalev, "Why Diversity Programs Fail," *Harvard Business Review*, July–August 2016. The authors note a significant positive correlation between the presence of mentoring programs and higher numbers of minorities in management roles.

[8] Catherine Tinsley and Robert Ely, "What Most People Get Wrong about Men and Women," *Harvard Business Review*, May–June 2018.

[9] See, for example, Lisa Burrell, "We Just Can't Handle Diversity," *Harvard Business Review*, July–August 2016.

[10] The Thomson Reuters Diversity and Inclusion Rating is an example of a broad index that tracks 24 separate items in four major categories: Diversity, Inclusion, News and Controversies, and People Development. It draws upon open information sources for publicly listed companies. https://www.refinitiv.com/content/dam/gl/en/documents/methodology/diversity-inclusion-rating-methodology.pdf

[11] Ashleigh Shelby Rosette of Duke University as quoted by Lisa Burrell, "We Just Can't Handle Diversity," *Harvard Business Review*, July–August 2016.

[12] Tomas Chamorro-Premuzic, "Does Diversity Actually Increase Creativity?", *Harvard Business Review*, June 28, 2017.

[13] "Of the six dimensions of diversity we considered, all showed a correlation with innovation. But the most significant gains came from changing the makeup of the leadership team in terms of the national origin of executives, range of industry backgrounds, gender balance, and career paths." Rocío Lorenzo, Nicole Voigt, Miki Tsusaka, Matt Krentz, and Katie Abouzahr, "How Diverse Leadership Teams Boost Innovation," *Boston Consulting Group*, January 2018, https://www.bcg.com/publications/2018/how-diverse-leadership-teams-boost-innovation

[14] See, for example, Roscoe Balter, Joy Chow, and Yin Jin, "What Diversity Metrics are Best Used to Track and Improve Employee Diversity," *Cornell University Industrial and Labor Relations School, DigitalCommons@ ILR*, Spring 2014, https://ecommons.cornell.edu/bitstream/handle/1813/74536/What_Diversity_Metrics_are_Best_Used_to_Track_and_Improve_Employee_Diversity.pdf?sequence=1&isAllowed=y

See also, Leah Smiley, "5 Must-Have Metrics for Diversity & Inclusion to Prove ROI," *The Society for Diversity*, October 10, 2016.

[15] Robert Austin and Gary Pisano, "Neurodiversity as a Competitive Advantage," *Harvard Business Review*, May–June 2017.

[16] For more information about the Inclusive Behaviors Inventory: https://www.globesmart.com/inclusive-behaviors-inventory/

[17] Sample items with low self-ratings are, "My knowledge of diverse customer needs enables me to achieve my objectives"; and, "When I work in a matrix relationship with others, I am skilled at getting them to contribute."

[18] This affirms the research cited previously that for diverse teams convergence, or alignment around decisions and joint implementation, is a critical challenge.

[19] Frank Dobbin and Alexandra Kalev, "Why Diversity Programs Fail," *Harvard Business Review*, July–August 2016.

[20] Rocío Lorenzo, Nicole Voigt, Miki Tsusaka, Matt Krentz, and Katie Abouzahr, "How Diverse Leadership Teams Boost Innovation," *Boston Consulting Group*, January 2018, https://www.bcg.com/publications/2018/how-diverse-leadership-teams-boost-innovation

[21] The ways that people react to directives are of course shaped by national and organizational cultures. Even very hierarchical cultures often have mechanisms for soliciting input or providing a measure of autonomy in the implementation process.

[22] An interview with Iris Bohnet by Gardiner Morse, "Designing a Bias-Free Organization," *Harvard Business Review*, July–August 2016.

[23] "Choice architecture" is one term for this type of approach to mitigating deeply-ingrained biases: "The idea is to deliberately structure how you present information and options. You don't take away individuals' right to decide or tell them what they should do. You just make it easier for them to reach more-rational decisions." Lisa Burrell, "We Just Can't Handle Diversity," *Harvard Business Review*, July–August 2016.

[24] Joan Williams and Marina Multhaup, "For Women and Minorities to Get Ahead, Managers Must Assign Work Fairly," *Harvard Business Review*, March 5, 2018.

[25] See, for example, Matt Krentz, "Survey: What Diversity and Inclusion Policies Do Employees Actually Want?", *Harvard Business Review*, March 5, 2019. Also, see Tracy Brower on the topic of work-life fulfillment in "We Need to Stop Striving for Work-Life Balance. Here's Why." *Fast Company*, February 16, 2019, https://www.fastcompany.com/90308095/why-you- should-stop-trying-to-achieve-work-life-balance

[26] See, for example, Kevin Sneader and Lareina Yee, "One is the loneliest number," *McKinsey Quarterly*, January 2019. https://www.mckinsey.com/featured-insights/gender-equality/one-is-the-loneliest-number. "When women find themselves alone in a group of men... they are far more likely than others to have their judgment questioned than women working in a more balanced environment (49 percent versus 32 percent), to be mistaken for someone more junior (35 percent versus 15 percent), and to be subjected to unprofessional and demeaning remarks (24 percent versus 14 percent). If they are treated like this, no wonder they get overlooked for promotion."

[27] Marcus Buckingham, *First, Break All The Rules: What the World's Greatest Managers Do Differently* (Gallup Press, 2016).

[28] Frank Dobbin and Alexandra Kalev, "Why Diversity Programs Fail," *Harvard Business Review*, July–August 2016. "Diversity managers sometimes put ineffective programs in place but have a positive impact overall—in part because managers know someone might ask them about their hiring and promotion decisions."

[29] See Ernest Gundling, Terry Hogan, and Karen Cvitkovich, *What is Global Leadership? 10 Key Behaviors that Define Successful Global Leaders* (Nicholas Brealey, 2011), Chapters 3–4.

[30] Renewal is a favorite theme, for example, of Satya Nadella, Microsoft's third-generation CEO, who has been lauded for his efforts to change the organization in response to market trends. Originally born in Hyderabad, India, Nadella is now the head of a company founded in the Pacific Northwest region of the U.S. with over 130,000 employees worldwide. Microsoft faces a classic renewal challenge as the personal computer market fades and new business opportunities such as cloud computing are fiercely contested.

BIBLIOGRAPHY

Adler, Nancy. *International Dimensions of Organizational Behavior*. 4th ed. Mason, OH: Thomson South-Western, 2002.

Aisch, Gregor, Larry Buchanan, Amanda Cox and Kevin Quealy. "Some Colleges Have More Students From the Top 1 Percent Than the Bottom 60. Find Yours." *The New York Times*, January 18, 2017.

Alexander, Michelle. *The New Jim Crow: Mass Incarceration in the Age of Colorblindness*. New York: New Press, 2020.

Austin, Robert, and Gary Pisano. "Neurodiversity as a Competitive Advantage." *Harvard Business Review*, May-June 2017.

Azar, Beth. "Your Brain on Culture." *American Psychological Association*, 41(10), November 2010.

Baldwin, James. *The Price of the Ticket: Collected Non-Fiction, 1948–1985*. New York: St. Martin's Press, 1985.

Balter, Roscoe, Joy Chow, and Yin Jin. "What Diversity Metrics are Best Used to Track and Improve Employee Diversity." *DigitalCommons@ILR. Cornell University Industrial and Labor Relations School*, Spring 2014.

Begley, Sharon. "West Brain, East Brain: What a Difference Culture Makes." *Newsweek*, February 18, 2010.

Bennis, Warren, and Robert Thomas. "Crucibles of Leadership." *Harvard Business Review*, 2002.

Bersin by Deloitte. "High-Impact and Inclusion: Diversity Models and Findings." 2017.

Booker, Salih, and Ari Rickman. "The Future is Africa, and the United States is Not Prepared." *The Washington Post*, June 6, 2018.

Brower, Tracy. "We Need to Stop Striving for Work-Life Balance. Here's Why." *Fast Company*, February 16, 2019.

Buckingham, Marcus. *First, Break All The Rules: What the World's Greatest Managers Do Differently*. Gallup Press, 2016.

Burrell, Lisa. "We Just Can't Handle Diversity." *Harvard Business Review*, July–August 2016.

Caligiuri, Paula. *Cultural Agility: Building a Pipeline of Successful Global Professionals*. San Francisco: Jossey-Bass, 2014.

Campbell, Michael C., and Sarah A. Tishkoff. "African Genetic Diversity: Implications for Human Demographic History, Modern Human Origins, and Complex Disease Mapping." *Annual Review of Genomics and Human Genetics*, Vol. 9, 403-433, September 22, 2008.

Casey, Mary E. and Shannon Murphy Robinson. *Neuroscience of Inclusion: New Skills for New Times*. Outskirts Press, 2017.

Catlin, Karen. *Better Allies: Everyday Actions to Create Inclusive, Engaging Workplaces.* Better Allies Press, 2019.

Chamorro-Premuzic, Tomas. "Does Diversity Actually Increase Creativity?" *Harvard Business Review*, June 28, 2017.

Cho, Karen. "How to Stimulate Creativity? Go Live Abroad." *INSEAD Knowledge*, June 12, 2009.

Cohen, Roger. "Tribalism Here, and There." *The New York Times*, March 10, 2008.

Corporate Leadership Council. "Creating Competitive Advantage Through Workforce Diversity." 2012.

Corporate Leadership Council. "The Global Leader." Corporate Executive Board report, 2012.

Coates, Ta-Nehisi. *Between the World and Me.* New York: Random House, 2015.

Crenshaw, Kimberlé. "Mapping the Margins: Intersectionality, Identity Politics, and Violence Against Women of Color." *Stanford Law Review*, 43 (6), July 1991.

Crenshaw, Kimberlé. "Why Intersectionality Can't Wait." *The Washington Post*, September 24, 2015.

de Bono, Edward. *Six Thinking Hats: An Essential Approach to Business Management.* Boston: Little, Brown and Company, 1985.

DeGruy, Joy. *Post-Traumatic Slave Syndrome: America's Legacy of Enduring Injury and Healing.* Joy DeGruy Publications Inc., 2017.

Diangelo, Robin. *White Fragility: Why it's so Hard for White People to Talk About Racism.* Boston: Beacon Press, 2018.

Dobbin, Frank, and Alexandra Kalev. "Why Diversity Programs Fail." *Harvard Business Review*, July–August 2016.

Dobbs, Richard, et al. "Urban world: The shifting global business landscape." *McKinsey Global Institute*, October 2013.

Drake, David. *Narrative Coaching: Bringing Our New Stories to Life.* Petaluma, CA: CNC Press, 2015.

Dyson, Michael Eric. *Long Time Coming: Reckoning with Race in America.* New York: St. Martin's Press, 2020.

Edmondson, Amy. "Psychological Safety and Learning Behavior in Work Teams." *Administrative Science Quarterly*, 44(2), June 1, 1999.

Financial Times. "Why 'emerging markets' is an outdated definition." August 4, 2015.

Freeman, Jonathan B., Nicholas O. Rule, Reginald B. Adams, Jr., and Nalini Ambady. "Culture shapes a mesolimbic response to signals of dominance and subordination that associates with behavior." *NeuroImage*, 47(1), 353–359, August 1, 2009.

Fuchs, Richard. "Germany is Not Shrinking." *Deutsche Welle*, February 2, 2017.

Gardenswartz, Lee, and Anita Rowe. "Diverse Teams at Work: Capitalizing on the Power of Diversity." *Society for Human Resource Management*, 2003.

Ghana Web. "Probe rape claim against GBA boss – FIDA." January 21, 2019.

Goldsmith, Marshall. *What Got You Here Won't Get You There*. New York: Hyperion, 2007.

Goleman, Daniel. *Emotional Intelligence: Why it Can Matter More than IQ*. New York: Bantam Books, 1995.

Goleman, Daniel. "What Makes a Leader?" *Harvard Business Review*, January 2004.

Gundling, Ernest, and Anita Zanchettin, eds. *Global Diversity: Winning Customers and Engaging Employees within World Markets*. Boston & London: Nicholas Brealey, 2008.

Gundling, Ernest, Christie Caldwell, and Karen Cvitkovich. *Leading Across New Borders: How to Succeed as the Center Shifts*. Hoboken, NJ: Wiley & Sons, 2015.

Gundling, Ernest, Terry Hogan, and Karen Cvitkovich. *What is Global Leadership? 10 Key Behaviors that Define Successful Global Leaders*. Boston & London: Nicholas Brealey, 2011.

Gundling, Ernest. *Working GlobeSmart: 12 People Skills for Doing Business Across Borders*. Boston & London: Davies-Black, 2003.

Gutchess, Angela H., Robert C. Welsh, Aysecan Boduroglu, and Denise Park. "Cultural differences in neural function associated with object processing." *Cognitive, Affective, & Behavioral Neuroscience*, 6(2), 102–109, 2006.

Hall, Edward. *The Silent Language*. Greenwich, CT: Fawcett Publications, Inc., 1959.

Hanson, Rick. *Hardwiring Happiness: The New Brain Science of Contentment, Calm, and Confidence*. New York: Harmony, 2016.

Hewlett, Sylvia Ann, Melinda Marshall, and Laura Sherbin. "How Diversity Can Drive Innovation." *Harvard Business Review*, December 2013.

Ibarra, Herminia. "The Authenticity Paradox." *Harvard Business Review*, January-February 2015.

Institute for Advanced Study. "Clifford Geertz: Work and Legacy." No date.

International Finance Corporation and AXA Group. "SheForShield: Insure Women to better protect all." September 2015.

Irving, Debby. *Waking up White, and Finding Myself in the Story of Race*. Elephant Room Press, 2014.

John, Charley-Kai. "Number of migrants in Germany hits record high." *Reuters World News*, April 12, 2018.

Kahneman, Daniel. *Thinking Fast and Slow*. New York: Farrar, Straus and Giroux, 2013.

Kelley, Tom. *The Ten Faces of Innovation*. New York: Doubleday, 2005.

Kennedy, Pagan. "William Gibson's Future is Now." *New York Times*, January 13, 2012.

Kim, Heejung, and Joni Sasaki. "Cultural Neuroscience: Biology of the Mind in Cultural Contexts." *Annual Review of Psychology*, Vol. 65, 487–514, January 2014.

Kimsey-House, Henry. Kimsey-House, Karen et al. *Co-Active Coaching*, Fourth Edition. Boston: Nicholas Brealey, 2018.

Kotter, John. *Corporate Culture and Performance*. New York: Free Press, 2011.

Kotter, John. *Leading Change*. Boston: Harvard Business Review Press, 2012.

Krentz, Matt. "Survey: What Diversity and Inclusion Policies Do Employees Actually Want?" *Harvard Business Review*, March 5, 2019.

Lorenzo, Rocío, Nicole Voigt, Miki Tsusaka, Matt Krentz, and Katie Abouzahr. "How Diverse Leadership Teams Boost Innovation." *Boston Consulting Group*, January 2018.

Lukianoff, Greg, and Jonathan Haidt. *The Coddling of the American Mind: How Good Intentions and Bad Ideas Are Setting Up a Generation for Failure*. New York: Penguin Press, 2018.

MacDonald, Heather. *The Diversity Delusion: How Race and Gender Pandering Corrupt the University and Undermine our Culture*. New York: St. Martin's Press, 2018.

McGregor, Jena. "The Business Brain in Close-up." *Bloomberg Businessweek*, July 22, 2007.

McKinsey Analysis. "Delivering Through Diversity." January 2018.

Molinsky, Andy. *Global Dexterity: How to Adapt Your Behavior Across Cultures without Losing Yourself in the Process*. Boston: Harvard Business Review Press, 2013.

Morse, Gardiner. Interview with Iris Bohnet. "Designing a Bias-Free Organization." *Harvard Business Review*, July–August 2016.

Mungai, Christine. "Pundits who decry 'tribalism' know nothing about real tribes." *The Washington Post*, January 30, 2019.

Nadella, Satya. *Hit Refresh: The Quest to Rediscover Microsoft's Soul and Imagine a Better Future for Everyone*. New York: HarperCollins, 2017.

Nielsen, Tinna, and Lisa Kepinski. *Inclusion Nudges Guidebook*. Edition 2, January 2016.

Pollock, David C., Ruth E. Von Reken, and Michael V. Pollock. *Third Culture Kids: Growing Up Among Worlds*, Third Edition. Boston & London: Nicholas Brealey, 2017.

Premium Times. "Ghana: Traders Association Protest Alleged Closure of 400 Nigerian-Owned Shops in Ghana." September 24, 2018.

Ritter, Simone, Rodica Damian, Dean Simonton, et al. "Diversifying Experiences Enhance Cognitive Flexibility." *Journal of Experimental Social Psychology*, February 21, 2012.

Rock, David. *Your Brain at Work*. New York: HarperCollins, 2009.

Ross, Howard. *Reinventing Diversity: Transforming Organizational Community to Strengthen People, Purpose, and Performance*. Lanham, Maryland: Rowman and Littlefield, 2011.

Ross, Howard. *Everyday Bias: Identifying and Navigating Unconscious Judgments in Our Daily Lives.* Lanham, Maryland: Rowman and Littlefield, 2014.

Schmid, Randolph E. "Africans have world's greatest genetic variation." *Science on NBCNews.com*, April 30, 2009.

Smiley, Leah. "5 Must-Have Metrics for Diversity & Inclusion to Prove ROI." *The Society for Diversity*, October 10, 2016.

Sneader, Kevin, and Lareina Yee. "One is the loneliest number." *McKinsey Quarterly*, January 2019.

Tapia, Andrés. *The Inclusion Paradox: The Post-Obama Era and the Transformation of Global Diversity*, Third Edition. Korn Ferry Institute, 2016.

The World Factbook. Washington, DC: Central Intelligence Agency, 2017.

Thomson Reuters. "Thomson Reuters Diversity and Inclusion Rating." 2018.

Tinsley, Catherine, and Robert Ely. "What Most People Get Wrong about Men and Women." *Harvard Business Review*, May–June 2018.

United Nations Department of Economic and Social Affairs. "The International Migration Report 2017." December 18, 2017.

Williams, Joan, and Marina Multhaup. "For Women and Minorities to Get Ahead, Managers Must Assign Work Fairly." *Harvard Business Review*, March 5, 2018.

Woetzel, Jonathan. Anu Madgavkar et al. "The power of parity: Advancing women's equality in Asia Pacific." *McKinsey & Company*, April 2018.

Young, Jeffrey. "Most Professors Think They're Above-Average Teachers. And That's a Problem." *EdSurge*, May 24, 2018.

Zaki, Jamil. *The War for Kindness: Building Empathy in a Fractured World.* New York: Broadway Books, 2019

Zhang, Jingzhu. "Test Review: The Intercultural Development Inventory Manual." *Journal of Psychoeducational Assessment*, February 20, 2014

RESOURCES

GlobeSmart Profile—Work smarter, faster, and more collaboratively by building awareness of style differences. Learn more about your unique work style and create a common vocabulary to address previously hidden biases. Understanding and adapting to work-style differences are key steps toward more inclusive leadership.

www.globesmart.com

INCLUSIVE BEHAVIORS INVENTORY℠

Inclusive Behaviors Inventory—Let inclusion power your workplace. Measure inclusion levels of employees and equip them with personalized action plans based on survey results. A 360 version is available for executives or for leadership teams.

www.globesmart.com/inclusive-behaviors-inventory

ABOUT THE AUTHORS

Ernest Gundling, Ph.D., is a co-founder and managing partner of Aperian Global. He assists clients in building strategic global approaches to leadership development, inclusion and diversity, and cross-border business relationships. He has lived and traveled extensively in Asia, Europe, Latin America, and the Middle East, including six years as an expatriate in Japan. A frequent keynote speaker and the author of five previous books—including *What is Global Leadership?, Global Diversity, and Leading Across New Borders*—he has also served for twenty-five years as a Lecturer at the Haas School of Business at the University of California, Berkeley.

Cheryl Williams, Ph.D., is a highly regarded subject matter expert on global workforce inclusion, diversity matters, cultural competency and leadership across boundaries. She spent over twenty-five years in leadership roles in the entertainment and high technology industries, where she managed employee education and training, recruitment, staffing, internal communications, employee relations, and community relations. She has worked extensively in over fifty countries, and serves as Professor Emeritus at Concordia University, Irvine, California.

ABOUT APERIAN GLOBAL

Aperian Global has provided consulting, training, and online learning tools to 40% of the Global Fortune 100. Aperian Global's employees are dedicated to helping clients work effectively across boundaries, both at home and abroad. The company provides scalable resources for building practical skills and knowledge that help individuals and organizations thrive in an increasingly diverse business landscape.

Aperian Global specializes in research-based inclusion practices—impactful in domestic work environments and adaptable to different world regions—along with strategic global mobility support and holistic cultural competence learning solutions.

GlobeSmart, the company's flagship online tool, has had more than one million users, and its work-style profile provides a way for team members to compare their styles and adjust to each other. The *Inclusive Behaviors Inventory*, available in both self-assessment and 360 versions, is also part of the GlobeSmart platform's assessment suite.

Aperian Global's products and services empower leaders at all levels to work in an inclusive way, engaging partners, colleagues, and employees from any background to deliver results through high-performance teamwork.

Founded in 1990, Aperian Global has offices in Bangalore, Boston, Kolding, Oakland, Paris, Raleigh, Shanghai, and Singapore, and staff and consultants on the ground in over 80 locations worldwide.

For more information, **visit www.aperianglobal.com**.

Made in the USA
Las Vegas, NV
09 August 2022

53009305R00157